LAW, CRIME AND LAW ENFORCEMENT

MASS SHOOTINGS AND GUN VIOLENCE IN AMERICA

ISSUES AND PERSPECTIVES

Law, Crime and Law Enforcement

Additional books in this series can be found on Nova's website under the Series tab.

Additional E-books in this series can be found on Nova's website under the E-book tab.

Criminal Justice, Law Enforcement and Corrections

Additional books in this series can be found on Nova's website under the Series tab.

Additional E-books in this series can be found on Nova's website under the E-book tab.

LAW, CRIME AND LAW ENFORCEMENT

MASS SHOOTINGS AND GUN VIOLENCE IN AMERICA

ISSUES AND PERSPECTIVES

JOHN C. ZANDLER
EDITOR

nova publishers
New York

For permission to use material from this book please contact us:
Telephone 631-231-7269; Fax 631-231-8175
Web Site: http://www.novapublishers.com

Library of Congress Cataloging-in-Publication Data

ISBN: 978-1-62618-893-8

Published by Nova Science Publishers, Inc. † New York

Contents

PREFACE

Shooting incidents such as the one at Sandy Hook Elementary School in December 2012 and the one at Aurora, CO, movie theater in July 2012 have focused attention on federal policy issues in the law enforcement, public health, and education arenas. The Congressional Research Service (CRS) has identified 78 public mass shootings that have occurred in the United States since 1983. These shootings have claimed almost 550 lives according to CRS estimates. Most gun owners buy their guns legally and use them safely, whether for self-defense, hunting, or sport shooting. Yet too often, irresponsible and dangerous individuals have been able to easily get their hands on firearms. Efforts must be strengthened to keep guns from falling into the wrong hands. This book focuses on mass shootings and gun violence in America with select implications they have for federal policy in the areas of public health and safety. While such crimes most directly impact particular citizens in very specific communities, addressing these violent episodes involves officials at all levels of government and professionals from numerous disciplines.

Chapter 1 - This report focuses on mass shootings and selected implications they have for federal policy in the areas of public health and safety. While such crimes most directly impact particular citizens in very specific communities, addressing these violent episodes involves officials at all levels of government and professionals from numerous disciplines. This report does not discuss gun control and does not systematically address the broader issue of gun violence. Also, it is not intended as an exhaustive review of federal programs addressing the issue of mass shootings.

Chapter 2 - The President's Plan to Protect Our Children and Our Communities by Reducing Gun Violence, released by the White House, January 16, 2013.

Chapter 3 - Statement of Senator Patrick Leahy, Chairman. Senate Judiciary Committee.

Chapter 4 - Statement of Senator Orrin G. Hatch, Senate Judiciary Committee.

Chapter 5 - Statement of Senator Ted Cruz, Senate Judiciary Committee.

Chapter 6 - Testimony of Captain Mark Kelly, Senate Judiciary Committee.

Chapter 7 - Testimony of David B. Kopel, Adjunct Professor of Advanced Constitutional Law, Denver University, Senate Judiciary Committee.

Chapter 8 - Testimony of Chief Jim Johnson, Baltimore County Police Department, Senate Judiciary Committee.

Chapter 9 - Testimony of Gayle S. Trotter, Senior Fellow, Senate Judiciary Committee.

Chapter 10 - Testimony of Wayne LaPierre, Executive Vice President, National Rifle Association, Senate Judiciary Committee.

Chapter 11 - Statement of Senator Patrick Leahy, Chairman, Senate Judiciary Committee.

Chapter 12 - Statement of Senator Orrin G. Hatch, Senate Judiciary Committee, Subcommittee on the Constitution, Civil Rights and Human Rights.

Chapter 13 - Statement of Senator Ted Cruz, Senate Judiciary Committee, Subcommittee on the Constitution, Civil Rights and Human Rights.

Chapter 14 - Statement of Senator Timothy J. Heaphy, U.S. Attorney, Department of Justice, Senate Judiciary Committee, Subcommittee on the Constitution, Civil Rights and Human Rights.

Chapter 15 - Testimony of Laurence H. Tribe, Carl M. Loeb University Professor, Harvard Law School, Senate Judiciary Committee, Subcommittee on the Constitution, Civil Rights and Human Rights.

Chapter 16 - Testimony of Daniel W. Webster, Professor and Director, Johns Hopkins Center for Gun Policy and Research, Senate Judiciary Committee, Subcommittee on the Constitution, Civil Rights and Human Rights.

Chapter 17 - Testimony of Sandra J. Wortham, Senate Judiciary Committee, Subcommittee on the Constitution, Civil Rights and Human Rights.

Chapter 18 - Statement of Charles J. Cooper, Partner, Cooper & Kirk, PLLC. Senate Judiciary Committee, Subcommittee on the Constitution, Civil Rights and Human Rights,

Chapter 19 - Testimony of Suzanna Hupp, Senate Judiciary Committee, Subcommittee on the Constitution, Civil Rights and Human Rights.

In: Mass Shootings and Gun Violence in America
Editor: John C. Zandler
ISBN: 978-1-62618-893-8

Chapter 1

PUBLIC MASS SHOOTINGS IN THE UNITED STATES: SELECTED IMPLICATIONS FOR FEDERAL PUBLIC HEALTH AND SAFETY POLICY*

Jerome P. Bjelopera, Erin Bagalman, Sarah W. Caldwell, Kristin M. Finklea and Gail McCallion

SUMMARY

This report focuses on mass shootings and selected implications they have for federal policy in the areas of public health and safety. While such crimes most directly impact particular citizens in very specific communities, addressing these violent episodes involves officials at all levels of government and professionals from numerous disciplines.

This report does not discuss gun control and does not systematically address the broader issue of gun violence. Also, it is not intended as an exhaustive review of federal programs addressing the issue of mass shootings.

Defining Public Mass Shooting

Policy makers may confront numerous questions about shootings such as the December 2012 incident at Sandy Hook Elementary School in Newtown, CT, that claimed 27 lives (not including the shooter). Foremost, what are the parameters of this threat? How should it be defined?

There is no broadly agreed-to, specific conceptualization of this issue, so this report uses its own definition for *public mass shootings*. These are incidents occurring in relatively public places, involving four or more deaths—not including the shooter(s)—and gunmen who select

* This is an edited, reformatted and augmented version of Congressional Research Service, Publication No. R43004, dated March 18, 2013.

victims somewhat indiscriminately. The violence in these cases is not a means to an end—the gunmen do not pursue criminal profit or kill in the name of terrorist ideologies, for example.

One Measure of the Death Toll Exacted by Public Mass Shootings

Applying this understanding of the issue, the Congressional Research Service (CRS) has identified 78 public mass shootings that have occurred in the United States since 1983.

This suggests the scale of this threat and is intended as a thorough review of the phenomenon but should not be characterized as exhaustive or definitive. According to CRS estimates, over the last three decades public mass shootings have claimed 547 lives and led to an additional 476 injured victims. Significantly, while tragic and shocking, public mass shootings account for few of the murders or non-negligent homicides related to firearms that occur annually in the United States.

Policymaking Challenges in Public Health and Safety

Aside from trying to develop a sense of this phenomenon's scope, policy makers may face other challenges when addressing this topic. To help describe some of the health and safety issues public mass shootings pose, this report discusses selected policy in three areas: *law enforcement*, *public health*, and *education*. While mass shootings may occur in a number of settings, the education realm is one that has received particular attention from policy makers, officials, and the public alike—at least since the 1999 shooting at Columbine High School in Littleton, CO. The tragedy at Sandy Hook Elementary has renewed such concerns for many.

In the areas of law enforcement, public health, and education, this report discusses some key efforts to *prevent* mass shootings as well as efforts geared toward *preparedness* and *response*. Policy measures that deal with *recovery* are also discussed within the context of education and public health initiatives.

Policy Effectiveness and Outlay of Resources

Many of the policymaking challenges regarding public mass shootings boil down to two interrelated matters: (1) a need to determine the effectiveness of existing programs and (2) figuring out where to disburse limited resources.

Finally, baseline metrics related to this problem are often unclear or unavailable. This lack of clarity starts with identifying the number of shootings themselves, since no broadly agreed-to definition exists. Several questions flow from this issue. How many people have such incidents victimized? How much does prevention of, preparedness for, and response to such incidents cost the federal government? What measurements can be used to determine the effectiveness of such programs?

INTRODUCTION

Shooting incidents such as the one at Sandy Hook Elementary School in December 2012 and the one at an Aurora, CO, movie theater in July 2012 have focused attention on federal policy issues in the law enforcement, public health, and education arenas, among others. The Congressional Research Service (CRS) has identified 78 public mass shootings that have occurred in the United States since 1983. These shootings have claimed almost 550 lives according to CRS estimates.[2]

President Obama's Plan to Reduce Gun Violence

On January 16, 2012, President Obama announced a slate of proposals aimed at reducing gun violence—not just public mass shootings, the topic of this report—in the United States.[1] The proposals focus on four areas:

- Closing background check loopholes,
- Banning military-style assault weapons and high-capacity magazines,
- Making schools safer, and
- Increasing access to mental health services.

Some of the President's proposals, such as encouraging better information sharing among and between states and federal agencies and providing incentives for police departments to use existing grants to hire school resource officers, can be addressed through executive actions. Other proposals, such as reinstating the assault weapons ban and providing funding for a range of mental health programs and services, require action by Congress. The President's proposals touch on a number of issues that public mass shootings raise for federal safety and public health policy.

How does the death toll tied to public mass shootings compare with figures related to the preeminent threat that federal law enforcement has confronted in the last decade? CRS estimates that since the terrible events of September 11, 2001 (9/11), Al-Qaeda-inspired homegrown terrorists have killed 14 people in two incidents in the United States.[3] Since 9/11, according to CRS estimates, 281 people have died in 38 public mass shootings.[4] Arguably, the comparatively low death toll associated with Al Qaeda-inspired incidents at least partly results from a large-scale federal focus on homeland security and counterterrorism efforts.

It is important to caution the reader that, while tragic and shocking, public mass shootings account for few of the murders[5] related to firearms that occur annually in the United States. According to the Federal Bureau of Investigation (FBI, the Bureau), in 2011, firearms were used to murder 8,583 people.[6] To provide further context, over the last two decades, the nation has experienced a general *decline* in violent crime. In 1992, 1.9 million violent crimes were reported, while 2011 saw 1.2 million.[7] In the same period, the national murder rate dropped from 9.3 to 4.7 per 100,000 inhabitants.[8]

ROADMAP FOR THE REPORT

As a starting point, this report delves into public mass shootings over the last three decades, exploring the nature of this threat. *Of note, this report does not focus on gun violence, writ large, nor does it discuss gun control.*[9]

In its broader discussion of related federal public health and safety issues, the report covers selected policy implications in three areas: *law enforcement*, *public health*, and *education*. While mass shootings may occur in a number of public settings, the education realm is one which has generated concern from policy makers, officials, and the public alike—at least since the 1999 shooting at Columbine High School in Littleton, CO. The tragedy at Sandy Hook Elementary has renewed such concerns for many. In this report, discussion of each of these is further broken down into efforts geared toward

- *prevention*—actions intended to reduce the likelihood of shootings.[10]
- *preparedness*—planning how to cope with potential shootings.
- *response*—structured efforts employed to react to an actual shooting.

Policy measures that deal with recovery are also discussed within the context of education and public health initiatives. Recovery entails helping institutions, communities, and individuals cope with the aftermath of a shooting.[11] This report is not intended as an exhaustive review of specific federal programs in these areas.

DEFINING AND IDENTIFYING PUBLIC MASS SHOOTINGS

This report attempts to refine the relatively broad concept of *mass shooting* (which could potentially involve a wide variety of actors targeting victims for any number of reasons) into a narrower formulation: *public mass shootings.* This has been done to focus discussion around a number of violent incidents that lie outside of specific crime issues such as terrorism, drug trafficking, gang activity, and domestic violence that have federal policies, law enforcement structures, and laws tailored in many instances to specifically address them.

Arriving at a Definition

In order to delineate a workable understanding of *public mass shooting* for this report, CRS examined scholarly journal articles, monographs, and government reports.[12] These sources discussed a variety of terms such as mass murder, mass shooting, mass killings, massacres, and multiple homicide. Definitions of these terms varied with regard to establishing the number of victims or fatalities involved, the weapons used, the motives of the perpetrator, and the timeframes within which the casualties or injuries occurred.

This report defines public mass shootings as *incidents occurring in relatively public places, involving four or more deaths—not including the shooter(s)—and gunmen who select victims somewhat indiscriminately. The violence in these cases is not a means to an end such as robbery or terrorism.*[13]

Relatively Public Places

For this report, public mass shootings happen in *relatively* public circumstances. Such settings can include schools, workplaces, restaurants, parking lots, public transit, even private parties that include at least some guests who are not family members of the shooter.[14]

Tallying Fatalities

Any definition of mass shootings requires a somewhat arbitrary threshold demarcating the number of victims killed per incident. This report's threshold is based on a definition of mass murder offered by the FBI.[15]An important caveat deserves mentioning. A compilation of incidents based on any such arbitrary threshold may fail to adequately describe the universe of incidents to which educators, public health professionals, and law enforcement have to react and for which they have to prepare.[16] One author has stated that gunmen "injure far more victims than they kill; however, they must certainly be considered mass murderers by obvious intentions of their actions."[17] In the critical early moments of a shooting, police, teachers, and rescue personnel do not necessarily know how many people are injured versus dead. Personnel and resources are initially mobilized in response to a shooting, regardless of the number of fatalities.

Indiscriminate Selection of Victims

For this report's definition, a killer's relationship to his or her victims is important. Driven by a desire for revenge and/or power, some killers may target family members or intimate friends.[18] In the incidents described as public mass shootings for this report, the gunmen cannot solely kill such individuals. This particularly rules out cases of domestic violence—instances only involving family members either inside or outside the home— from consideration as public mass shootings. Thus, for this report, the gunmen in public mass shootings somewhat indiscriminately select their victims. For example, a student assailant involved in a public mass shooting plans on killing particular teachers, while simultaneously staging a wider assault on his school.

Violence Not a Means to an End

For this report, a public mass shooter's agenda certainly may stem from his specific personal experiences and psychological conditions. However, as implied in the above definition, the shooters who perpetrated the incidents counted in this report did not have broad socio-political objectives, such as using violence to advocate the fall of a regime.[19]

Thus, gunmen acting in the name of a terrorist organization or a clearly framed philosophy of hate typically were not considered public mass shooters. Also, shootings largely motivated by criminal profit were not counted. Based on the purpose undergirding the assailant's violence, the following examples do not fit the definition of public mass shooting used for this report.

- In December 2012, Dwayne Moore was convicted of *home invasion, armed robbery*, and four counts of first-degree murder in Massachusetts. He reportedly gunned down four victims, including a child, in a September 2010 drug-related incident in Boston, MA.[20]
- A mass murder that has been widely reported as a *hate-motivated* incident occurred on the morning of August 5, 2012, when Wade Michael Page shot to death six people at the Sikh Temple of Wisconsin in Oak Creek—near Milwaukee, WI.[21] According to the FBI, police responding to the scene returned fire, wounding Page. He then took his own life by shooting himself.[22]

- U.S. Army Major Nidal Hasan was charged in a shooting at Fort Hood, TX, on November 5, 2009. The mass murder, which has been described as a *terrorist incident*, killed 13 and injured more than 40 others.[23]

Identifying Incidents

To identify incidents of public mass shootings, CRS reviewed descriptions of mass shooting events found in scholarly journal articles, monographs, lists created by government entities and advocacy organizations, and news accounts.[24]

It is important to note that while every effort was made to be thorough in reviewing the sources used, the incidents identified by CRS should not be considered as constituting an exhaustive list of public mass shootings.[25]

Readers are also cautioned against tying this report's definition of public mass shootings directly to specific federal policy responses. In other words, the policy responses discussed below are not restricted to preventing or reacting to public mass shootings as defined in this report. For instance, many of the policy measures discussed herein respond to shooting events or threats that could include fewer than four deaths or shooters with specific ideologies and targets. The shooting definition offered in this report is meant to help illustrate the nature and breadth of a threat that lacks an agreed-upon conceptualization among experts, capturing some of the most extreme shooting cases over the last three decades.

Describing Public Mass Shootings

For many years, mass shootings have been of interest and concern to a variety of experts— including psychologists, sociologists, criminologists, public health experts, policy makers, and students of popular culture—who have written much on the topic.

Journalists have tracked such killings for a long time as well. For example, a case involving gunman Howard B. Unruh in September 1949 received national attention.[26] There were over 50 news articles in more than a dozen major newspapers in the United States in the month after the shooting occurred.

- In what was reported at the time as the biggest mass murder in U.S. history, Unruh killed 13 people in a 20-minute-long incident in Camden, NJ. He shot people he knew as well as strangers. His victims included three children.[27]

All of this interest in such shootings has produced a wide variety of terms and concepts that address an assortment of issues. Categorizing types of murder—and mass shootings, more narrowly—can be tricky. In many cases, individual incidents involving assailants who kill one, two, or three people are described as single, double, or triple murder.

However, when the number of victims rises or the case involves complicating circumstances such as the killer assailing individuals in different locations or a string of murders committed over a period of days, months, or years, efforts to define and understand murder can grow much more difficult.

Placing Them within a Broader Context

Most scholarly and expert sources suggest that mass shootings are rare violent crimes. One study has described them as "very low-frequency and high intensity event[s]."[28] The 78 public mass shootings between 1983 and 2012 that CRS has identified claimed 547 lives (see Figure 1).[29]

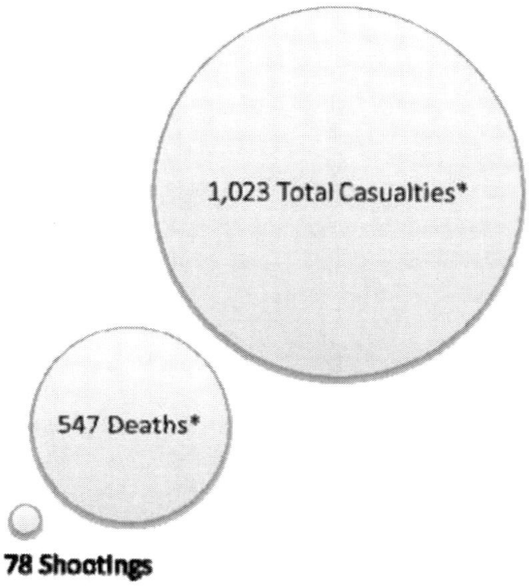

Source: CRS, based on analysis of mass shooting incidents identified by CRS.
Notes: * "Deaths" do not include shooters. "Total Casualties" include deaths and victims who suffered nonlethal injuries from gunshots.

Figure 1. Public Mass Shootings in the United States 1983-2012; Deaths and Total Casualties.

A Subset of Multiple Murder

Public mass shootings, as defined by this report, can be viewed as part of the larger issue of "multiple murder." A lexicon has emerged since the 1980s to describe instances of multiple murder.[30] Qualitatively broader than cases of single, double, or triple murder, instances of multiple murder can be divided into a number of categories including serial or mass killings.[31]

Figure 2 lays out how this report frames the issue of public mass shootings. Starting at the top of Figure 2, *serial murders* involve multiple victims killed by the same offender or offenders in separate events over a period of days, months, or years.[32] For this report, *mass murders* involve four or more people killed—not including the shooter(s)—in less than one day by the same offender or offenders.

Mass murder can then be divided into subcategories—that may or may not involve gunmen—such as massacres perpetrated by people interested in genocide, cult killings, terrorist plots, the slaying of people during the course of drug trafficking, and, as conceptualized in this report, public mass shootings.[33]

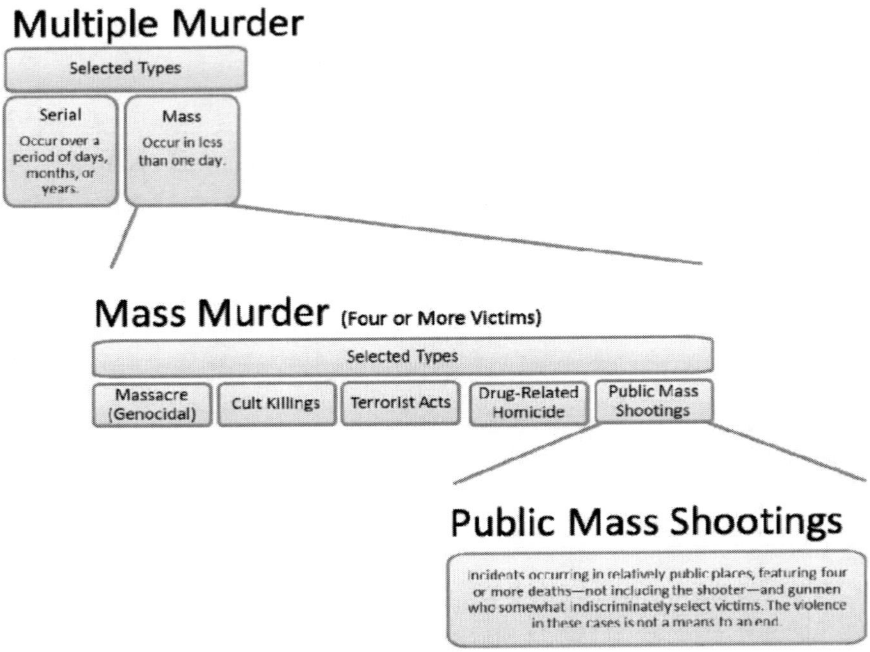

Sources: Graphic constructed by CRS, adapted from concepts highlighted in: James Alan Fox and Jack Levin, *Extreme Killing: Understanding Serial and Mass Murder*, 2nd ed. (Los Angeles: Sage, 2012), p. 19; James L. Knoll, IV, "The 'Pseudocommando' Mass Murderer: Part I, The Psychology of Revenge and Obliteration," *Journal of the American Academy of Psychiatry and the Law,* vol. 38, no. 1 (2010) pp. 87-89; Federal Bureau of Investigation, *Serial Murder: Multi-Disciplinary Perspectives for Investigators*, 2008, p. 8; John E. Douglas, Ann W. Burgess, and Robert K. Ressler, *Crime Classification Manual: A Standard System for Investigating and Classifying Violent Crimes,* 2nd ed. (San Francisco: Jossey-Bass, 2006) p. 96; Grant Duwe, "A Circle of Distortion: The Social Construction of Mass Murder in the United States," *Western Criminology Review,* vol. 6, no. 1 (2005) p. 59. Paul E. Mullen, "The Autogenic (Self-Generated) Massacre," *Behavioral Sciences and the Law,* vol. 22, no. 3 (2004) pp. 311-314; Grant Duwe, Tomislav Kovandzic, and Carlisle E. Moody, "The Impact of Right-to-Carry Concealed Firearm Laws on Mass Public Shootings," *Homicide Studies,* vol. 6, no. 4 (2002) p. 273; Michael D. Kelleher, *Flash Point: The American Mass Murderer,* (Westport, CT: Praeger, 1997) p. 2.

Notes: For this graphic, "public mass shootings" involve four or more deaths from gunshot wounds, not including the perpetrator of the violence. "Murder" implies the willful killing of one human being by another.

Figure 2. Placing Public Mass Shootings into Context.

Public Mass Shootings—Settings

Among the 78 public mass shootings since 1983 that CRS has identified, 26 occurred at workplaces where the shooter was employed either at the time of the incident or prior to it. The next largest number of public mass shootings occurred at places of education (12).[34]

- In 2000 in Wakefield, MA, Michael McDermott took three guns to Edgewater Technology Inc., where he was employed, and shot seven coworkers.[35]
- In 2006 Charles Roberts entered a one-room Amish schoolhouse in Lancaster County, PA, where he shot and killed five students and injured five others.[36]

As the above implies, the public mass shootings identified by CRS involve a high level of localization. A mass shooter usually targets individuals in one location or, as the examples below demonstrate, in a small handful of closely clustered geographic sites.

- In 1988 Michael Hayes shot at people randomly as he roamed his neighborhood in Winston Salem, NC, killing four and injuring five.[37]
- In 2009 Michael McLendon shot his mother before driving to the nearby town of Samson, GA, where he shot five more people. He then drove to another neighboring town, Geneva, where he shot several more people before killing himself. In total McLendon killed 10 people and injured six.[38]

Public Mass Shootings—Perpetrators

Many experts agree that a workable, detailed profile of mass shooters does not exist.[39] However, there are some observations that can be made regarding public mass shooters. For instance, among the public mass shooting incidents reviewed by CRS, the gunmen generally acted alone, were usually white and male, and often died during the shooting incident. The average age of the shooters in the incidents identified by CRS was 33.5 years.

Only on rare occasions was more than one perpetrator involved in a public mass shooting. CRS has identified three such incidents since 1983.

- In 1993, Juan Luna and James Degorski killed seven employees at a restaurant in Palatine, IL.[40]
- In 1998, Andrew Golden and Mitchell Johnson killed five people and injured 10 at their middle school in Jonesboro, AR.[41]
- In 1999 Dylan Klebold and Eric Harris killed 13 and injured 23 at their high school in Littleton, CO, and then killed themselves.[42]

Source: CRS, based on analysis of mass shooting incidents identified by CRS.

Figure 3. Age of Perpetrators in Public Mass Shootings 1983-2012; Grouped in 10-Year Intervals.

Of the public mass shooting incidents identified by CRS for which information on the race of the perpetrator(s) was available, over half of the shooters were reportedly white.[43]

Almost always, the shooters were male. Of the incidents compiled by CRS, only one involved a female assailant. In January 2006, Jennifer Sanmarco shot to death seven individuals—six were fatally wounded in a U.S. postal facility in Goleta, CA. One death occurred near Sanmarco's condominium, also in Goleta. She killed herself as well.[44] It was common for the gunmen involved in the shootings identified by CRS to kill themselves during their assaults. Forty-one of 81 shooters killed themselves. In 10 instances, law enforcement officers killed the gunmen involved.[45] The shooters identified by CRS ranged in age from 11 to 66 years old. All but 10 were age 20 or older. Most of them were in their 20s, 30s, or 40s (see Figure 3).

Law Enforcement Implications

When considering law enforcement's role in coping with public mass shootings, policy makers and the public likely are most aware of how police forces react when they learn of an incident. Public mass shootings typically trigger a rapid police response, followed by an investigation and, potentially, prosecutions and sentencing. Also, while a shooting incident may spur an immediate law enforcement response, the *potential* for such a scenario impacts law enforcement prevention and preparedness measures. Police are not typically involved in recovery efforts. From a law enforcement perspective, mass shootings tend to be single-jurisdiction issues involving a particular community. As such, while the federal government may not play a direct role in formulating specific state and local practices, it may influence these practices through the availability of grants. For example, the Department of Homeland Security (DHS) offers funding via its Homeland Security Grant Program to "fund a range of preparedness activities, including planning, organization, equipment purchase, training, exercises, and management and administration."[46] Although Department of Justice (DOJ) grants are not necessarily framed in terms of prevention, preparedness, or response, they can certainly address these issues regarding mass shootings.[47]

Federal Framework for Emergency Management

U.S. emergency management is largely decentralized, potentially involving public, private, and nongovernmental agencies. Nonetheless, there exists a federal framework for managing domestic incidents. Within this framework, the National Incident Management System (NIMS) is an all-hazards, national approach to incident management.[48] It is built on

- continuous preparedness,
- flexible communications and information systems,
- standardized resource management,
- incident management and coordination (built, in part, on the Incident Command System), and
- ongoing updating of NIMS concepts and principles.

All federal departments and agencies are required to adopt NIMS.[49] In addition, state, local, and tribal organizations must adopt NIMS in order to be eligible for federal preparedness grants.

One foundational question is what, if anything, does the federal government want to influence in the states via grant funding related to law enforcement? Should the federal government enhance interagency information sharing and coordination on procedures to evaluate and deal with shooting threats?[50] Should it increase law-enforcement-related grant funding to bolster school resource officer training or the number of metal detectors in academic settings? In this area, the Obama Administration's January 16, 2013 report, *Now Is the Time: The President's Plan to Protect Our Children and Our Communities by Reducing Gun Violence* (*The President's Plan*), included a commitment to using the Community Oriented Policing Services (COPS) program to incentivize police departments to hire more school resource officers. The plan also indicates that DOJ will develop a model—including best practices— for using school resource officers.[51]

Of course, such issues potentially involve a variety of specialists—not only police officials but also public health experts and educators, among others. Grants impacting preparedness may shape first responder training, and grants influencing response could affect the development of law enforcement protocols for responding to mass shootings. Some policy makers may wish to incentivize the establishment and training of tactical emergency medical services (EMS) teams to support law enforcement during instances of mass shootings or related events. These teams could provide medical threat assessments, deliver medical care, and promote law enforcement safety, among other things. Little research has evaluated the effectiveness of such tactical EMS teams in the civilian domain, and policy makers may wish to request additional research in this arena.[52] Congress may debate which elements of law enforcement prevention, preparedness, and response—if any—the federal government could try to influence in the states and localities.[53]

In addition to providing financial assistance and incentives for certain law enforcement activities, the federal government may provide assistance in the form of manpower. Policy makers may debate whether federal law enforcement has sufficient authority and resources to assist state and local entities—if requested and if appropriate—in preparing for and responding to mass shootings and related incidents. For example, *The President's Plan* calls for additional funding for the federal government to train law enforcement, school officials, and others to respond to scenarios involving shooters.

Prevention

While law enforcement's role in crime control traditionally has been viewed as largely *reactive*, there has been a trend toward enhancing *proactive* law enforcement efforts. Thus, in the past three decades, much of the policing world has incorporated investigative strategies bent on preventing crimes in addition to solving crimes that have already occurred.[54] However, the effectiveness of proactive law enforcement techniques in preventing public mass shootings is unclear. As modern policing has evolved, several prominent philosophies and techniques—including community policing and intelligence-led policing—have focused on law enforcement preventing rather than solely responding to crime.

Community Policing

As laid out by DOJ, "[c]ommunity policing is a philosophy that promotes organizational strategies, which support the systematic use of partnerships and problem-solving techniques, to proactively address the immediate conditions that give rise to public safety issues such as crime, social disorder, and fear of crime."[55] Community policing can employ a range of techniques to control crime, and these techniques can be tailored to the specific needs of individual communities. The federal government has incentivized community policing efforts through DOJ's COPS office.[56]

Research on community policing generally speaks to its impact on overall crime rates, and CRS has not identified any comprehensive research on how community policing may be used to specifically address mass shootings. Policy makers may question whether community policing efforts are useful in targeting a specific type of crime (mass shootings) in a specific setting (public places).

Intelligence-Led Policing

Based in part on community policing and problem solving efforts, intelligence-led policing initiatives, originally developed in Great Britain, have emerged throughout the nation.[59] After 9/11, intelligence operations were transformed at the federal level as well as at the state and local levels. More and more, intelligence-led policing is not a single methodology, but a framework that encompasses much of modern operational police activity.[60] Similar to community policing, intelligence-led policing relies upon information input (as the basis for intelligence analysis), two-way communications with the public, scientific data analysis (using the basic formula that information plus analysis equals intelligence), and problem solving.[61]

Intelligence-Led Policing and Fusion Centers

Gunmen involved in public mass shootings may not be targets easily preempted from wrongdoing by intelligence-led policing. However, there still may be roles that fusion centers[57] can play in countering this threat. (Such centers have been highlighted as tools to enhance intelligence-led policing.) Fusion centers may be able to help contextualize this issue. For instance, the Commonwealth Fusion Center based in Massachusetts launched the "Targeting Violent Crime Initiative," sponsored by DOJ, to examine firearms offenses in Massachusetts. This effort has focused on issues such as determining the source of firearms used in gun crimes in Massachusetts; understanding potential links between the illegal gun markets; and delving into gun crime trends throughout the state.[58] As such, policy makers may be interested in whether fusion centers have anything to offer in the way of intelligence-led policing to address mass shootings.

The impact of intelligence-led policing cannot yet be fully evaluated because "long term studies of police forces that have fully implemented and adopted intelligence-led policing have yet to be conducted."[62] Further, like research on community policing efforts, available information on intelligence-led policing does not address whether intelligence-led policing may be an effective approach to use in addressing mass shootings.

Using intelligence-led policing to thwart mass shooters may be especially challenging for a number of reasons.

- Mass shooters most often act alone and share few of their plans with others.[63] Typically, they do not engage in ongoing conspiracies that can be infiltrated by undercover police officers or monitored by informants.[64]

- There may be too few public mass shooting incidents to establish detailed geographic patterns (hot spots) for law enforcement to exploit.[65]

Offender Profiling for Public Mass Shootings: Not a Preventive Tool

Researchers and policy makers have questioned whether law enforcement can develop a profile of a mass shooter to help identify at-risk individuals before a shooting incident occurs. No effective mass shooter profile exists for law enforcement to use to proactively identify potential suspects. One researcher has succinctly noted that "the predictors [for mass murder] are invariably far more common than the event we hope to predict, and mass murder is very rare. Although mass murderers often do exhibit bizarre behavior, most people who exhibit bizarre behavior do not commit mass murder."[66] Aside from usually but not always being male, there are few other characteristics across mass murderers that would be reliable or valid for creating a general profile for individuals most likely to engage in a public mass shooting. This also holds true when examining individuals who carry out mass shootings in specific settings; for instance, "[t]here is no accurate or useful profile of 'the school shooter.'"[67]

Also of note, criminal profiling is generally utilized *after* a crime has been committed, and not usually as a preventive tool.[68] In the course of investigating serial crimes by a repeat offender such as a serial murderer, it could be utilized as a proactive tool to narrow the pool of potential offenders before a subsequent crime is committed. However, because mass shooters generally do not have the opportunity to commit a second crime—they are most typically either killed or captured after the mass shooting—investigative analysis would be most commonly employed after the mass shooting to understand how it happened rather than as a tool to identify potential shooters before an incident occurs.

All of this does not mean that preventing public mass shootings is wholly beyond the scope of federal law enforcement. For instance, to enhance law enforcement efforts in the violent crime domain, DHS, DOJ, and the FBI have been working to "identify measures that could be taken to reduce the risk of mass casualty shootings."[69]

Preparedness and Prevention Combined—Threat Assessments

Alternatively, what has come to be known as "threat assessment" may be more appropriately suited to prepare for the threat of potential shooters and to prevent them from harming others. Federal law enforcement has been involved in providing threat assessment approaches to frontline professionals, such as educators, who may encounter potential shooters. Threat assessments are used after a potentially harmful individual has come to the attention of authorities. The assessment process evaluates the threat he or she poses. Certainly, threat assessments may be used to prevent a mass shooting. Law enforcement efforts to train front-line professionals in the assessment process can be seen as an effort geared toward preparing these individuals to cope with threats.

The National Threat Assessment Center (NTAC), which is part of the U.S. Secret Service, provides research on threat assessment as well as on targeted violence.[70] The threat assessment approach used by the U.S. Secret Service was developed as part of its broader intelligence activities designed to protect the President and other officials. Nonetheless, it "can be applied with some modification to evaluating risk for other forms of targeted violence."[71] It does not rely upon "profiles" of potential malicious actors (as profiles have not proven to be reliable predictors for actual threat), nor does it depend on stated threats as a starting point for evaluating risk (because not every person who makes a threat poses a true risk, and not all persons who pose risks make threats).[72] Within this threat assessment framework, it has been suggested that information be collected relating to: (1) facts that bring the subject to the attention of authorities, (2) the subject of interest, (3) attack-related behaviors, (4) possible motives, and (5) potential targets.[73] Of note, law enforcement may not be the only authorities involved in evaluating information and conducting such a threat assessment, but the assessment framework may be one of several tools that law enforcement relies upon in an attempt to prevent targeted violence, including mass shootings. Policy makers may wonder whether threat assessment has proved to be a viable tool for law enforcement to use in preventing incidents of mass shootings. Further, they may question if the threat assessment framework could be modified to better serve law enforcement and other professionals who collaborate on efforts to prevent targeted violence.

If threat assessments can effectively identify potential mass shooters, policy makers may debate how law enforcement could use this information. One potential option could be to create a criminal watchlist, similar to the Terrorist Screening Database,[74] or terrorist watchlist, to be used in background checks for firearms, among other things.[75] Similar to questions regarding the threshold for placing a suspected individual on the terrorist watchlist, one of the relevant issues would involve establishing criteria for the addition of potential mass shooters to a violent criminal watchlist. There may also be questions about if or how law enforcement may engage with others such as mental health professionals and community leaders in decisions to place someone on such a watchlist. (For a discussion of how the federal government coordinates preparedness efforts for incidents involving mass casualties see "Preparedness" under the "Public Health Implications" section of this report).

As another means of preparing for mass shootings, some law enforcement agencies have participated in tailored trainings. DHS, for instance, sponsors preparedness courses for shootings as well as webinars, and workshops.[76] The California Highway Patrol has taken advantage of these opportunities and, between August 2012 and January 2013, "has led 18 active shooter trainings on campuses across Northern California."[77] In these two-day classes, officers participate in simulated scenarios; they are trained to respond to a reported incident, bring a shooter under control, and ensure the safety of building occupants.

Response

Federal Response to a Local Crime

From a law enforcement perspective, public mass shootings are often highly localized incidents involving lone gunmen acting near where they live. Thus, these cases largely do not involve conspiracies or the extensive crossing of jurisdictions. As such, mass shootings generally may be considered a local concern. Nonetheless, federal law enforcement—most notably the FBI—has historically provided assistance, when requested, to state and local law enforcement in the investigation of crimes that do not automatically fall under the jurisdiction of federal law enforcement.[78]

Some have expressed concerns that without official authority to respond to such incidents that fall primarily under a single state's jurisdiction, the federal response to these incidents could be slowed from questions of jurisdiction.[79] However, in practice, federal law enforcement has routinely assisted state and local law enforcement in a variety of capacities. The FBI's Office of Law Enforcement Coordination (OLEC), for one, is the liaison between the FBI and the greater law enforcement community. FBI assistance includes a variety of criminal justice information and research, background checks and security clearances, and disaster and hazardous material response teams. Of note, the 112th Congress passed legislation (P.L. 112-265) that formally authorizes the Attorney General to provide investigative assistance to states in instances of violent crimes in public venues, including attempted and actual mass killings. Some may question whether this authority will change federal law enforcement involvement in responding to and investigating instances of public mass shootings or whether it will simply formalize an already well-established practice.

Definitional Implications for Criminal Justice Process

As noted, the definition of a mass shooting is not always consistent across the scholarly, policy, and law enforcement realms. Within the law enforcement realm, a clear definition of mass shootings may be more critical during certain phases of the criminal justice process than others. Take, for instance, the question of who counts as a "victim" of a mass shooting. Is a victim

- Only someone who was killed at the scene of the crime?
- Someone who was shot and hospitalized in critical condition for an extended period of time?
- Someone who was caught in the cross-fire but not critically injured by bullets?
- Someone who died or was injured in attempting to escape the situation, but who did not die from a gunshot wound?

The individual circumstances involving victims are quite varied, but in certain steps of the criminal justice process, the need for a concrete definition may be more pressing.

The fact that law enforcement will respond to a public mass shooting may not depend on the ability to pinpoint the exact number of dead or injured victims. However, the details regarding victimization may more greatly impact how the incident is investigated and prosecuted after the conclusion of the mass shooting. Once an investigation begins, information about individuals considered "victims" may be of special interest to investigators and prosecutors. If the shooter survives the incident and is prosecuted, whether or not a victim dies as a result of the mass shooting will influence the charges brought against the shooter. These charges may include actual and attempted homicide, manslaughter, and assault, among others.[80] The charges can, in turn, influence the length of sentence a shooter may receive if convicted of the charges brought against him. A gunman's motives influence how police investigate shootings. A shooter's motives may also drive the charges ultimately brought against him, if he survives the incident. While some cases may be instances of relatively indiscriminate killing, others involve assailants driven by particular hatreds that lead to the targeting of specific groups and can be considered hate crimes and investigated and prosecuted accordingly. Still others can involve ideologically-motivated killing, leading to terrorism-related investigations and charges. In considering a shooter's motives and intentions, law enforcement may question whether it is the shooter's resolve to die along with his victims, either in an act of self-inflicted suicide or through "suicide-by-cop," what some have termed "suicide by mass murder."[81] When law enforcement officers respond to a report of a shooter, they are faced with multiple concerns in attempting to disarm and arrest the shooter. Will they have to use lethal force on the suspect? Will the suspect take his own life? Will the suspect try to prolong his life and his rampage through the use of body armor and other defensive tactics?

PUBLIC HEALTH IMPLICATIONS[82]

From a public health policy perspective, public mass shootings are mass casualty incidents (MCI) that cause both injury and death.[83] Although public mass shootings are infrequent, the health sector[84] has considerable related experience to bring to bear on preparing for and responding to these events.

The health sector addresses mass shootings as it does any other health threat, through (1) prevention, (2) preparedness, (3) response, and (4) recovery over the long term. Prevention focuses on the perpetrators of mass shooting. The other three components of the health sector approach concentrate on the victims of such incidents. Public health options to thwart mass shootings are likely limited. Of these four components, the effectiveness of preventive efforts may be most unclear. Fundamentally, this area likely lacks strong evidence regarding what might successfully stop potential shooters from becoming actual shooters. This evidence could come from evaluation of new or existing policies. Such efforts could help fill a gap in knowledge about what is effective. In terms of preparedness, response, and recovery, proven approaches exist. However, policy makers may wish to consider how existing capacities (or policies to increase capacity) vary across geographic areas and populations. Also, the ability to rapidly evaluate the effectiveness of existing programs and/or deploy resources may hinge on the flexibility of funding structures.

Prevention

Public health interventions are often based on research with large-scale datasets and rigorous information collection regimens.[85] The effectiveness of this approach may be limited largely because public mass shootings are rare, *potential* perpetrators cannot be identified accurately, and no systematic means of intervening are known to be effective. Regardless, a public health-oriented discussion of prevention of mass shootings should consider the field's traditional approach to stemming any cause of injury or death, highlighting some of the ways that this approach may or may not address public mass shootings.

Public health professionals address prevention of injury and death via a three-step process focused on understanding and stemming health-related problems:

- First, systematic collection of data (*surveillance*)[86] may help define the scope of the problem, identify an outbreak of the problem, and detect trends related to the problem.
- Second, research may identify characteristics associated with higher rates of injury or death attributed to the problem (called *risk factors* and *protective factors*,

respectively). Such research may be based on surveillance or other sources of information.

- Third, efforts to reduce risk factors and enhance protective factors may be developed to stem the problem. These are founded on research pursued in the previous step of this process. Called *preventive interventions* within the context of public health, such undertakings traditionally focus on victims. However, as mentioned above, in the case of public mass shootings, the focus of prevention is generally on the gunmen involved.[87]

Surveillance May Not Be Necessary to Identify Public Mass Shootings

Mass shootings are rare, high-profile events, rather than broad trends that require systematic data collection to understand. The public health system does not conduct surveillance specifically for public mass shootings as defined in this report. Some broader information about shootings is collected (e.g., from death certificates[88]); however, this information is largely about victims rather than assailants, limiting its usefulness for research into the prevention of mass shootings. For example, the Centers for Disease Control and Prevention's (CDC's) National Violent Death Reporting System (NVDRS) enables participating states to supplement death certificates with information from law enforcement agencies, crime laboratories, coroner or medical examiner reports, health providers, and other state and local agencies. The NVDRS is currently in operation in fewer than half the states.[89] *The President's Plan* proposes expanding the NVDRS to all 50 states at a cost of $20 million.[90]

Difficulty in Identifying Risk and Protective Factors

According to the parameters of this CRS analysis, the victims of public mass shootings are essentially random. Thus, health research into risk and protective factors tied to these incidents would likely focus on things that would either boost or lower the chances that one might become a gunman. One obstacle in identifying such factors is the relatively small data pool available for research (several dozen tragedies over the last thirty years in the United States).

Gun violence broadly, rather than public mass shootings, accounts for many more instances of death and injury per year and yields a far larger pot of observable information. This information may be used in research to identify risk and protective factors. Therefore, potential risk and protective factors may have more utility when public health professionals confront the much broader phenomenon of gun violence, not just public mass shootings. Consequently, potential risk factors such as mental illness, substance abuse, exposure to violence, and easy access to guns are all addressed to some extent in *The President's Plan,* which covers the wider issue of gun violence.[91] *The President's Plan* also responds to the suggestion by some that health research related to gun violence has been hampered by a statutory prohibition on the use of certain funding to "advocate or promote gun control."[92] *The President's Plan* states that research into gun violence is not advocacy,[93] and a Presidential Memorandum directs the Health and Human Services (HHS) Secretary to "conduct or sponsor research into the causes of gun violence."[94]

The Effectiveness of Preventive Interventions Is Unclear

Prevention of public mass shootings in a public health context would in theory involve interventions targeted at potential perpetrators, not potential victims. These interventions would be founded on well-tested risk and protective factors, which—as noted above—do not currently exist. If relatively unproven factors were to be used in the development of preventive interventions, this would likely yield many misidentifications. Because the number of public mass shootings in the United States may be too small to offer substantive analysis that could produce effective interventions, it may be most feasible to address gunmen involved in such incidents as a subset of violent offenders. Preventive interventions directed at potential violent offenders may target populations, at-risk subgroups, or high-risk individuals. These approaches may or may not prove effective within the broader context of gun violence, and what effect (if any) they would have on mass shootings is unclear as well. *The President's Plan* provides examples of each approach:

- Population-wide interventions include finalizing regulations for mental health parity in private health insurance and ensuring that Medicaid plans are in compliance with parity requirements.[95]
- Interventions targeting at-risk subgroups include a clarification that doctors are permitted to talk about gun safety with patients who have access to guns and efforts to make mental health and conflict resolution services available specifically for students who have been exposed to violence.[96]
- Interventions targeting high-risk individuals include a clarification that health professionals are permitted to report to law enforcement violent threats that patients may make.[97] Also, on January 15, 2013, the HHS Office of Civil Rights issued a letter to health care providers to clarify that federal health privacy laws do not prohibit them from disclosing "necessary information about a patient to law enforcement, family members of the patient, or other persons, when [they] believe the patient presents a serious danger to himself or other people."[98] Interventions focused on high-risk individuals can also involve training law enforcement officers to work with mental health professionals to intervene with students in crisis.

Preparedness

The federal government has supported coordinated mass casualty incident (MCI) preparedness efforts in large cities since 1997[99] and in all 50 states, territories, and the District of Columbia since 2002,[100] through federal grants and contracts to public health agencies. These agencies are required to develop plans to integrate responding entities—including federal, state, and local law enforcement; emergency medical services (EMS); private sector health care facilities; and others. These federal grants and contracts support the rapid establishment of interdisciplinary communications (e.g., emergency operations centers) and periodic exercises that bring key responders together to practice before an actual incident, among other things. Although these federal grants and contracts were established in response to concerns about terrorism, they may also help local agencies prepare for MCIs such as public mass shootings. Some are concerned about whether these programs are sufficiently dispersed to enable rural areas to prepare for an MCI.[101] Certain aspects of the health care delivery system, such as the capacity and proximity of critical facilities to a mass shooting, can affect survival from a public mass shooting. Three components of the health care delivery system contribute to MCI readiness: (1) emergency medical services (EMS), (2) hospital-based emergency departments (EDs), and (3) trauma care.

Emergency medical services (EMS) include 911 call centers, medical care that occurs at the scene of an emergency, the transportation of victims to hospitals, and any treatment that occurs on the way. EMS systems vary by locality—some are operated by municipal or county governments, others by fire departments, and still others by private for-profit companies. This may mean that response times, quality, availability, and preparedness vary by locality. Federal responsibility for EMS is shared across the Department of Transportation, DHS, and HHS,[102] which raises potential concerns about coordination and sustainability.[103] Also, an HHS grant program administered by the Health Resources and Services Administration (HRSA) supports an effort to ensure that emergency medical services are appropriate for children.[104]

Hospital-based emergency departments (ED) vary by locality, and not all hospitals have an ED. Rural areas in particular may have both fewer hospitals overall and fewer hospitals that offer emergency care. In both urban and rural areas, some EDs may not function optimally on a day-to-day basis, which would affect their ability to respond to an MCI. EDs may be overcrowded, may "board" patients when inpatient beds are unavailable, and may divert ambulances because they are operating at capacity.[105] The federal government supports EDs through a variety of mechanisms including hospital preparedness grants, interagency coordination, and training of emergency health providers.[106] Through the Medicare and Medicaid programs, the federal government provides payments to hospitals that deliver care to uninsured patients in hospital EDs.[107] These payments (called disproportionate share payments) are an important source of a financial support for EDs.

Trauma centers are specialized hospitals with the resources and equipment needed to treat severely injured patients.[108] They provide specialized care that is beyond the capability of the typical ED. Trauma centers are classified into four levels, with lower numbers (I, II) providing more specialized care. Trauma centers may play a role in responding to MCIs, but not all areas have the patient volume to support a trauma center. Distance to the nearest trauma center may be an issue in some MCIs. The federal government provides some funding for trauma centers through grants authorized under HHS, but not of all these programs have received funding.[109] In addition, the CDC is working to raise awareness of trauma centers and has produced research showing the importance of access to trauma care in surviving a severe injury.[110]

Response

The medical response to an MCI involves triage[111] and limited treatment of victims on-site, as well as the transfer of victims to appropriate health care facilities for definitive treatment. As described above, federal preparedness funding aims to ensure: (1) that the medical components of MCI response work as well as possible when needed, (2) that individual components are as capable as they can be in response, and (3) that medical responders can coordinate and communicate well with each other and with other response sectors such as law enforcement and public education. However, when an incident occurs, local authorities and health systems are largely on their own during the initial phases of a response. The federal government, through HHS (and, when needed, the Department of Defense), can support local efforts to respond to MCIs, making available mobile medical teams, mobile field hospitals, medical supply and pharmaceutical caches, and medical evacuation and transport.[112] In general, however, mass shootings resolve quickly, often before federal operational assistance can be delivered. In the event of a public mass shooting or other MCI, as with any emergency medical situation, delaying treatment while determining a patient's insurance status or ability to pay for health care services may prove fatal. The Emergency Medical Treatment and Active Labor Act (EMTALA) protects against such a delay.[113] EMTALA requires a hospital that receives Medicare payments (as the vast majority of hospitals do) to screen a patient for emergency medical conditions without regard for the patient's ability to pay. If the screening identifies an emergency medical condition, EMTALA requires the hospital to stabilize the patient. In instances where a patient's injuries are too severe to be treated at an ED, a patient may be sent to a trauma center. EMS or local EDs may determine whether a transfer to a trauma center is needed. Trauma centers are also subject to EMTALA (if the hospitals receive Medicare payments) and are required to accept transfers when an ED has determined that the trauma center possesses the specialized services that the patient needs but the ED lacks.

Recovery

Recovery of affected individuals and communities over the long term may require ongoing services to meet the physical and mental health care needs of both victims and responders. Ongoing services may involve inpatient and outpatient medical care; psychosocial interventions such as pastoral or peer counseling; and population-level interventions such as public announcements about common reactions to traumatic events (which can help normalize people's experiences and reduce anxiety around symptoms that are likely to be transient) or information about how to discuss an incident with children.[114] The availability of such services in a timely and accessible manner may also be important for reducing long-term consequences such as posttraumatic stress disorder.[115] Although federal resources generally focus on the immediate aftermath of an MCI, the federal government may fund public health interventions as well as programs that support the physician and behavioral health workforce and other infrastructure. The federal government also has a role in providing and financing health services that victims and responders may access.[116]

For an individual's long-term recovery from a public mass shooting, lack of insurance or inability to pay for health care services may limit the treatment options available (e.g., physical rehabilitation or counseling). Thus, financial support may play a key role in long-term recovery.[117]

Education Implications

Schools are unique institutions. They have a mission of great importance to our nation—they are responsible for keeping our children safe while educating them and helping prepare them to be responsible and productive citizens. All levels of government are involved to some extent in this mission.[118] As mentioned earlier in this report, twelve of the 78 public mass shootings identified by CRS occurred in academic settings. Eight of these happened at primary or secondary education facilities. One incident, the December 14, 2012, shooting deaths of 20 children and 6 adults[119] at Sandy Hook Elementary School in Newtown, CT, has heightened congressional interest in school security.[120] Policy makers are examining whether school security can be further enhanced, and if so, how best to accomplish that goal.[121]

Four of the 12 public mass shootings in education settings involved high school or middle school students as assailants.[122] The federal government has supported efforts to preempt students from engaging in gun violence at school. More broadly, it has promoted policies to curb violence in schools, such as anti-bullying programs, which may or may not stem public mass shootings by student perpetrators. This section of the report focuses on those federal programs and initiatives administered by the Department of Education that may be relevant in the event of a public mass shooting in a school setting.

The President's Plan was released following the Newtown tragedy—it includes several provisions specifically related to schools.[123] However, funding for these provisions may not be sufficient to provide meaningful assistance to all schools that could potentially benefit. Difficult decisions confront policy makers. They must consider how to make the greatest possible improvements in student safety while likely being faced with limited federal resources to devote to safety initiatives. Policy makers may have to decide whether funds should be spread across many activities so that each activity gets some additional funding, or whether funding should be concentrated in fewer programs believed to be most cost effective. This decision is made even more difficult because research on effectiveness is limited for many school security programs. This may lead to consideration of whether more funding should be provided for research into program effectiveness, and if so, whether it would restrict funding for existing school security programs. Policy makers must also consider the importance of continuity of funds for local program success. It can be difficult for local school districts to plan, develop and implement programs if they cannot be certain of a reliable funding stream. In recent years much of the dedicated funding for school safety programs provided by the Department of Education has been cut.[124] Some programs were cut because they were perceived as too small to make a difference. Others were cut because they failed to demonstrate their effectiveness. For example, funding for the Safe and Drug Free Schools and Communities Act (SDFSCA) program, the federal government's primary program aimed at preventing drug abuse and violence in and around public schools, has declined from $435 million in FY2009 to $65 million in FY2012.[125]

Department of Education guidance has divided the crisis management process for schools into four phases. Those four phases, in sequential order are: prevention, preparedness, response, and recovery.[126] Because emergency planning at institutions of higher education occurs in a significantly different environment and context, this report focuses on emergency planning at the elementary and secondary school level.[127]

Prevention

Prevention (and mitigation) involves broadly structured efforts to help schools reduce the need to respond to crises including mass shootings. This stage of crisis management is critical for educators. If students do not feel safe at school, they will not be able to focus their energy on the most important task before them—learning. According to the Department of Education, this first stage of crisis management should include the following activities:

- connecting with community responders to identify potential hazards,
- reviewing the most recent school safety audit,
- determining who is responsible for overseeing violence prevention at the school,
- soliciting staff input on the crisis plan,
- reviewing school incident data,
- determining major crime and violence problems at the school and assessing how effectively they are currently being addressed, and
- conducting an assessment to determine how existing threats may impact the school's vulnerability to particular crises.[128]

School Climate

Improving school climate is one strategy for mitigating and preventing a variety of crises, including mass shootings (if the perpetrators involved in these incidents are students). A CDC report states that a positive school climate is "characterized by caring and supportive interpersonal relationships; opportunities to participate in school activities and decision-making; and shared positive norms, goals, and values."[129] Research has indicated that one of the most important elements in a positive school climate is for students to have a feeling of school connectedness. School connectedness is defined as "the belief by students that adults and peers in the school care about their learning as well as about them as individuals."[130]

The Department of Education's Office of Special Education Programs funds a Technical Assistance Center on Positive Behavioral Interventions and Supports. The Center provides capacity-building information and technical assistance to schools, districts, and states who are implementing a school climate protocol called *School-wide Positive Behavioral Interventions and Supports* (SWPBIS). SWPBIS is a three-tiered prevention-based approach to improving school-wide disciplinary practices. According to the Center, SWPBIS is used in more than 9,000 schools across 40 states.[131] SWPBIS has been linked to reductions in student suspensions and office discipline referrals.[132]

Bullying prevention is also an important aspect of improving school climate. The Federal government recognizes the importance of this issue and has become increasingly involved in bullying prevention initiatives in recent years.[133]

Research indicates that both victims of bullying and those who engage in bullying behavior can experience both short and long-term effects resulting in psychological difficulties and social relationship problems. A GAO literature review of seven meta-analyses on the impact of bullying on victims found that bullying could result in psychological, physical, academic, and behavioral issues.[134] In addition, a Secret Service study on school safety and school attacks found that "Many attackers felt bullied, persecuted or injured by others prior to the attack."[135]

School Resource Officers

The SDFSCA defines school resource officers as career law enforcement officers assigned by a local law enforcement agency to work with schools and community based organizations to:

> (A) educate students in crime and illegal drug use prevention and safety; (B) develop or expand community justice initiatives for students; and (C) train students in conflict resolution, restorative justice, and crime and illegal drug use awareness.[136]

The President's Plan would provide an incentive for DOJ's Community Oriented Policing Services (COPS) grants to be used to hire more school resource officers in the current year,[137] and would seek $150 million in funding for a new Comprehensive Safety Grants program. This new grant program would provide school districts and law enforcement agencies with funding to hire new school resource officers and school psychologists. This new funding stream could also be used to purchase school safety equipment, develop or expand school safety proposals, and to train crisis intervention teams of law enforcement officers to respond and assist students in a crisis.

School resource officers are popular with the public. A recent Pew research study found that 64% of those surveyed supported having armed security guards or police in more schools.[138] However, some researchers and civil rights organizations have expressed concern about increasing the presence of school resource officers in schools, arguing that the presence of law enforcement can have a negative impact on the learning environment, and may lead to more school suspensions and referrals to the juvenile justice system.[139] On December 12, 2012, the Senate Judiciary Subcommittee on the Constitution, Civil Rights and Human Rights, held a hearing titled "Ending the School-to-Prison Pipeline." In his opening statement Chairman Richard Durbin stated that:

> For many young people, our schools are increasingly a gateway to the criminal justice system. This phenomenon is a consequence of a culture of zero tolerance that is widespread in our schools and is depriving many children of their fundamental right to an education.[140]

Preparedness and Emergency Planning

Preparedness involves marshaling the necessary resources to ensure that they are available in the event of a crisis, including shooting incidents. This involves

- confirming that the school's current emergency plan is consistent with the National Incident Management System,
- acquiring the necessary equipment and first aid resources to address a potential crisis,
- establishing procedures to account for the location of all students,
- developing procedures to communicate with staff, families and the media,
- ensuring all school staff are familiar with the school's layout, safety features, utility shutoffs, etc., and
- conducting practice drills for students and staff.[141]

One of the proposals included in *The President's Plan* would provide $30 million in one-time grants to school districts to help them develop and implement Emergency Management plans. In addition, a current SDFSCA program—Readiness and Emergency Management for schools (REMS) provides competitive grants to LEAs to strengthen and improve their emergency response and crisis plans. No grants were awarded in FY2012.[142]

The Department of Education has developed resources and training materials that are available online to help schools develop emergency plans and respond to crises.[143] However, these resources are not limited to addressing a school shooting crisis; they are intended to be applicable to a range of potential crises that could impact a school (e.g., natural disaster, pandemics, terrorism).

Indicators of School Crime and Safety data show that many schools have been increasing measures intended to improve school safety. In school year 1999-2000, 54.1% of surveyed students (ages 12-18) reported that their school had security guards and/or assigned police officers; this percentage had increased to 68.1% by school year 2009-2010. Other school security measures that have increased between school year 1999-2000 and school year 2009-2010 include the use of security cameras (from 19.4% to 61.1%); locking or monitoring doors (from 74.6% to 91.7%); and requiring faculty and staff to wear badges or IDs (from 25.4% to 62.9%).[144] *The President's Plan* would set up an interagency group to release a model set of emergency management plans for schools, houses of worship, and institutions of higher education. It would also require the Department of Education to collect and disseminate best practices for addressing school discipline.

Maintaining crisis response capacity is required of schools by 92% of states.[145] Press accounts of school shootings have provided anecdotal evidence indicating that school emergency planning (lock-down procedures and practice drills, etc.) may have minimized deaths and injuries in incidents of mass shootings. However, federal legislation does not regulate the content or quality of these plans, and the comprehensiveness and implementation of these plans vary considerably across school districts.

Response

An organized and coordinated response to a crisis is based in large part on the prevention and preparedness activities that schools have adopted and implemented. According to the Department of Education, during a crisis (which can include mass shootings), schools should undertake the following activities:

- identifying the type of crisis that is occurring,
- activating the incident management system,
- identifying the appropriate response to the crisis (e.g., evacuation, shelter in place, lockdown, etc.),
- implementing the plans and procedures established in the preparation phase,
- ensuring that important information is being communicated to staff, students and parents, and
- ensuring that emergency first aid is being provided to the injured.[146]

Many school shootings last only minutes—as a consequence, teachers and school staff become the immediate responders out of necessity in many crises, sometimes heroically sacrificing their own lives to protect the children in their care. Community first responders, including law enforcement and emergency medical personnel, are also key to ending a crisis as quickly as possible. Among their many tasks, they must immediately subdue the shooter, if he is still alive; and they most coordinate all the emergency services that are required by survivors of the shooting.

Recovery

Recovery efforts are focused on returning students to the learning environment as soon as possible. These efforts include

- restoring school facilities,
- identifying the supports and services needed by students, staff, and families to help them recover from the crisis,
- connecting individuals to services, including mental health and counseling services, and
- allowing sufficient time for recovery and deciding how to commemorate the event.[147]

The primary Department of Education program available to schools to assist recovery efforts following a crisis is Project SERV (School Emergency Response to Violence). This program provides education-related services to schools that have been disrupted by a violent or traumatic crisis. Local educational agencies and institutions of higher education (IHEs) are eligible to apply for these grants.[148] Project SERV funds may be used for a wide variety of activities, including mental health assessments, referrals, and services for victims and witnesses of violence; enhanced school security; technical assistance in developing a response to the crisis; and training for teachers and staff in implementing the response.[149]

School counselors can also play an important role in facilitating a school community's recovery following a crisis. School counselors can provide an avenue for students to be heard by a caring adult, and can provide needed services or make referrals for services to community providers.[150]

The President's Plan includes several provisions that would increase student access to mental health services. It seeks $150 million in funding for a new *Comprehensive Safety Grants* program. One of the authorized uses of this program would be to hire school counselors. In addition, the proposal seeks $50 million to train 5,000 additional mental health professionals to serve youth in schools and communities, and $25 million to provide mental health services for trauma, conflict resolution, and other school-based violence prevention strategies. The proposal would also provide $55 million for a new Project AWARE which would train teachers and other adults to recognize and help youth with mental illness and work with a variety of community agencies and organizations to ensure youth who need help are connected to service providers.

CONCLUSION

When addressing public mass shootings, many of the policymaking challenges may boil down to two interrelated concerns: (1) a need to determine the effectiveness of existing programs— particularly preventive efforts—and (2) figuring out where to disburse limited resources.

The law enforcement and public health fields have lengthy histories of applying preventive approaches to their work. However, the utility of widely employed preventive measures in these areas to fight public mass shootings is far from clear. For example, it appears that intelligence-led policing fails to address this threat. Likewise, preventive public health approaches reliant on research drawn from large data sets, covering broad populations, and examining general trends may not adequately address relatively rare—though devastating—public mass shootings. Given this, policy makers may be interested in supporting the development of useful preventive schemes in the law enforcement and public health arenas.

In the area of education, preventive efforts may be more effective. Fostering a positive school climate can be seen as a key element in preventing shootings. Additionally, the use of school resource officers as a preventive measure is popular among Americans. Yet, there are those who question the impact of such officers on the learning environment.

Policy makers confront the task of disbursing resources among a wide assortment of programs to tackle public mass shootings. Which efforts are more important than others? For example, should prevention trump response in most cases? Should programs that have multiple uses be favored over others that may be seen as more focused (or vice versa)? For example, which should receive more support related to dealing with mass shootings: EMS or efforts to cultivate positive school climate? Which untested programs or approaches should be evaluated thoroughly? Who should evaluate them? How long should funding exist to tackle the threat of mass shootings?

All of this hints at an overarching difficulty confronting experts interested in crafting policy to address mass shootings. Essentially, baseline metrics gauging the effectiveness of policies to thwart public mass shootings are often unclear or unavailable. This lack of clarity starts with identifying the number of shootings, themselves, since no broadly agreed-to definition exists. Several questions flow from this issue. How many people have such incidents victimized? How much does prevention of, preparedness for, and response to such incidents cost the federal government? What measurements can be used to determine the effectiveness of such efforts? In other words, and most importantly, how will we measure our successes or determine our failures in fighting this problem?

End Notes

[1] The White House, *Now Is the Time: The President's Plan to Protect Our Children and Our Communities by Reducing Gun Violence*, January 16, 2013, http://www.whitehouse.gov /sites/default/files/docs/wh_now_is_ the_time_full.pdf. Hereafter: *The President's Plan.*

[2] For more information on this report's approach regarding the concept of "public mass shooting," please see the section titled "Defining and Identifying Public Mass Shootings."

[3] Incidentally, these deaths stemmed from two shooting incidents in which the gunmen were likely motivated by ideology tied to Al Qaeda. For more information, please see CRS Report R41416, *American Jihadist Terrorism: Combating a Complex Threat*, by Jerome P. Bjelopera.

[4] This count does not include shooters killed in these incidents.

[5] For this report, murder implies the willful killing of one human being by another.

[6] Federal Bureau of Investigation, *Uniform Crime Reports, Crime in the United States, 2011,* Table 8, "Expanded Homicide Data," http://www.fbi.gov/about-us/cjis/ucr/crime-in-the-u.s/2011/crime-in-the-u.s.-2011/tables

/expandedhomicide-data-table-8. The Federal Bureau of Investigation (FBI, the Bureau) counts what it describes as "murder and nonnegligent manslaughter" for these statistics. Preliminary figures for 2012 suggest "an increase of 1.9 percent in the number of violent crimes ... for the first 6 months of 2012 when compared with figures reported for the same time in 2011." See Federal Bureau of Investigation, *Uniform Crime Reports, Crime in the United States, 2012, January-June Preliminary Semiannual Uniform Crime Report,* http://www.fbi.gov/about-us/cjis/ucr/crime-in-theu.s/2012/preliminary-semiannual-uniform-crime-report-january-june-2012. It is unknown, however, whether this preliminary reported increase in violent crimes was coupled with an increase in firearm-related homicides.

[7] Federal Bureau of Investigation, *Uniform Crime Reports, Crime in the United States, 2011,* Table 1, "Crime in the United States by Volume and Rate per 100,000 Inhabitants, 1992–2011," http://www.fbi.gov/about-us/cjis/ucr/crimein-the-u.s/2011/crime-in-the-u.s.-2011/ tables/table-1.

[8] According to the FBI these figures include "murder and nonnegligent manslaughter." See ibid.

[9] For more information on this see CRS Report RL32842, *Gun Control Legislation*, by William J. Krouse.

[10] Some policies and programs discussed in this report may also help *mitigate* the impact of actual shootings. For example, while the presence of school resource officers may help prevent a school shooting, such an officer could feasibly mitigate the impact of a shooting by intervening after a gunman began his assault.

[11] To some degree these concepts—prevention, preparedness, response, and recovery—correspond with ideas that guide federal emergency management. In this report, these concepts are used only to help describe issues involved in devising policy related to public mass shootings. For more on federal emergency management, see CRS Report R42845, *Federal Emergency Management: A Brief Introduction*, coordinated by Bruce R. Lindsay.

[12] James Alan Fox and Jack Levin, *Extreme Killing: Understanding Serial and Mass Murder*, 2nd ed. (Los Angeles: Sage, 2012), p. 19. Hereafter: Fox and Levin, *Extreme Killing*. James L. Knoll, IV, "The 'Pseudocommando' Mass Murderer: Part I, The Psychology of Revenge and Obliteration," *Journal of the American Academy of Psychiatry and the Law,* vol. 38, no. 1 (2010) pp. 87-89; Federal Bureau of Investigation, *Serial Murder: Multi-Disciplinary Perspectives for Investigators*, 2008, p. 8; John E. Douglas, Ann W. Burgess, and Robert K. Ressler, *Crime Classification Manual: A Standard System for Investigating and Classifying Violent Crimes,* 2nd ed. (San Francisco: Jossey-Bass, 2006) p. 96; Grant Duwe, "A Circle of Distortion: The Social Construction of Mass Murder in the United States," *Western Criminology Review,* vol. 6, no. 1 (2005) p. 59. Paul E. Mullen, "The Autogenic (Self-Generated) Massacre," *Behavioral Sciences and the Law,* vol. 22, no. 3 (2004) pp. 311-314. Hereafter: Mullen, "The Autogenic." Grant Duwe, Tomislav Kovandzic, and Carlisle E. Moody, "The Impact of Right-to-Carry Concealed Firearm Laws on Mass Public Shootings," *Homicide Studies,* vol. 6, no. 4 (2002) p. 273; Michael D. Kelleher, *Flash Point: The American Mass Murderer,* (Westport, CT: Praeger, 1997) p. 2. Hereafter: Kelleher, *Flash Point.*

[13] This report only includes incidents that occurred in the 50 states, Puerto Rico, and the District of Columbia.

[14] For a general discussion of violence in the workplace, see Federal Bureau of Investigation, *Workplace Violence: Issues in Response,* (2004). Hereafter: Federal Bureau of Investigation, *Workplace Violence.*

[15] The FBI has defined mass murder as "[a] number of murders (four or more) occurring during the same incident, with no distinctive time period between the murders. These events typically involved a single location, where the killer murdered a number of victims in an ongoing incident." This report allows for instances of mass murder to involve more than one specific location. For the FBI definition, see Federal Bureau of Investigation, *Serial Murder,* p. 8. For a different definition, see Fox and Levin, *Extreme Killing,* p. 19. While this report focuses a great deal on the timing involved in serial and mass murder to differentiate the two categories, Fox and Levin emphasize motivation. The 112th Congress passed legislation (P.L. 112-265) that formally authorizes the Attorney General to provide investigative assistance to states in instances of violent crimes in public venues, including attempted and actual mass killings. For the purposes of P.L. 112-265, the term "mass killings" means three or more killings in a single incident and relies on the definition of "place of public use" from 18 U.S.C. 2332f(e)(6).

[16] One expert has written: "A common definition of mass murder requires the intentional death of at least four individuals in a single incident. Another interpretation of the term reduces the number of slain victims to three for the crime to be considered mass murder. Both of these definitions are obviously arbitrary and focus exclusively on the number of victims killed." Kelleher, *Flash Point,* p. 2.

[17] Ibid.

[18] See Fox and Levin, *Extreme Killing,* pp. 23-25 for a discussion.

[19] For more on terrorism-related incidents in the United States see CRS Report R41416, *American Jihadist Terrorism: Combating a Complex Threat*, by Jerome P. Bjelopera and CRS Report R42536, *The Domestic Terrorist Threat: Background and Issues for Congress*, by Jerome P. Bjelopera.

[20] Brian Ballou et al., "Dwayne Moore Convicted of Four Counts of First-Degree Murder in Mattapan Slaying Trial," *Boston Globe,* December 17, 2012, http://www.boston.com /metrodesk/2012/12/17/dwayne-moore-found-guiltymattapan-massacre/ETijeAnjXDGR98 symtVy1K/story.html.

[21] John Diedrich et al., "FBI: Seeking Second 'Person of Interest' in Oak Creek Sikh Temple Shooting," *Milwaukee Journal Sentinel*, August 6, 2012, http://www.jsonline.com/news /crime/shooter-wade-page-was-army-vet-whitesupremacist-856cn28-165123946.html. Dinesh Ramde and Todd Richmond, "Motive Sought for Mass Shooting at Wis. Sikh Temple," *Associated Press,* August 6, 2012, http://news.yahoo.com/motive-sought-6-slain-wis-sikh-temple083039570.html. A Sikh temple is also called a gurdwara.

[22] William Branigin and Michael Laris, "Wade Michael Page Committed Suicide, FBI Says," *Washington Post,* August 8, 2012, http://www.washingtonpost.com/politics/wade-michael-pages-ex-girlfriend-arrested/2012/08 /08/00c99f72-e10a-11e1-a19c-fcfa365396c8_story. html.

[23] See U.S. Congress, Senate Committee on Homeland Security and Governmental Affairs, *A Ticking Time Bomb: Counterterrorism Lessons from the U.S. Government's Failure to Prevent the Fort Hood Attack*, 112th Cong., 1st sess., February 2011, p. 53, http://hsgac.senate.gov/public/_files/Fort_Hood/FortHoodReport.pdf. "Fort Hood Shooting Suspect to Remain Confined," *Associated Press State and Local Wire,* in *msnbc.com,* November 21, 2009, http://www.msnbc.msn.com/id/34084622; "Fort Hood Shooting Suspect Out of Intensive Care," *CNN.com,* December16, 2009, http://www.cnn.com /2009/CRIME/12/16/texas.fort. hood.hasan /index.html?iref=allsearch.

[24] Connecticut Office of Legislative Research, "Weapons Used in Mass Shootings," January 18, 2013, http://www.cga.ct.gov/2013/rpt/2013-R-0057.htm; Counterterrorism Bureau of the New York City Police Department, "Active Shooter: Recommendations and Analysis for Risk Mitigation," 2012 edition, http://www.nyc.gov/html/nypd/ downloads/pdf /counterterrorism/ActiveShooter2012Edition.pdf; James Alan Fox and Jack Levin, "Table 19.1: Deadliest Mass Murders in the United States Since 1900," in *Extreme Killing,* p. 230; Citizens Crime Commission of New York City, "Mass Shooting Incidents in America (1984-2012)," http://www.nycrimecommission.org/initiative1- shootings.php; Brady Campaign to Prevent Gun Violence, "Mass Shootings in the United States Since 2005," December, 14, 2012, http://www.brady campaign.org/xshare/pdf/major-shootings.pdf; Mark Follman, Gavin Aronsen, and Deanna Pan, "US Mass Shootings, 1982-2012: Data from Mother Jones' Investigation," *Mother Jones*, December 28, 2012, http://www.motherjones. com/politics/2012/12/mass-shootings-mother-jones-full-data. Mayors Against Illegal Guns, "Mass Shootings Since January 20, 2009," http://libcloud.s3.amazonaws.com /9/f8/9 /1098/1/ mass_shootings_2009-13_-_jan_29_12pm.pdf; Michael Kelleher, "Chapter 11: A Survey of Mass Murderers" in *Flash Point,* pp. 173-181. Searches of U.S. newspapers and wire services using LexisNexis were conducted in many instances in order to confirm information or gather more details about incidents listed in the sources consulted.

[25] While other sources and methods (relying on the FBI's Supplementary Homicide Reports, for example) can be applied in defining this issue and counting the number of incidents, the approach used for this report was selected based on a careful evaluation of this report's objectives and CRS resources. Our definition encompasses a count of fatalities along with information about motivation for a shooting and where it occurs spatially. While it would be possible to use FBI data to generate counts of incidents involving the requisite number of fatalities for inclusion in an estimate of mass shootings, the additional research needed to assess the motivational and spatial criteria that must be met for inclusion would require a very large undertaking. We expect our estimates provide a good approximation of the frequency and scale of mass shootings, but note that more comprehensive approaches could be taken to improve the precision of the estimates.

[26] Richard Goldstein, "Howard Unruh, 88, Dies; Killed 13 of His Neighbors in Camden 1949," *New York Times,* October 29, 2009. Unruh, who reportedly suffered from paranoid schizophrenia, never stood trial for the murders. He died after being confined for six decades in the Trenton Psychiatric Hospital. In 1950, reporter Meyer Berger received a Pulitzer Prize for his coverage of Unruh's mass shooting.

[27] Ibid. See also "N.J. Vet Killed 13 in 1949 in Biggest U.S. Mass Murder," *Boston Globe,* April 16, 1953. Meyer Berger, "Veteran Kills 12 in mad Rampage on Camden Street," *New York Times,* September 8, 1949.

[28] J. Reid Meloy, et. al., "A Comparative Analysis of North American Adolescent and Adult Mass Murderers," Behavioral Sciences and the Law, vol. 22, no. 3 (2004) p. 307.

[29] Not including shooters who died in the course of a shooting.

[30] There is no universally agreed to or legally codified number of victims per incident that distinguishes multiple murder from other types of murder.

[31] "Qualitatively broader" is intended to suggest that there are qualitative factors surrounding incidents of multiple murder that help to distinguish them from single, double, or triple murders. This conceptualization of multiple murder does not necessarily require multiple murders to include four or more deaths. Characterizing multiple murders involves examining some of the circumstances surrounding a killer's actions.

[32] The FBI has offered what can be seen as a broad definition of serial murder: "The unlawful killing of two or more victims by the same offender(s), in separate events." The Bureau also dismisses the key distinction between serial and spree killing. Spree killing can be defined as: "two or more murders committed by an offender or offenders, without a cooling-off period." The lack of a "cooling off period" theoretically distinguishes spree killing from serial murder. However, a majority of experts convened by the FBI in 2005 to discuss serial killing determined that the concept of a cooling off period was too vague to be useful, thus minimizing spree killing as a distinct type of murder. For this report, crimes that some may consider spree killings also can fall under the category of "public mass shooting," if the shootings occur during one day or less. See Federal Bureau of Investigation, *Serial Murder: Multi-Disciplinary Perspectives for Investigators*, 2008, p. 9. Hereafter: Federal Bureau of Investigation, *Serial Murder.* Serial killing is defined in federal law as: "a series of three or more killings, not less than one of which was committed within the United States, having common characteristics such as to suggest the reasonable possibility that the crimes were committed by the same actor or actors." See 28 U.S.C. § 540B.

[33] For a discussion of the variety of mass killings see Mullen, "The Autogenic" p. 313.

[34] Not all of the incidents CRS identified took place exclusively at one location. The numbers given here reflect incidents that occurred in part or in full at the type of location described.

[35] Brian MacQuarrie and Rick Klein, "Slaughter at the Office: Man Held in Deaths of 7 Colleagues in Wakefield," *Boston Globe*, December 27, 2000.

[36] Cindy Stauffer et al., "Horror in Schoolhouse: 5 Amish Girls Killed, 5 Critically Wounded in Shocking Massacre," *Lancaster New Era*, October 3, 2006.

[37] Paul Nowell, "Four Killed, Five Injured in Shooting Spree," Associated Press, July 18, 1988.

[38] Shaila Dewan, "Gunman Kills 10 in Alabama, Then Takes His Life," *New York Times*, March 10, 2009.

[39] In this instance, "workable" is intended to convey a profile with the discerning ability to proactively identify individuals planning to engage in a shooting. In the case of school shootings, the FBI has stated that, an effective profile or checklist that can predict who will become an assailant does not exist. See Mary Ellen O'Toole, *The School Shooter: A Threat Assessment Perspective,* (Federal Bureau of Investigation, 2000) p. 1. See also Federal Bureau of Investigation, *Workplace Violence,* pp. 21, 25, 26; Mullen, "The Autogenic," p. 322; Robert A. Fein et al., *Threat Assessment in Schools: A Guide to Managing Threatening Situations and to Creating Safe School Climates*, (Secret Service, Department of Education, May 2002) p. 17.

[40] Jeff Coen, Eric Ferkenhoff, and Flynn McRoberts, "Brown's Suspects Charged: 'They Are People without a Soul,' Police Chief Says," *Chicago Tribune*, May 19, 2002.

[41] John Kifner et al., "From Wild Talk and Friendship to Five Deaths in a Schoolyard," *New York Times*, March 29, 1998.

[42] Patricia Callahan, "Dream Turns to Nightmare," *Denver Post*, April 22, 1999, p. A1.

[43] While a range of demographic information on the perpetrators (including shooter gender and age) was noted in multiple sources reviewed by CRS, perpetrator race was often noted by just a single source, if at all. As such, CRS is not confident in presenting more nuanced data on the race of the shooters involved in public mass shootings identified for this report.

[44] Steve Chawkins and Jill Leovy, "7 Victims of Goleta Rampage," *Los Angeles Times,* February 2, 2006.

[45] Whether these gunmen intended to die at the hands of law enforcement (an act commonly described as "suicide by cop") is unclear. For more on this issue see Anthony J. Pinizzotto, Edward F. Davis, and Charles E. Miller III, "Suicide by Cop" *FBI Law Enforcement Bulletin,* vol. 74, no. 2 (February 2005), pp. 8-20.

[46] The State Homeland Security Program (part of the Homeland Security Grant Program) "supports the implementation of state Homeland Security Strategies to address the identified planning, organization, equipment, training, and exercise needs to prevent, protect against, mitigate, respond to, and recover from acts of terrorism and other catastrophic events." See http://www.fema.gov/fy-2012-homeland-security-grant-program#0.

[47] A number of existing grant programs may be used as vehicles to incentivize state and local law enforcement. For more information on the history and purpose areas of the Edward Byrne Memorial Justice Assistance Grant (JAG) Program, see CRS Report RS22416, *Edward Byrne Memorial Justice Assistance Grant (JAG)*

Program, by Nathan James. For information on the Community Oriented Policing Services (COPS) program, see CRS Report RL33308, *Community Oriented Policing Services (COPS): Background and Funding*, by Nathan James. For information on the various juvenile justice grant programs, see CRS Report RL33947, *Juvenile Justice: Legislative History and Current Legislative Issues*, by Kristin M. Finklea.

[48] NIMS enables relevant entities to "prevent, protect against, respond to, recover from, and mitigate the effects of incidents, regardless of cause, size, location, or complexity, in order to reduce the loss of life and property and harm to the environment." It is a flexible system, adaptable to the spectrum of potential incidents, and one that provides standardized framework to foster coordination and cohesion between relevant agencies. Federal Emergency Management Agency, "National Incident Management System," December 2008, http://www.fema.gov/pdf/ emergency/nims/NIMS_brochure.pdf. NIMS is administered by the Department of Homeland Security (DHS), and through the National Integration Center, the Secretary of DHS "publishes the standards, guidelines, and compliance protocols for determining whether a Federal, State, tribal, or local government has implemented NIMS." See Federal Emergency Management Agency, "About National Incident Management System," July 20, 2012, http://www.fema.gov/about-national-incident-management-system.

[49] This is required by Homeland Security Presidential Directive 5 (HSPD-5), issued by former President George W. Bush on February 28, 2003.

[50] Many such questions involve law enforcement as well as other experts with key roles to play in this area. As a case in point, policy makers may debate whether the federal government should encourage states to provide preventative mental health services to individuals at risk of committing violent crimes. Determining who could benefit from such services potentially involves police officers as well as medical professionals and teachers. Several juvenile justice grant programs have purpose areas that could be used to provide mental health services to at-risk youth. Congress may also consider incentivizing law enforcement training that includes a focus on mental health offender issues. The JAG program, for one, provides grant money for a variety of purpose areas, including law enforcement training broadly. Within programs such as this, funds could be utilized for specialized training.

[51] See *The President's Plan*. While resource officers may be described as a preventive law enforcement measure, this report covers them as part of prevention efforts in the realm of education. See the discussion under the heading "School Resource Officers" in this report.

[52] See Nelson Tang and Gabor D. Kelen, "Invited Commentary: Role of Tactical EMS in Support of Public Safety and the Public Health Response to a Hostile Mass Casualty Incident," *Disaster Medicine and Public Health Preparedness*, vol. 1, suppl. 1, (2007), pp. s55-s56. See Michael J. Feldman, Brian Schwartz, and Laurie J. Morrison, "Effectiveness of Tactical Emergency Medical Support: A Systematic Review," June 6, 2006.

[53] Beyond guiding or shaping local policing, federal grant programs can also reinforce existing state and local practices or subsidize actions that state and local governments had planned to pursue on their own, among other things.

[54] These investigative strategies include community policing, problem-oriented policing, intelligence-led policing, and predictive policing. See Lois M. Davis et al., *Long-Term Effects of Law Enforcement's Post-9/11 Focus on Counterterrorism and Homeland Security*, RAND, 2010, pp. 2-4, http://www.rand.org/pubs /monographs /2010/ RAND_ MG1031.pdf.

[55] Department of Justice, *Community Policing Defined*, http://www.cops.usdoj.gov/default. asp?item=36. See also Bureau of Justice Assistance, "Understanding Community Policing: A Framework for Action," August 1994, https://www.ncjrs.gov/pdffiles/commp.pdf.

[56] For more information on the Community Oriented Policing Services (COPS) program within DOJ, see CRS Report R40709, *Community Oriented Policing Services (COPS): Current Legislative Issues*, by Nathan James and CRS Report RL33308, *Community Oriented Policing Services (COPS): Background and Funding*, by Nathan James.

[57] Fusion centers are a "collaborative effort of two or more Federal, state, local, or tribal government agencies that combines resources, expertise, or information with the goal of maximizing the ability of such agencies to detect, prevent, investigate, apprehend, and respond to criminal or terrorist activity." See P.L. 110-53, Aug. 3, 2007, §511, 121 STAT. 322. Amends Homeland Security Act of 2002 by adding §210A(j).

[58] David Lambert, Federal Bureau of Investigation, "Intelligence-Led Policing in a Fusion Center," *FBI Law Enforcement Bulletin*, vol. 79, no. 12 (December 2010), pp. 1-6.

[59] Bureau of Justice Assistance, "Intelligence-Led Policing: The New Intelligence Architecture," September 2005, https://www.ncjrs.gov/pdffiles1/bja/210681.pdf.

[60] Jerry H. Ratcliffe, *Intelligence-Led Policing*, (Portland, OR: Willan Publishing, 2008), p. 6.

[61] Department of Justice, "Intelligence-Led Policing: The Integration of Community Policing and Law Enforcement Intelligence," *Law Enforcement Intelligence: A Guide for State, Local, and Tribal Law Enforcement Agencies*, http://www.cops.usdoj.gov/pdf/e09042536_ Chapter_04.pdf.

[62] Jerry Ratcliffe, "What is Intelligence-Led Policing," http://jratcliffe.net/research/ilp.htm.

[63] This is not meant to suggest that mass shooters are always silent regarding their plans. Rather, they may not typically involve others in orchestrating their schemes.

[64] Whereas criminal groups may engage in activities that could produce intelligence information for law enforcement to exploit, such as communicating to one another via email regarding their schemes, lone gunmen or mass shooters often do not. Minus any ideological underpinnings for their actions, public mass shooters may in some ways be likened to terrorist suspects who act alone, often described as "lone wolves." One FBI official has said, "The lone wolf is arguably one of the biggest challenges to American law enforcement. How do you get into the mind of a terrorist? The FBI does not have the capability to know when a person gets up in middle America and decides: 'I'm taking my protest poster to Washington or I'm taking my gun.'" See Gary Fields and Evan Perez, "FBI Seeks to Target Lone Extremists," *Wall Street Journal,* June 15, 2009, http://online.wsj.com/article/SB124501849215613523.html. For more on lone wolves, see CRS Report R42536, *The Domestic Terrorist Threat: Background and Issues for Congress*, by Jerome P. Bjelopera.

[65] Hot spot analysis is one technique that may be involved in intelligence-led policing. For more information about mapping crime, see National Institute of Justice, "Mapping Crime: Understanding Hot Spots," August 2005.

[66] Richard J. McNally, "Why Psychiatrists Can't Predict Mass Murderers," *Salon.com*, January 12, 2011.

[67] National Institute of Justice, "Preventing School Shootings: A Summary of a U.S. Secret Service Safe School Initiative Report," *NIJ Journal*, 2002. The notion of profiling "may be an effective strategy for limiting the field of suspects after a crime has occurred," but it is generally not considered effective for *proactively* identifying an individual who may be a greater risk for committing a targeted act of violence, including a public mass shooting. See Randy Borum, Robert Fein, Bryan Vossekuil, et al., "Threat Assessment: Defining an Approach for Evaluating Risk of Targeted Violence," *Behavioral Sciences and the Law*, vol. 17 (1999), p. 328. Hereafter: Borum et al., "Threat Assessment."

[68] The FBI and its behavioral analysts in the Behavioral Science Unit developed what is often referred to as criminal "profiling," or criminal investigative analysis. It was advanced as an investigative technique to narrow the field of potential offenders based on analyses of the crimes committed. Today, much of the criminal investigative analysis at the FBI is conducted by agents and analysts in the Behavioral Analysis Units at the National Center for the Analysis of Violent Crime. Federal Bureau of Investigation, "Criminal Profiling Part 1 of 7," http://vault.fbi.gov/ Criminal%20Profiling/Criminal%20Profiling%20Part %201% 20of%207/view. The National Center for the Analysis of Violent Crime is a component of the Critical Incident Response Group at the FBI. For more information, see http://www.fbi.gov/about-us/cirg/investigations-and-operations-support/investigations-operations-support#cirg_ncavc.

[69] Components of such risk reduction involve prevention, protection, response, education, and research/evaluation. Department of Homeland Security, "Statement by Secretary Napolitano on President Obama's Proposal to Combat Gun Violence," press release, January 16, 2013, http://www.dhs.gov/news/2013/01/16/statement-secretary-napolitanopresident-obama%E2%80%99s-proposal-combat-gun-violence.

[70] See Secret Service, "National Threat Assessment Center," http://www.secretservice.gov/ntac. shtml.

[71] Borum et al., "Threat Assessment," p. 327. In 1992, the Secret Service, along with the Federal Bureau of Prisons and National Institute of Justice, undertook a 5-year Exceptional Case Study Project (ECSP) to study individuals who have attacked or attempted to attack public officials and figures in the United States. For specific ECSP findings, see Robert A. Fein and Bryan Vossekuil, "Threat Assessment Investigations: A Guide for State and Local Law Enforcement Officials," July 1998.

[72] Borum et al., "Threat Assessment," p. 372.

[73] Ibid., p. 330.

[74] For more information on the Terrorist Screening Database, see http://www.fbi.gov/about-us/nsb/tsc.

[75] For more information on terrorist watchlist screenings and background checks for firearms, see CRS Report R42336, *Terrorist Watch List Screening and Brady Background Checks for Firearms*, by William J. Krouse.

[76] See Department of Homeland Security, "Active Shooter Preparedness," http://www.dhs.gov /activeshooter.

[77] Kaci Poor, "Active Shooter Training Prepares Local Law Enforcement for Sandy Hook Situation," *The Times-Standard*, January 25, 2013.

[78] One of the FBI's top ten priorities is to "support federal, state, local and international partners." See http://www.fbi.gov/about-us/quick-facts. Of course, other federal law enforcement agencies, such as the

Bureau of Alcohol Tobacco, Firearms, and Explosives, can help local police with mass shooting investigations.

[79] Jerry Seper, "FBI Agents Back Bill Allowing Feds to Help Probe Mass Killings," *The Washington Times*, January 2, 2013.

[80] Federal crimes of attempted and actual homicide and manslaughter are codified at 18 U.S.C. § 1111-1113.

[81] Rachel Kalish and Michael Kimmel, "Suicide by Mass Murder: Masculinity, Aggrieved Entitlement, and Rampage School Shootings," *Health Sociology Review*, vol. 19, no. 4 (2010).

[82] This section includes contributions from Sarah A. Lister, Specialist in Public Health and Epidemiology (public health, prevention, preparedness and response), and Elayne J. Heisler, Analyst in Health Services (emergency departments, trauma care).

[83] Casualties can include victims or responders who die from their injuries; victims or responders who survive with physical injuries (not limited to gunshot wounds); and victims, responders, bystanders, and community members who experience psychological repercussions. The most severe injuries are less common than minor injuries such as sprains and strains. See Department of Health and Human Services (HHS), Centers for Disease Control and Prevention (CDC), *Emergency Preparedness and Response: Injuries and Mass Casualty Events*, http://www.bt.cdc.gov/masscasualties/ injuriespro.asp Traumatic events can have both short- and long-term consequences. See Centers for Disease Control and Prevention, *Emergency Preparedness and Response: Coping with a Traumatic Event*, http://www.bt.cdc.gov/ masscasualties/copingpro.asp.

[84] According to DHS, in the context of critical national infrastructure, the health care and public health sector (referred to as "the health sector" in this report) consists of a variety of health care facilities and transportation services, products manufacture and distribution, financing and data management systems, governmental public health agencies, and nongovernmental organizations. Department of Homeland Security, *Healthcare and Public Health Sector-Specific Plan: An Annex to the National Infrastructure Protection Plan*, 2010, Executive Summary, p. 1, http://www.dhs.gov/xlibrary/ assets/nipp-ssp-healthcare-and-public-health-2010.pdf.

[85] For examples of public health surveillance systems, see Centers for Disease Control and Prevention, National Center for Health Statistics, *Surveys and Data Collection Systems*, http://www.cdc.gov/nchs/surveys.htm.

[86] This does not include what may be considered surveillance within law enforcement contexts, i.e., covertly gathered information about suspects.

[87] Centers for Disease Control and Prevention, Injury Center, *Violence Prevention, The Public Health Approach to Violence Prevention*, http://www.cdc.gov/ViolencePrevention/overview /publichealthapproach.html. The approach is discussed in the context of school violence in U.S. Congress, House Committee on Education and the Workforce, Subcommittee on Early Childhood, Youth and Families, *School Violence: Protecting Our Children*, 106th Cong., 1st sess., March 1, 1999, H.Hrg.106-9 (Washington: GPO, 1999), pp. 44-58. The CDC describes a four-step process; this CRS report combines the last two steps (intervention evaluation and implementation) into one step, resulting in the three-step process described in the text.

[88] Both the legal authority for maintaining registries of deaths and the responsibility for issuing death certificates reside with individual states, territories, and two cities (Washington, DC, and New York, NY). Information collected in death certificates is aggregated at the federal level by the National Center for Health Statistics (NCHS, within CDC) in the National Vital Statistics System (NVSS); see http://www.cdc.gov/nchs/nvss.htm. NCHS extracts information from NVSS to create the National Death Index (NDI), a data set that can be combined with other data sets for research purposes; see http://www.cdc.gov /nchs/data_ access/ndi/about_ndi.htm. Information about non-fatal shootings is included in the CDC's National Electronic Injury Surveillance System – All Injury Program (NEISS-AIP), which collects data from a sample of U.S. hospital emergency departments; NEISS-AIP data can be used to generate national estimates of nonfatal injuries. See Centers for Disease Control and Prevention, *Injury Prevention & Control: Data & Statistics*, http://www.cdc.gov/injury/wisqars/index.html. Additionally, the National Conference of State Legislatures reports that 40 states have statutes establishing statewide trauma registries that collect data about trauma, including both fatal and non-fatal gunshot wounds; the data collected and the source of the data (e.g., emergency medical service or trauma centers) vary by state. See Hollie Hendrikson, *The Right Patient, the Right Place, the Right Time: A Look at Trauma and Emergency Medical Services Policy in the States*, National Conference of State Legislatures, Washington, DC, September 2012, http://www.ncsl.org/documents/health /NCSLTraumaReport812.pdf.

[89] Centers for Disease Control and Prevention, *National Violent Death Reporting System*, http://www.cdc.gov/ violenceprevention/nvdrs.

[90] *The President's Plan*.

[91] *The President's Plan*.

[92] CDC appropriations from FY1997 through FY2011 included a prohibition on the use of funds "to advocate or promote gun control." This prohibition has been extended to all HHS agencies for FY2012 and FY2013. See CRS Report WSLG375, *Is Gun Violence Research Advocacy? Appropriations Restrictions on Using HHS Funds to "Advocate or Promote Gun Control,"* by Kathleen S. Swendiman, January 23, 2013. See also Jay Dickey and Mark Rosenberg, "'Senseless' is not studying gun violence," *The Washington Post*, July 29, 2012, and Michael Luo, "Sway of N.R.A. Blocks Studies, Scientists Say," *The New York Times*, January 25, 2011.

[93] *The President's Plan.*

[94] U.S. President (Obama), "Engaging in Public Health Research on the Causes and Prevention of Gun Violence," *Public Papers of the Presidents of the United States* (Washington: GPO, 2013).

[95] *The President's Plan.* See CRS Report R41768, *Mental Health Parity and Mandated Coverage of Mental Health and Substance Use Disorder Services After the ACA*, by Amanda K. Sarata. Mental health parity generally refers to the concept that health insurance coverage for mental health services should be offered on par with covered medical and surgical benefits.

[96] *The President's Plan.*

[97] *The President's Plan.*

[98] Letter from Leon Rodriguez, Director, Health and Human Services, Office of Civil Rights, "Message to Our National Health Care Providers," January 15, 2013, http://www.hhs.gov/ocr. The letter clarifies requirements of the Health Insurance Portability and Accountability Act (HIPAA) Privacy Rule, 45 CFR § 164.512(j).

[99] Metropolitan Medical Response System contracts required more than 120 cities to establish and exercise mass casualty management plans. National Research Council, *Preparing for Terrorism: Tools for Evaluating the Metropolitan Medical Response System Program*, Washington, D.C., The National Academies Press, 2002, http://www.nap.edu /catalog.php?record_id=10412. The program, originally managed by HHS, is now a component of the Federal Emergency Management Agency (FEMA) Homeland Security Grant Program (HSGP). It received dedicated appropriations from FY1997 through FY2011. For FY2012, its purposes are allowable, but no longer required, of grantees receiving HSGP funds. Federal Emergency Management Agency, FY2012 Homeland Security Grant Program, http://www.fema.gov/fy-2012-homeland-security-grant-program.

[100] Department of Health and Human Services, Public Health Emergency, "Hospital Preparedness Program," http://www.phe.gov/preparedness/planning/hpp/pages/default.aspx.

[101] Kristin Viswanathan, Theresa Wizemann, and Bruce M. Altevogt, "Improving Rural Mass Casualty Response in the United States," in *Preparedness and Response to a Rural Mass Casualty Incident* (Washington, DC: National Academies Press, 2011), pp. 77-86.

[102] Institute of Medicine, *Future of Emergency Care: Emergency Medical Services at the Crossroads* (Washington, DC: The National Academies Press, 2007).

[103] The National Conference of State Legislatures suggests that state-level organization of EMS services also impedes coordination. See Hollie Hendrikson, *The Right Patient, the Right Place, the Right Time: A Look at Trauma and Emergency Medical Services Policy in the States*, National Conference of State Legislatures, Washington, DC, September 2012, p. 9, http://www.ncsl.org/documents/health/NCSLTraumaReport812.pdf.

[104] This program is described in CRS Report R41278, *Public Health, Workforce, Quality, and Related Provisions in PPACA: Summary and Timeline*, coordinated by C. Stephen Redhead and Erin D. Williams. The funding for this program is described in CRS Report R41390, *Discretionary Spending in the Patient Protection and Affordable Care Act (ACA)*, coordinated by C. Stephen Redhead.

[105] U.S. Government Accountability Office, *Hospital Emergency Departments: Crowding Continues to Occur, and Some Patients Wait Longer than Recommended Time Frames*, 09-347, April 30, 2009, http://www.gao.gov/products/ GAO-09-347; Institute of Medicine, *Emergency Medical Services at the Crossroads* (Washington, DC: The National Academies Press, 2007); and Institute of Medicine, *Hospital-Based Emergency Care: At the Breaking Point* (2007).

[106] For more information about HHS programs to train emergency providers, see CRS Report R41278, *Public Health, Workforce, Quality, and Related Provisions in PPACA: Summary and Timeline*, coordinated by C. Stephen Redhead and Erin D. Williams. For more about the Hospital Preparedness Program see Department of Health and Human Services, Public Health Emergency, "Hospital Preparedness Program," http://www.phe.gov/preparedness /planning/hpp/ pages/default.aspx; and Department of Health and Human Services, Assistant Secretary for Preparedness and Response, *Healthcare Preparedness Capabilities: National Guidance for Healthcare System Preparedness*, January 2012, p. 24, http://www.phe.gov /Preparedness /planning/hpp/reports/Documents/capabilities.pdf.

[107] CRS Report R42865, *Medicaid Disproportionate Share Hospital Payments*; and CRS Report R41196, *Medicare Provisions in the Patient Protection and Affordable Care Act (PPACA): Summary and Timeline*, by Alison Mitchell.

[108] Centers for Disease Control and Prevention, "Access to Trauma Care: Getting the Right Care, at the Right Place, at the Right Time," August 24, 2010, http://www.cdc.gov /traumacare/access_trauma.html. Hereafter: Centers for Disease Control and Prevention," "Access to Trauma Care."

[109] For information about regional trauma programs, see CRS Report R41278, *Public Health, Workforce, Quality, and Related Provisions in PPACA: Summary and Timeline*, coordinated by C. Stephen Redhead and Erin D. Williams. For information about funding of regional trauma programs, see CRS Report R41390, *Discretionary Spending in the Patient Protection and Affordable Care Act (ACA)*, coordinated by C. Stephen Redhead.

[110] Centers for Disease Control and Prevention, "Access to Trauma Care."

[111] This involves identifying "the severity and type of injury and determin[ing] which hospital or other facility would be the most appropriate to meet the needs of the patient." See Centers for Disease Control and Prevention, "Field Triage," http://www.cdc.gov/fieldtriage/.

[112] For information, see Department of Health and Human Services, Assistant Secretary for Preparedness and Response, "Medical Assistance," http://www.phe.gov/Preparedness /support/medicalassistance/Pages/default. aspx; and Archived CRS Report RL33095, *Hurricane Katrina: DOD Disaster Response*, by Steve Bowman, Amy Belasco, and Lawrence Kapp.

[113] The Emergency Medical Treatment and Active Labor Act (EMTALA) was enacted as part of the Consolidated Omnibus Budget Reconciliation Act of 1985 (P.L. 99-272). For more information on EMTALA, see CRS Report RS22738, *EMTALA: Access to Emergency Medical Care*, by Edward C. Liu.

[114] Centers for Disease Control and Prevention, *Emergency Preparedness and Response: Mass Casualty Event Preparedness and Response*, http://www.bt.cdc.gov/masscasualties.

[115] See James Hawdon et al., "Social Solidarity and Wellbeing after Critical Incidents: Three Cases of Mass Shootings," *Journal of Critical Incident Analysis*, vol. 3, no. 1 (Fall 2012), pp. 2-25.

[116] For example, the Substance Abuse and Mental Health Services Administration (SAMHSA) has programs that may provide access to mental health services for victims (see http://www.samhsa.gov/), and the Health Resources and Services Administration trains mental health providers and has programs to place providers in rural and other underserved areas (see http://nhsc.hrsa.gov/ and http://bhpr.hrsa.gov/grants/mentalbehavioral /index. html). Under certain circumstances (e.g., if the infrastructure damage approached $1 million), the Governor might request that the President declare a major disaster area under the Robert T. Stafford Disaster Relief and Emergency Assistance Act of 1974 (the Stafford Act). Under a Stafford declaration, FEMA would be authorized to fund (among other things) a Crisis Counseling Assistance and Training Program (CCP); see 42 U.S.C. §5183. Alternatively, the President might consider a mass shooting event to be a "uniquely federal responsibility" and declare an emergency on that basis. Programs such as the CCP could be an adjustment made to the declaration under the President's authority, providing supplemental resources to state, local, and/or private mental health organizations. Such a declaration could also arguably provide assistance to safety forces (e.g., overtime pay) and provide other essential assistance requested by the state. See CRS Report RL33579, *The Public Health and Medical Response to Disasters: Federal Authority and Funding, by Sarah A. Lister*; Archived CRS Report RL33738, *Gulf Coast Hurricanes: Addressing Survivors' Mental Health and Substance Abuse Treatment Needs,* by Ramya Sundararaman, Sarah A. Lister, Erin D. Williams; and CRS Report RL33053, *Federal Stafford Act Disaster Assistance: Presidential Declarations, Eligible Activities, and Funding,* by Francis X. McCarthy.

[117] The coverage of mental health services under private health insurance plans, Medicare, and Medicaid may be particularly relevant for the long-term recovery of victims of an MCI. For more information about mental health coverage under private health insurance and Medicaid, see CRS Report R41249, *Mental Health Parity and the Patient Protection and Affordable Care Act of 2010,* by Amanda K. Sarata.

[118] States and school districts have primary responsibility for the provision of elementary and secondary education in the United States. The vast majority of funding for schools is also provided by states and localities; the federal government contributes approximately 9% to the overall funding of elementary and secondary education. Nevertheless, the United States Department of Education (Department of Education) performs numerous functions, including promoting educational standards and accountability; gathering education data; disseminating research on important education issues; and administering federal education programs and policies. One of the most important priorities for the Department of Education in elementary and secondary education is improving academic outcomes for all students; particularly disadvantaged students, students with disabilities, English language learners, Indians, Native Hawaiians, and Alaska Natives.

[119] The gunman also killed himself and his mother. She was not shot at the school.

[120] For public health resources specifically addressing the Newtown tragedy see http://www.phe.gov/emergency/events/ newtown/Pages/default.aspx.

[121] In December, 2012, a group of 9 violence prevention researchers and practitioners developed a position statement on the Newtown shootings that has been endorsed by a wide variety of organizations and individuals. See http://www.ccbd.net/sites/default/files/OFFICIAL %20FOR%20DISSEMINATION-Connecticut%20School%20Shooting%20Position%20 Statement%2012-19-2012-2%20pm%20ET.pdf.

[122] Of the eight remaining shootings: a) three involved non-students targeting elementary schools, b) one involved a gunman targeting people at the high school he formerly attended, c) four occurred on college campuses and involved either active or former students. CRS did not identify a public mass shooting involving a student attending elementary school who acted as an assailant in an incident at his or her own school.

[123] Schools continue to be among the safest places for children. Out of 1,579 homicides of youth ages 5-18 in the 2008- 2009 year (most recent data available), approximately 1% (17), were school associated homicides. This percentage has remained consistently at less than 2% since the survey began in school year 1992-1993. These data do not indicate the weapon used. National Center for Education Statistics, Department of Education, and Bureau of Justice Statistics, Office of Justice Programs, Department of Justice, *Indicators of School Crime and Safety: 2011*, Washington, D.C. February, 2012.

[124] One of the Safe and Drug Free Schools and Communities Act programs (SDFSCA) that is continuing to receive funding is the Safe Schools/Healthy Students (SS/HS) grant program. It is funded jointly by the Department of Education and SAMHSA. The program is administered by the Department of Education, SAMHSA, and DOJ. The SS/HS initiative is a discretionary grant program that provides schools and communities with federal funding to implement an enhanced, coordinated, comprehensive plan of activities, programs, and services that focus on healthy childhood development and the prevention of violence and alcohol and drug abuse. Grantees are required to establish partnerships with local law enforcement, public mental health, and juvenile justice agencies/entities. The program received $17 million in Department of Education funding for FY2012. These grants are awarded to state education agencies (SEAs), high-need local educational agencies (LEAs) and their partners.

[125] As authorized, the SDFSCA is divided into two major programs: State Formula Grants and National Programs. The majority of State Formula Grant funding was distributed first by formula to states and then also by formula to LEAs. However, FY2009 is the last year that funding was provided for State Formula Grants. Presently, funding is only provided for National Programs. Funding for the State Grant Formula program was eliminated in part because it was believed that the amount of money reaching LEAs was too small to implement effective programing. For more information on the SDFSCA program see CRS Report RL34496, *Safe and Drug-Free Schools and Communities Act: Program Overview and Reauthorization Issues*, by Gail McCallion.

[126] The Department of Education has a variety of resources to help schools and communities develop an emergency management plan. See http://www2.ed.gov/admins/lead/safety /emergencyplan/crisisplanning.pdf. See also http://rems.ed.gov/CreatingAndUpdating SchoolEmergencyManagementPlans.aspx.

[127] For a discussion of school safety issues at Institutions of Higher Education, see CRS Report RL33980, *School and Campus Safety Programs and Requirements in the Elementary and Secondary Education Act and Higher Education Act*, by Gail McCallion and Rebecca R. Skinner.

[128] A Secret Service study indicated that conducting threat assessments may help schools be better prepared to address potential problems. The study was based on information regarding 37 school shootings involving 41 attackers. It concluded that there is no accurate or useful 'profile' of a school shooter. In contrast, it indicated that threat assessment may be useful if it is: "a fact-based investigative and analytical approach that focuses on what a particular student is doing and saying, and not on whether the student 'looks like' those who have attacked schools in the past. Threat assessment emphasizes the importance of behavior and communications for identifying, evaluating and reducing the risk posed by a student who may be thinking about or planning for a school-based attack." Bryan Vossekuil et al., *The Final Report and Findings of the Safe School Initiative: Implications for the Prevention of School Attacks in the United States*. Department of Education and Secret Service, Washington D.C. 2004. p. 41. For more on threat assessments, see "Preparedness and Prevention Combined—Threat Assessments " in this report.

[129] Centers for Disease Control and Prevention, *School Connectedness: Strategies for Increasing Protection Factors Among Youth.* Atlanta, GA, Department of Health and Human Services, 2009, p. 7.

[130] Ibid., p. 3.

[131] *The President's Plan* requests $50 million to help 8,000 additional schools implement strategies to improve school climate. In addition to assistance provided through the Technical Assistance Center, the Department of Education is currently providing funding to 11 Safe and Supportive Schools grantees ($47.5 million in FY2012). SEAs, high-need LEAs and their partners can apply for this grant. Funding is used to develop and implement programs that measure and improve conditions for learning based on local needs.

[132] Catherine Bradshaw, et al., "Examining the Effects of Schoolwide Positive Behavioral Interventions and Supports on Student Outcomes," *Journal of Positive Behavior Interventions*, vol. 12, no. 3 (July 2010).

[133] Representatives from the U.S. Departments of Agriculture, Defense, Education, Health and Human Services, the Interior, Justice, the Federal Trade Commission and the White House Initiative on Asian Americans and Pacific Islanders have come together to form a Federal Partners in Bullying Prevention Steering Committee. The Federal Partners work to coordinate policy, research, and communications on bullying topics. The Federal Partners have created a website, http://www.stopbullying.gov, which provides extensive resources on bullying, including information on how schools can address bullying. In addition, with leadership the Department of Education, the Federal Partners have sponsored three antibullying summits attended by education practitioners, policy makers, researchers, and federal officials.

[134] Government Accountability Office, School Bullying: *Extent of Legal Protections for Vulnerable groups Needs to Be More Fully Assessed*, GA0-12-349, May 2012, pp. 8-10, http://www.gao.gov/assets/600/591202.pdf.

[135] Bryan Vossekuil, et al., *The Final Report and Findings of the Safe School Initiative: Implications for the Prevention of School Attacks in the United States*, Department of Education and Secret Service, Washington D.C. 2004, p. 12.

[136] 20 USC 7161. Another version of the federal conceptualization of the role of a school resource officer is "a career law enforcement officer, with sworn authority, deployed in community-oriented policing, and assigned by the employing police department or agency to work in collaboration with schools and community-based organizations" for a variety of purpose areas. See 42 U.S.C. § 3796dd-8. Purpose areas are: "(A) to address crime and disorder problems, gangs, and drug activities affecting or occurring in or around an elementary or secondary school; (B) to develop or expand crime prevention efforts for students; (C) to educate likely school-age victims in crime prevention and safety; (D) to develop or expand community justice initiatives for students; (E) to train students in conflict resolution, restorative justice, and crime awareness; (F) to assist in the identification of physical changes in the environment that may reduce crime in or around the school; and (G) to assist in developing school policy that addresses crime and to recommend procedural changes." As such, the broad notion of a school resource officer may not be uniform across states and localities.

[137] This proposal can be implemented through executive action, it will not require congressional action. For more information on the COPS program see CRS Report R40709, *Community Oriented Policing Services (COPS): Current Legislative Issues*, by Nathan James.

[138] The Pew survey was based on phone interviews with a national sample of 1,502 adults during January 9-13, 2013. The Pew Research Center for the People and the Press, *Gun Rights Proponents More Politically Active: In Gun Control Debate, Several Options Draw Majority Support,* January 14, 2013.

[139] Data indicate that suspensions for all students have been increasing over time, however, there has been a disproportionate increase for non-Whites, particularly African American students. "The Black/White gap has grown from 3 percentage points in the 1970s to over 10 percentage points in the 2000s. Blacks are now over three times more likely than Whites to be suspended." Daniel Losen and Russell Skiba, *Suspended Education: Urban Middle Schools in Crisis*, The Civil Rights Project, Los Angeles, CA, September 13, 2010, p. 3.

[140] http://durbin.senate.gov/public/index.cfm/pressreleases?ID=7dcaee2b-b40e-4199-bf20-557b4 b1bc650.

[141] http://www2.ed.gov/admins/lead/safety/emergencyplan/crisisplanning.pdf.

[142] LEAs that receive a REMS grant are required to form partnerships and collaborate with community organizations, local law enforcement agencies, heads of local government, and offices of public safety, health, and mental health as they review and revise these plans. Plans are required to be coordinated with state or local homeland security plans and must support the implementation of NIMS (for more on NIMS please see the text box titled "Federal Framework for Emergency Management" at the beginning of the "Law Enforcement Implications" section of this report.) REMS grants may be used for training school safety teams and students, conducting facility audits, informing families about emergency response policies, implementing an Incident Command System, conducting drills and tabletop simulation exercises, preparing and distributing copies of crisis plans, and, to a limited extent, for purchasing school safety equipment. Grantees under this program may receive support in managing and implementing their projects and

sustaining their efforts over time from the Readiness and Emergency Management for Schools Technical Assistance Center.

[143] The Department of Education's website includes information on all stages of crisis management: prevention/mitigation, preparedness, response, and recovery. See http://www2.ed.gov/admins/lead/safety/emergencyplan/index.html. The Department of Education emphasizes the importance of schools ensuring that their emergency plans and potential responses are coordinated and aligned with first responders and with NIMS.

[144] These data are based on responses from school principals or persons most knowledgeable about crime and safety issues at the school. National Center for Education Statistics, Department of Education, and Bureau of Justice Statistics, Office of Justice Programs, Department of Justice, *Indicators of School Crime and Safety: 2011*, Washington, D.C. February, 2012.

[145] See "Executive Summary" *Journal of School Health,* vol. 78, no. 2 (February 2008), p. 110. The federal SDFSCA State Formula Grant program required LEAs receiving funding under the program to have a comprehensive plan, including *"a crisis management plan for responding to violent or traumatic incidents on school grounds ... "* However, FY2009 was the last year that funding was provided for State Formula Grants, and as a consequence this federal requirement has lapsed.

[146] See http://www2.ed.gov/admins/lead/safety/crisisplanning.pdf.

[147] See http://www2.ed.gov/admins/lead/safety/emergencyplan/crisisplanning.pdf.

[148] Project SERV provides grants of up $50,000 for short term needs (up to six months); and grants of up to $250,000 for extended services (for a period of up to 18 months). LEAs and IHEs may apply for both Immediate Services funding and Extended Services funding; however, a separate application must be submitted for each.

[149] Appropriations for this program are requested on a no-year basis, to remain available for obligation at the federal level until expended. Thus, funds can be carried over from year to year in the event that there are no school-related crises in a given year.

[150] The Elementary and Secondary School Counseling program received funding of $52 million in FY2012. It provides competitive grants to LEAs to establish or expand elementary and secondary school counseling programs. Grantees that receive funding under this program must meet several requirements, including having a program that is comprehensive in addressing the counseling and educational needs of all students; increases the range, availability, quality, and quantity of counseling services; expands services through qualified staff; involves public and private entities in collaborative efforts to enhance the program and promote integrated services; and provides appropriate staff training. The President did not request any FY2013 funding for this program, instead proposing to a fund a broader Successful, Safe, and Healthy Students program. In addition to the Elementary and Secondary School Counseling program there are two other mental health programs authorized by the Elementary and Secondary Education Act; however they are no longer receiving funding. The Grants for the Integration of Schools and Mental Health Systems program authorizes the Secretary to award competitive grants or enter into contracts or cooperative agreements with SEAs, LEAs, or Indian tribes for the purpose of increasing student access to quality mental health care by developing innovative programs to link local school systems with the local mental health system. The program last received funding of $6 million in FY2010. The second program is the Promotion of School Readiness through Early Childhood Emotional and Social Development (Foundations for Learning). The Secretary, in consultation with the Secretary of Health and Human Services, is permitted to award Foundations for Learning Grants to LEAs, local councils, community-based organizations, and other public or nonprofit private entities to assist eligible children with school readiness. The program last received funding of $1 million in FY2010.

In: Mass Shootings and Gun Violence in America
Editor: John C. Zandler
ISBN: 978-1-62618-893-8

Chapter 2

NOW IS THE TIME: THE PRESIDENT'S PLAN TO PROTECT OUR CHILDREN AND OUR COMMUNITIES BY REDUCING GUN VIOLENCE*

White House Staff

INTRODUCTION

Our nation has suffered too much at the hands of dangerous people who use guns to commit horrific acts of violence. As President Obama said following the Sandy Hook Elementary School tragedy, "We won't be able to stop every violent act, but if there is even one thing that we can do to prevent any of these events, we have a deep obligation, all of us, to try."

Most gun owners are responsible and law-abiding, and they use their guns safely. The President strongly believes that the Second Amendment guarantees an individual right to bear arms. But to better protect our children and our communities from tragic mass shootings like those in Newtown, Aurora, Oak Creek, and Tucson, there are four common-sense steps we can take right now. The president's plan includes :

- Closing background check loopholes to keep guns out of dangerous hands;
- Banning military-style assault weapons and high-capacity magazines, and taking other common-sense steps to reduce gun violence;
- Making schools safer; and
- Increasing access to mental health services.

While no law or set of laws will end gun violence, it is clear that the American people want action. If even one child's life can be saved, then we need to act. Now is the time to do the right thing for our children, our communities, and the country we love.

---

* This plan was released by the White House, January 16, 2013.

1. Closing Background Check Loopholes to Keep Guns Out of Dangerous Hands

Most gun owners buy their guns legally and use them safely, whether for self-defense, hunting, or sport shooting.

Yet too often, irresponsible and dangerous individuals have been able to easily get their hands on firearms. We must strengthen our efforts to keep guns from falling into the wrong hands.

Require Background Checks for All Gun Sales

The single most important thing we can do to prevent gun violence and mass shootings, like the one in Newtown, is to make sure those who would commit acts of violence cannot get access to guns. A critical tool in achieving that goal is the National Instant Criminal Background Check System, which was created by the Brady Act to ensure that guns are not sold to those prohibited from buying them, including felons and those convicted of domestic violence.

Over the last 14 years it has helped keep more than 1.5 million guns out of the wrong hands. It is able to make 92 percent of background check determinations on the spot. However, too many guns are still sold without a background check and too many individuals prohibited from having a gun slip through the cracks. We need to strengthen the system by requiring every gun buyer to go through a background check and ensuring that the background check system has complete information on people prohibited from having guns. We should:

- Require criminal background checks for all gun sales: Right now, federally licensed firearms dealers are required to run background checks on those buying guns, but studies estimate that nearly 40 percent of all gun sales are made by private sellers who are exempt from this requirement. A national survey of inmates found that only 12 percent of those who used a gun in a crime acquired it from a retail store or pawn shop, where a background check should have been run. Congress should pass legislation that goes beyond just closing the "gun show loophole" to require background checks for all firearm sales, with limited, common-sense exceptions for cases like certain transfers between family members and temporary transfers for hunting and sporting purposes.
- Call on licensed dealers and private sellers to do their part through executive action: Private sellers can already choose to sell their guns through licensed dealers so the dealer can run a background check on the buyer, and the Administration is calling on them to do so. The Bureau of Alcohol, Tobacco, Firearms, and Explosives (ATF) will send an open letter to licensed dealers giving them guidance on how best to facilitate these checks.

Strengthen the Background Check System

The background check system is the most efficient and effective way to keep guns out of the hands of dangerous individuals, but we need to make sure it has access to complete information about these individuals.

For example, although the number of mental health records available to the system has increased by 800 percent since 2004, a recent report by the Government Accountability Office found that there are still 17 states that have made fewer than 10 mental health records available.

We need to make sure reliable data on prohibited purchasers is available to the background check system.

The Administration is announcing four new executive actions to enhance the system's ability to identify dangerous people and stop them from getting guns:

- *Address unnecessary legal barriers that prevent states from reporting information about those prohibited from having guns*: Some states have cited concerns about restrictions under the Health Insurance Portability and Accountability Act as a reason not to share relevant information on people prohibited from gun ownership for mental health reasons. The Administration will begin the regulatory process to remove any needless barriers, starting by gathering information about the scope and extent of the problem.
- *Improve incentives for states to share information with the background check system*: States are a critical source for several key categories of relevant records and data, including criminal history records and records of persons prohibited from having guns for mental health reasons. The Department of Justice will invest $20 million in FY2013 to give states stronger incentives to make this data available. The Administration is also proposing $50 million for this purpose in FY2014, and will look for additional ways to ensure that states are doing their part to provide relevant information.
- *Hold federal agencies accountable for sharing reliable information with the background check system*: Some federal agencies also have relevant records. The President is issuing a Presidential Memorandum holding agencies to requirements that they identify these records, make them available to the background check system, and regularly report that those records are complete and up-to-date.
- *Make sure dangerous people are prohibited from having guns*: The background check system is designed to keep guns out of the hands of those forbidden by law to have them. But we need to make sure our laws are effective at identifying the dangerous or untrustworthy individuals that should not have access to guns. The President will direct the Attorney General, in consultation with other relevant agencies, to review the laws governing who is prohibited from having guns and make legislative and executive recommendations to ensure dangerous people aren't slipping through the cracks.

2. Banning Military-Style Assault Weapons and High-Capacity Magazines, and Taking Other Common-Sense Steps to Reduce Gun Violence

We need to do more to prevent easy access to instruments of mass violence. We also need to provide law enforcement with additional tools to prevent gun violence, end the freeze on gun violence research, make sure health care providers know they can report credible threats of violence and talk to their patients about gun safety, and promote responsible gun ownership.

Get Military-Style Assault Weapons and High-Capacity Magazines off the Streets

A 2010 survey by the Police Executive Research Forum found that more than one-third of police departments reported an increase in criminals' use of assault weapons and high-capacity magazines since the prohibition on high-capacity magazines and assault weapons expired in 2004. To protect law enforcement and enhance public safety, we must redouble our efforts to:

- *Reinstate and strengthen the ban on assault weapons*: The shooters in Aurora and Newtown used the type of semiautomatic rifles that were the target of the assault weapons ban that was in place from 1994 to 2004. That ban was an important step, but manufacturers were able to circumvent the prohibition with cosmetic modifications to their weapons. Congress must reinstate and strengthen the prohibition on assault weapons.
- *Limit ammunition magazines to 10 rounds*: The case for prohibiting high-capacity magazines has been proven over and over; the shooters at Virginia Tech, Tucson, Aurora, Oak Creek, and Newtown all used magazines holding more than 10 rounds, which would have been prohibited under the 1994 law.

These magazines enable any semiautomatic weapon to be used as an instrument of mass violence, yet they are once again legal and now come standard with many handguns and rifles. Congress needs to reinstate the prohibition on magazines holding more than 10 rounds.

- *Finish the job of getting armor-piercing bullets off the streets*: It is already illegal to manufacture and import armor-piercing ammunition except for military or law enforcement use.

But it is generally still not illegal to possess or transfer this dangerous ammunition. Congress should finish the job of protecting law enforcement and the public by banning the possession of armor-piercing ammunition by, and its transfer to, anyone other than the military and law enforcement.

Give Law Enforcement Additional Tools to Prevent and Prosecute Gun Crime

In order to prevent and respond to gun violence, we must give law enforcement every tool they need to keep us safe. That includes passing stronger laws to stop those who would put guns into the hands of criminals, keeping 15,000 cops on the street, and eliminating restrictions that keep federal law enforcement from doing its job.

- *Create serious punishments for gun trafficking*: Today, criminals can easily buy guns from unlicensed dealers, or acquire them with the help of so-called "straw purchasers" who pass the required background check to buy guns from licensed dealers. But there is no explicit law against straw purchasing, so straw purchasers and others who traffic guns can often only be prosecuted for paperwork violations. We cannot allow those who help put guns into the hands of criminals to get away with just a slap on the wrist. Congress should close these loopholes with new gun trafficking laws that impose serious penalties for these crimes.
- *Help communities across the country keep 15,000 cops on the street*: One of the most important steps we can take to reduce gun violence is to keep police officers at their posts in our neighborhoods and communities. The President is calling on Congress to act on the Administration's $4 billion proposal to help keep 15,000 cops on the street in cities and towns across the country.
- *Take executive action to enhance tracing data*: When law enforcement recovers a gun during a criminal investigation, they can trace that gun's path from its manufacturer, to the dealer who sold it, to its first purchaser. This gun tracing process helps law enforcement solve violent crimes by generating leads in specific cases and can reveal gun trafficking patterns when large amounts of tracing data are combined. However, not all federal law enforcement agencies are uniformly required to trace all guns they recover and keep in custody. The President will issue a Presidential Memorandum requiring them to trace all such firearms.
- *Take executive action to help law enforcement avoid returning guns to the wrong hands*: Law enforcement should never be put in the position of unknowingly returning a gun to an individual who is prohibited from having it. Currently, when law enforcement must return firearms seized as part of an investigation, they do not have the ability to conduct a full background check on the owner. The Administration will propose regulations to ensure that law enforcement has access to the database needed for complete background checks.
- *Finally give the Bureau of Alcohol, Tobacco, Firearms, and Explosives (ATF) a confirmed director*: The ATF has not had a confirmed director for six years. There is no excuse for leaving the key agency enforcing gun laws in America without a leader. It is time for Congress to confirm an ATF director.
- *Eliminate restrictions that force the ATF to authorize importation of dangerous weapons simply because of their age*: ATF is required to authorize the importation of certain "curio or relic" firearms, and outdated regulations include all firearms manufactured more than 50 years ago in the definition of "curio or relic." But today, firearms manufactured more than 50 years ago include large numbers of

semiautomatic military-surplus rifles, some of which are easily convertible into machine guns or otherwise appealing for use in crime. Congress should get rid of restrictions that prevent ATF from changing this definition, enabling ATF to ensure that firearms imported as curios or relics are actually of interest as collectibles, rather than letting these rules be used as a way to acquire fully functional and powerful military weapons.

- *Maximize enforcement efforts to prevent gun violence and prosecute gun crime*: The Attorney General will work with all United States Attorneys to continue to ensure that every appropriate resource is focused on preventing gun violence. To this end, the Attorney General will ask all U.S. Attorneys to consider whether supplemental efforts would be appropriate in their districts, in areas such as prosecutions of people who have been convicted of a felony and illegally seek to obtain a firearm, or people who attempt to evade the background check system by providing false information.
- *Analyze information on lost and stolen guns and make it widely available to law enforcement*: The Department of Justice will publish an annual report on lost and stolen guns to ensure that data collected by ATF is available. This report will include state-by-state statistics about guns reported as missing. Making this data available will provide valuable information to law enforcement about how to target its resources, and give states and cities the information they need to pass laws and take other effective steps to make sure that lost and stolen guns are reported. The Department will also identify best practices that are working today and encourage states and cities to follow those models.
- *Provide effective training for active shooter situations for 14,000 law enforcement officers, first responders, and school officials*: One of the best ways to minimize the loss of life in a mass shooting is to make sure law enforcement, first responders, school officials, and others are prepared to respond to an active shooter. The Administration will immediately expand access to federal training, and federal agencies will ensure that protocols for responding to active shooter situations are consistent. And Congress should provide an additional $14 million to help train 14,000 more police officers and other public and private personnel to respond to active shooter situations.

End The Freeze on Gun Violence Research

There are approximately 30,000 firearm-related homicides and suicides a year, a number large enough to make clear this is a public health crisis. But for years, the Centers for Disease Control (CDC) and other scientific agencies have been barred by Congress from using funds to "advocate or promote gun control," and some members of Congress have claimed this prohibition also bans the CDC from conducting any research on the causes of gun violence. However, research on gun violence is not advocacy; it is critical public health research that gives all Americans information they need.

- Conduct research on the causes and prevention of gun violence, including links between video games, media images, and violence: The President is issuing a

Presidential Memorandum directing the Centers for Disease Control and scientific agencies to conduct research into the causes and prevention of gun violence. It is based on legal analysis that concludes such research is not prohibited by any appropriations language. The CDC will start immediately by assessing existing strategies for preventing gun violence and identifying the most pressing research questions, with the greatest potential public health impact. And the Administration is calling on Congress to provide $10 million for the CDC to conduct further research, including investigating the relationship between video games, media images, and violence.

- Better understand how and when firearms are used in violent death: To research gun violence prevention, we also need better data. When firearms are used in homicides or suicides, the National Violent Death Reporting System collects anonymous data, including the type of firearm used, whether the firearm was stored loaded or locked, and details on youth gun access. Congress should invest an additional $20 million to expand this system from the 18 states currently participating to all 50 states, helping Americans better understand how and when firearms are used in a violent death and informing future research and prevention strategies.

Preserve the Rights of Health Care Providers to Protect Their Patients and Communities from Gun Violence

We should never ask doctors and other health care providers to turn a blind eye to the risks posed by guns in the wrong hands.

- *Clarify that no federal law prevents health care providers from warning law enforcement authorities about threats of violence:* Doctors and other mental health professionals play an important role in protecting the safety of their patients and the broader community by reporting direct and credible threats of violence to the authorities. But there is public confusion about whether federal law prohibits such reports about threats of violence. The Department of Health and Human Services is issuing a letter to health care providers clarifying that no federal law prohibits these reports in any way.
- *Protect the rights of health care providers to talk to their patients about gun safety:* Doctors and other health care providers also need to be able to ask about firearms in their patients' homes and safe storage of those firearms, especially if their patients show signs of certain mental illnesses or if they have a young child or mentally ill family member at home. Some have incorrectly claimed that language in the Affordable Care Act prohibits doctors from asking their patients about guns and gun safety. Medical groups also continue to fight against state laws attempting to ban doctors from asking these questions. The Administration will issue guidance clarifying that the Affordable Care Act does not prohibit or otherwise regulate communication between doctors and patients, including about firearms.

Encourage Gun Owners to Live up to Their Responsibility to Store Guns Safely

The President believes that the Second Amendment guarantees an individual right to bear arms, and he respects our nation's rich hunting and sport shooting traditions and the millions of responsible Americans who participate in them every year. But this right comes with a responsibility to safely store guns to prevent them from accidentally or intentionally being used to harm others. The Administration is encouraging gun owners to take responsibility for keeping their guns safe and encouraging the development of technology that will make it easier for gun owners to meet this responsibility, and the Consumer Product Safety Commission is assessing the need for new standards for gun locks.

- *Launch a national responsible gun ownership campaign:* The Administration will encourage gun owners to take responsibility for keeping their guns safe with a national campaign. The campaign will promote common-sense gun safety measures like the use of gun safes and trigger locks, separate storage of guns and ammunition, and the reporting of lost and stolen weapons to law enforcement.
- *Review and enhance as warranted safety standards for gun locks and gun safes:* We also need to make sure that gun locks and gun safes work as intended. Several gun locks have been subject to recall due to their failure to function properly; that is not acceptable. The Chair of the Consumer Product Safety Commission (CPSC) intends to review the effectiveness of gun locks and gun safes, including existing voluntary industry standards, and take any steps that may be warranted to improve the standards as well as to protect the public from unreasonable risks of injury or death that arise when those products within the CPSC's jurisdiction fail.
- *Encourage the development of innovative gun safety technology:* Despite rapid advances in technologies in recent years, there are few readily available firearms that utilize these new technologies to help guard against unauthorized access and use. The President is directing the Attorney General to work with technology experts to review existing and emerging gun safety technologies, and to issue a report on the availability and use of those technologies. In addition, the Administration will issue a challenge to the private sector to develop innovative and cost-effective gun safety technology and provide prizes for those technologies that are proven to be reliable and effective.

3. Making Schools Safer

We need to make our schools safer, not only by enhancing their physical security and making sure they are prepared to respond to emergencies like a mass shooting, but also by creating safer and more nurturing school climates that help prevent school violence. Each school is different and should have the flexibility to address its most pressing needs. Some schools will want trained and armed police; others may prefer increased counseling services. Either way, each district should be able to choose what is best to protect its own students.

Put up to 1,000 More School Resource Officers and Counselors in Schools and Help Schools Invest in Safety

Putting school resource officers and mental health professionals in schools can help prevent school crime and student-on-student violence. School resource officers are specially trained police officers that work in schools. When equipped with proper training and supported by evidence-based school discipline policies, they can deter crime with their presence and advance community policing objectives. Their roles as teachers and counselors enable them to develop trusting relationships with students that can result in threats being detected and crises averted before they occur. School psychologists, social workers, and counselors can help create a safe and nurturing school climate by providing mental health services to students who need help. Not every school will want police officers or additional school counselors, but we should do what we can to help schools get the staff they determine they need to stay safe.

- *Take executive action to provide incentives for schools to hire school resource officers*: COPS Hiring Grants, which help police departments hire officers, can already be used by departments to fund school resource officers. This year, the Department of Justice will provide an incentive for police departments to hire these officers by providing a preference for grant applications that support school resource officers.
- *Put up to 1,000 new school resource officers and school counselors on the job*: The Administration is proposing a new Comprehensive School Safety program, which will help school districts hire staff and make other critical investments in school safety. The program will give $150 million to school districts and law enforcement agencies to hire school resource officers, school psychologists, social workers, and counselors. The Department of Justice will also develop a model for using school resource officers, including best practices on age-appropriate methods for working with students.
- *Invest in other strategies to make our schools safer*: School districts could also use these Comprehensive School Safety Grants to purchase school safety equipment; develop and update public safety plans; conduct threat assessments; and train "crisis intervention teams" of law enforcement officers to work with the mental health community to respond to and assist students in crisis. And the General Services Administration will use its purchasing power to help schools buy safety equipment affordably.

Ensure Every School Has a Comprehensive Emergency Management Plan

In the unthinkable event of another school shooting, it is essential that schools have in place effective and reliable plans to respond. A 2010 survey found that while 84 percent of public schools had a written response plan in the event of a shooting, only 52 percent had drilled their students on the plan in the past year. We must ensure that every school has a high-quality plan in place and that students and staff are prepared to follow it.

- *Give schools and other institutions a model for how to develop and implement reliable plans:* The Departments of Education, Justice, Health and Human Services, and Homeland Security will release—by May 2013—a set of model, high-quality emergency management plans for schools, houses of worship, and institutions of higher education, along with best practices for developing these plans and training students and staff to follow them. In addition, the Department of Homeland Security, in coordination with the Department of Justice, will assist interested schools, houses of worship, and institutions of higher education in completing their own security assessments.
- *Help schools develop and implement emergency plans*: Congress should provide $30 million of one-time grants to states to help their school districts develop and implement emergency management plans. But schools also need to take responsibility for getting effective plans in place. Going forward, Congress should require states and school districts that receive school safety funding from the Department of Education to have comprehensive, up-to-date emergency plans in place for all of their schools.

Create a Safer Climate at Schools Across the Country

A report issued by the U.S. Secret Service and the Department of Education after the Columbine shooting found that one of the best things schools can do to reduce violence and bullying is to improve a school's climate and increase trust and communication between students and staff.

Fortunately, we already have evidence-based strategies which have been found to reduce bullying and other problem behaviors like drug abuse or poor attendance, while making students feel safer at school and improving academic performance.

- *Help 8,000 schools create safer and more nurturing school climates:* With technical assistance from the Department of Education, 18,000 schools have already put in place evidence-based strategies to improve school climate. These strategies involve certain steps for the whole school (like consistent rules and rewards for good behavior), with more intensive steps for groups of students exhibiting at-risk behavior, and individual services for students who continue to exhibit troubling behavior. The Administration is proposing a new, $50 million initiative to help 8,000 more schools train their teachers and other school staff to implement these strategies. The Administration will also develop a school climate survey, providing reliable data to help schools implement policies to improve climate.
- *Share best practices on school discipline*: Students who are suspended or expelled are far more likely to repeat a grade, not graduate, or become involved in the juvenile justice system. As a result, effective school discipline policies are critical to addressing school and community crime and violence issues. The Department of Education will collect and disseminate best practices on school discipline polices and help school districts develop and equitably implement their policies.

4. IMPROVING MENTAL HEALTH SERVICES

As President Obama said, "We are going to need to work on making access to mental health care as easy as access to a gun." Today, less than half of children and adults with diagnosable mental health problems receive the treatment they need. While the vast majority of Americans with a mental illness are not violent, several recent mass shootings have highlighted how some cases of mental illness can develop into crisis situations if individuals do not receive proper treatment. We need to do more than just keep guns out of the hands of people with serious mental illness; we need to identify mental health issues early and help individuals get the treatment they need before these dangerous situations develop.

Make Sure Students and Young Adults Get Treatment for Mental Health Issues

Three-quarters of mental illnesses appear by the age of 24, yet less than half of children with diagnosable mental health problems receive treatment. And several recent mass shootings, including those at Newtown, Tucson, Aurora, and Virginia Tech, were perpetrated by students or other young people.

- *Reach 750,000 young people through programs to identify mental illness early and refer them to treatment:* We need to train teachers and other adults who regularly interact with students to recognize young people who need help and ensure they are referred to mental health services. The Administration is calling for a new initiative, Project AWARE (Advancing Wellness and Resilience in Education), to provide this training and set up systems to provide these referrals. This initiative, which would reach 750,000 young people, has two parts:
  - *Provide "Mental Health First Aid" training for teachers*: Project AWARE includes $15 million for training for teachers and other adults who interact with youth to detect and respond to mental illness in children and young adults, including how to encourage adolescents and families experiencing these problems to seek treatment.
  - *Make sure students with signs of mental illness get referred to treatment*: Project AWARE also includes $40 million to help school districts work with law enforcement, mental health agencies, and other local organizations to assure students with mental health issues or other behavioral issues are referred to the services they need. This initiative builds on strategies that, for over a decade, have proven to decrease violence in schools and increase the number of students receiving mental health services.
- *Support individuals ages 16 to 25 at high risk for mental illness*: Efforts to prevent school shootings and other gun violence can't end when a student leaves high school. Individuals ages 16 to 25 are at high risk for mental illness, substance abuse, and suicide, but they are among the least likely to seek help. Even those who received services as a child may fall through the cracks when they turn 18. The

Administration is proposing $25 million for innovative state-based strategies supporting young people ages 16 to 25 with mental health or substance abuse issues.

- *Help schools address pervasive violence*: Twenty-two percent of 14 to 17 year olds have witnessed a shooting in their lifetime. Research shows that exposure to community violence can impact children's mental health and development and can substantially increase the likelihood that these children will later commit violent acts themselves. To help schools break the cycle of violence, Congress should provide $25 million to offer students mental health services for trauma or anxiety, conflict resolution programs, and other school-based violence prevention strategies.
- *Train more than 5,000 additional mental health professionals to serve students and young adults*: Experts often cite the shortage of mental health service providers as one reason it can be hard to access treatment. To help fill this gap, the Administration is proposing $50 million to train social workers, counselors, psychologists, and other mental health professionals. This would provide stipends and tuition reimbursement to train more than 5,000 mental health professionals serving young people in our schools and communities.
- *Launch a national conversation to increase understanding about mental health:* The sense of shame and secrecy associated with mental illness prevents too many people from seeking help. The President is directing Secretaries Sebelius and Duncan to launch a national dialogue about mental illness with young people who have experienced mental illness, members of the faith community, foundations, and school and business leaders.

Ensure Coverage of Mental Health Treatment

While most mental illnesses are treatable, those with mental illness often can't get needed treatment if they don't have health insurance that covers mental health services. The Affordable Care Act will provide one of the largest expansions of mental health coverage in a generation by extending health coverage to 30 million Americans, including an estimated 6 to 10 million people with mental illness. The Affordable Care Act will also make sure that Americans can get the mental health treatment they need by ensuring that insurance plans cover mental health benefits at parity with other benefits.

- *Finalize requirements for private health insurance plans to cover mental health services:* The Administration will issue final regulations governing how existing group health plans that offer mental health services must cover them at parity under the Mental Health Parity and Addiction Equity Act of 2008. In addition, the Affordable Care Act requires all new small group and individual plans to cover ten essential health benefit categories, including mental health and substance abuse services. The Administration intends to issue next month the final rule defining these essential health benefits and implementing requirements for these plans to cover mental health benefits at parity with medical and surgical benefits.
- *Make sure millions of Americans covered by Medicaid get quality mental health coverage*: Medicaid is already the biggest funder of mental health services, and the

Affordable Care Act will extend Medicaid coverage to as many as 17 million hardworking Americans. There is some evidence that Medicaid plans are not always meeting mental health parity requirements today, an issue that will only become more important as Medicaid is expanded. The Administration is issuing a letter to state health officials making clear that these plans must comply with mental health parity requirements.

Learn more at whitehouse.gov/now-is-the-time

In: Mass Shootings and Gun Violence in America
Editor: John C. Zandler
ISBN: 978-1-62618-893-8

Chapter 3

STATEMENT OF SENATOR PATRICK LEAHY, CHAIRMAN, SENATE JUDICIARY COMMITTEE. HEARING ON "WHAT SHOULD AMERICA DO ABOUT GUN VIOLENCE?"*

On December 14, America's heart was broken when 20 young children and six dedicated educators were murdered. This is the first Judiciary Committee hearing of the 113th Congress. I ask all assembled here today to join in the discussion as part of a collective effort to find solutions to help ensure that no family, no school, and no community ever has to endure such a grievous tragedy again.

We must come together today as Americans seeking common cause. Let us forego sloganeering, demagoguery and partisan recriminations. This is too important for all that. We all abhor the recent tragedies – in just the last two years – in an elementary school in Connecticut, in a movie theater in Colorado, in a sacred place of worship in Wisconsin, and in front of a shopping mall in Arizona.

Americans are looking to us for solutions and for action. This Committee is a focal point for that process. I have introduced a measure to provide law enforcement agencies with stronger tools against illegal gun trafficking. Others have proposed restrictions on military style weapons and the size of ammunition clips. Others have proposed modifications to the background check systems to keep guns out of the wrong hands, while not unnecessarily burdening law-abiding citizens.

I know gun store owners in Vermont. They follow the law and conduct background checks to block the conveyance of guns to those who should not have them. They wonder why others who sell guns do not have to follow these same protective rules. I agree with these responsible business owners. If we can all agree that criminals and those adjudicated as mentally ill should not buy firearms, why should we not try to plug the loopholes in the law that allow them to buy guns without background checks? It is a simple matter of common sense. And if we agree that the background check system is worthwhile, should we not try to improve its content and use so it can be more effective? What responsible gun owner objects to improving the background check system?

---

* This is an edited, reformatted and augmented version of a statement presented January 30, 2013 before the Senate Judiciary Committee.

At the outset of this hearing, I note that the Second Amendment is secure and will remain secure and protected. In two recent cases, the Supreme Court has confirmed that the Second Amendment, like other aspects of our Bill of Rights, secures a fundamental individual right. Americans have the right to self-defense and to have guns in their homes to protect their families. No one can or will take those rights or our guns away. Second Amendment rights are the foundation on which our discussion rests. They are not at risk. But lives are at risk when responsible people fail to stand up for laws that will keep guns out of the hands of those who will use them to commit mass murder. I ask that we focus our discussion on additional statutory measures to better to protect our children and all Americans. Ours is a free society, an open society. We come together today to consider how to become a safer and more secure society.

No one begrudges the government assistance provided to victims of mass tragedies made possible by the law we passed after the bombing at Oklahoma City. The bill I introduced last week against gun trafficking will similarly prove helpful and become an accepted part of our crime control framework. It, too, is a commonsense reform. It fills a hole in our law enforcement arsenal so that straw purchasers who acquire weapons for criminals can be prosecuted more effectively.

Last Thursday the President nominated the U.S. Attorney from Minnesota to direct the Federal Bureau of Alcohol, Tobacco, Firearms and Explosives. I trust that all Senators will cooperate in a prompt hearing and action on that nomination and will join in good faith to strengthen our law enforcement efforts against gun violence and to protect public safety.

As a responsible gun owner and someone who cherishes all of our constitutional rights; as a Senator who has sworn an oath to uphold those rights, and as a father and grandfather; and as a former prosecutor who has seen the results of gun violence first hand, I undertake these efforts with hope that this hearing can build consensus around commonsense solutions. Previous measures to close the gun show loophole or to improve the background check system have been bipartisan. I hope in this new Congress, further improvements will also become bipartisan. I have said what kinds of measures I can support. I challenge other Senators to come forward and do so, as well. I will ask our witnesses what legislative proposals they support to make America safer, and I thank everyone for joining today's discussion.

In: Mass Shootings and Gun Violence in America
Editor: John C. Zandler
ISBN: 978-1-62618-893-8

Chapter 4

STATEMENT OF SENATOR ORRIN G. HATCH. HEARING ON "WHAT SHOULD AMERICA DO ABOUT GUN VIOLENCE?"*

The recent mass shootings in this country have left us heartbroken and searching for answers. There has been a call to act by the Obama Administration, Members of Congress and the American public to find legislative solutions to curb gun violence. If we are to deal with this very complex problem via legislative solution, any legislation must meet three criteria. First and foremost, the legislation must be consistent with honoring the Second Amendment. Secondly, we must provide policy that draws from past legislative experience. Thirdly, we must consider and address all possible contributing factors to identify the root causes of this problem. Any legislation that fails to meet all three criteria is destined to be ineffective and a disservice to victims and their family members.

To date, legislative efforts have been a single-minded approach to the problem, additional gun control measures to include banning so-called assault weapons, banning so-called high capacity magazines and heavier penalties for straw-purchasers.

Going forward, each of these legislative efforts will be individually analyzed to determine whether they are consistent with the principles of the Second Amendment. Any review of this legislation will include applying the principles discussed in recent decisions of the U.S. Supreme Court and debated by Members of Congress. Whether they comport with the Second Amendment remains to be seen. However, what is certain is that all of the current proposals fail to satisfy the second and third criteria.

All of these legislative efforts fail to recognize the lessons learned from past legislative experience in this area, the second necessary criteria for a successful solution. History has shown that gun control legislation has had little to no effect on stemming these types of incidents. A 10 year federal ban on assault weapons resulted in no discernible decrease in gun violence. Each and every one of the current proposals ignores the evidence and data that stricter gun control does not lead to a decrease in gun violence. The renewed efforts for stricter gun control are a waste of time, effort and resources as they have been proven ineffective.

* This is an edited, reformatted and augmented version of a Statement Presented January 30, 2013 before the Senate Judiciary Committee.

In addition, these legislative actions fail to satisfy the third criteria, which is to consider and address all of the possible contributing factors to identify the root causes of this problem. Experts in the area of these types of shootings have identified common contributing causes, some of which include various issues with mental illness and treatment, violence in our culture through media, breakdown of the family unit, breakdowns in background checks for weapons purchases, response times of law enforcement, and the emergency action plans for schools. None of the identified contributing factors have been considered by the current proposals.

As we move forward, we must focus on a carefully considered, comprehensive approach that includes all of the factors discussed above. Anything less is a disservice to victims and their families.

In: Mass Shootings and Gun Violence in America
Editor: John C. Zandler
ISBN: 978-1-62618-893-8

Chapter 5

STATEMENT OF SENATOR TED CRUZ. HEARING ON "WHAT SHOULD AMERICA DO ABOUT GUN VIOLENCE?"*

This country was rightfully shocked by the tragedy at Shady Hook Elementary on December 14, 2012. Every parent was understandably horrified by the senseless murder of 20 children and 6 adults that day in Newtown, Connecticut.

We are now appropriately engaged in a national discussion about mental illness and how state and local governments can prevent future tragedies. But politicians should not be exploiting the tragic murder of children as an excuse to push an extreme anti-gun agenda.

Gun control would not have stopped the massacre of the 26 innocent Americans at Newtown. But it would restrict the constitutional rights of every American. We cannot outlaw evil, but we can remain vigilant in working to deter and punish violent criminals. And we should vigorously defend the constitutional right of law-abiding citizens to arm and protect themselves and others from deadly attacks.

Study after study has shown that strict gun control does not reduce violence. When DC banned handguns, homicides went up. When Chicago banned handguns, homicides went up. When Australia banned guns, violent crime went up. And after Great Britain banned guns, its violent crime rate was more than four-times higher than the rate in the United States.

We should not pass legislation that the evidence has proven is utterly ineffective. In particular, the Department of Justice has already concluded that the so-called "assault weapons ban," when it was in effect, had no impact on reducing crime. This is unsurprising, because real assault weapons—machine guns--have been functionally illegal since 1934. All an "assault weapons ban" would do is restrict cosmetic features of firearms, in effect, banning "scary-looking guns." Instead of passing ineffective show legislation—sound and fury, signifying nothing—we should be acting to deter and punish violent criminals and to prevent those with dangerous mental illness from illegally acquiring firearms.

There is wide agreement that guns should not be in the hands of the mentally ill. Current law seeks to identify those individuals, but it relies on states submitting relevant medical records. Not all states are doing this. We should make sure current state law is enforced and

* This is an edited, reformatted and augmented version of a statement presented January 30, 2013 before the Senate Judiciary Committee.

work with states to help them get past the challenges that prevent them from providing more robust data. This is an area of bipartisan agreement and a direct way to address the real problem of the mentally ill getting guns.

I look forward to our discussion today and to future hearings that will address the best strategies for preventing violent crimes and preserving the constitutional rights of every American.

In: Mass Shootings and Gun Violence in America
Editor: John C. Zandler
ISBN: 978-1-62618-893-8

Chapter 6

TESTIMONY OF CAPTAIN MARK KELLY, AMERICANS FOR RESPONSIBLE SOLUTIONS. HEARING ON "WHAT SHOULD AMERICA DO ABOUT GUN VIOLENCE?"*

Thank you Chairman Leahy and Ranking Member Grassley for inviting me here today. I look forward to a constructive dialogue with your committee. I also want to take the opportunity to congratulate Gabby's friend and much respected former colleague, Jeff Flake, on his new role as Arizona's junior Senator.

***

As you know, our family has been immeasurably affected by gun violence. Gabby's gift for speech is a distant memory. She struggles to walk, and she is partially blind. Her right arm is completely paralyzed. And a year ago she left a job she loved serving the people of Arizona.

But in the past two years, we have watched Gabby's determination, spirit, and intellect conquer her disabilities.

We aren't here as victims. We're speaking to you today as Americans.

We're a lot like many of our fellow citizens following this debate about gun violence:

- We're moderates. Gabby was a republican long before she was a democrat.
- We're both gun owners, and we take that right and the responsibilities that come with it very seriously.
- And we watch with horror when the news breaks to yet another tragic shooting. After 20 kids and six of their teachers were gunned down in their classrooms at Sandy Hook, we said, this time must be different. Something needs to be done.

We are simply two reasonable Americans who realize we have a problem with gun violence, and we need Congress to act.

---

* This is an edited, reformatted and augmented version of a testimony presented January 30, 2013 before the Senate Judiciary Committee.

***

At 10:10am on January 8, 2011, a young man walked up to Gabby at her constituent event at a Safeway in Tucson, leveled his gun, and shot her through the head. He then turned down the line and continued firing. In 15 seconds, he emptied his magazine. It contained 33 bullets; there were 33 wounds.

As the shooter attempted to reload, he fumbled. A woman grabbed the next magazine, and others tackled and restrained him.

Gabby was the first victim. Christina-Taylor Green, nine years old, born on 9/11 2001, was shot with the thirteenth bullet or after. And others followed.

The killer in the Tucson shooting suffered from severe mental illness. He is a paranoid schizophrenic who had been deemed unqualified for service in the United States Army and exhibited increasingly bizarre behavior as he spiraled toward murder. At Pima Community College, his disruptions led to run-ins with the campus police and his expulsion, but he was never reported to mental health authorities.

On November 30, 2010, he walked into a sporting goods store, passed a federal NICS background check, and walked out with a Glock 19 semiautomatic handgun. He had never been legally adjudicated as mentally ill, and, even if he had, Arizona at the time had over 121,000 records of disqualifying mental illness it had not submitted to the background check system.

Looking back, we can't say with certainty, "Only if we had done this, it wouldn't have happened." There isn't a single action or law that could have elegantly prevented the Tucson shooting from being written into the history books.

Gabby is one of roughly 100,000 victims of gun violence in America every year. Behind every victim lays a matrix of failure and inadequacy – in our families, communities, and values; in our society's approach to poverty, violence, and mental illness; and, yes, in our politics and in our gun laws.

One of our messages is simple: The breadth and complexity of the problem of gun violence great, but it is not an excuse for inaction.

* * *

As you know, there's another side to our story. Gabby is a gun owner. I am a gun owner.

We have our firearms for the same reasons millions of Americans just like us have guns – to defend ourselves, our family, and our property, and to go hunting or target shooting.

We believe wholly and completely in the Second Amendment of our Constitution – and that it confers upon all Americans the right to own a firearm for protection, collection, and recreation.

We take that right very seriously, and we would never, ever give it up – just like Gabby would never relinquish her gun, and I would never relinquish mine.

But rights demand responsibility. And this right does not extend to terrorists. It does not extend to criminals. It does not extend to the mentally ill.

When dangerous people get guns, we are all vulnerable – at the local movie theater, worshipping at church, conducting our everyday business, exercising our civic responsibilities as Americans, and – time after time after time – at school, on our campuses, in our children's classrooms.

When dangerous people get dangerous guns, we are all the more vulnerable. Dangerous people with weapons specifically designed to inflict maximum lethality upon others have turned every corner of our society into places of carnage and gross human loss.

* * *

Our rights are paramount. But our responsibilities are serious. And as a nation we are not taking responsibility for the gun rights our founders conferred upon us.

Gabby and I are pro-gun ownership. We are anti-gun violence.

And we believe that in this debate Congress should look not toward special interests and ideology, which push us apart, but toward compromise, which brings us together. We believe whether you call yourself pro-gun or anti-gun violence, or both – that you can work together to pass laws that save lives.

We have some ideas for you.

Fix background checks. Currently up to 40 percent of all gun transfers are made through private sales and without background checks. Not surprisingly, 80 percent of criminals reported obtaining their weapons through private sales with no background check. This makes a mockery of our background check system. Congress should close the private sales loophole and strengthen the background check system by requiring states and the federal government to supply the necessary records.

Remove the limitations on the CDC and other public health organizations on collecting data and conducting scientific research on gun violence. As a fighter pilot and astronaut, I saw the value of using data to achieve our military and scientific objectives. We wouldn't have gotten to the Moon or built the International Space Station without robust use of data to make informed decisions. It is simply crazy that we limit gun violence data collection and analysis when we could use that knowledge to save lives.

Enact a federal gun trafficking statute with real penalties for people in the business of helping criminals get guns. Let's get law enforcement the tools they need to stop violent criminals from killing people with illegal guns.

And, finally, let's have a careful and civil conversation about the lethality of the firearms we permit to be legally bought and sold. You can't just walk into a store and buy a machine gun, but you can easily buy a semi-automatic high velocity assault rifle and/or high capacity ammunition magazines. We should come together and decide where to draw that line in such a way that it protects our rights and communities alike.

* * *

This country and this Congress can find a commonsense consensus on preventing gun violence and protecting our inviolable Second Amendment rights. We went to the Moon and back within a decade of deciding we were going to do it. We have prevailed over adversaries big and small. Surely when the safety of our communities, our schools, and our children is at stake, our politics can provide a path toward compromise, and not an obstacle that can't be overcome.

Thank you.

In: Mass Shootings and Gun Violence in America
Editor: John C. Zandler
ISBN: 978-1-62618-893-8

Chapter 7

TESTIMONY OF DAVID B. KOPEL, ADJUNCT PROFESSOR OF ADVANCED CONSTITUTIONAL LAW, DENVER UNIVERSITY. HEARING ON "WHAT SHOULD AMERICA DO ABOUT GUN VIOLENCE?"*

"[W]e cannot clearly credit the [1994 'assault weapons'] ban with any of the nation's recent drop in gun violence."—U.S. Department of Justice 2004 study.[2]

"Passing a law like the assault weapons ban is a purely symbolic move in that direction [to disarm the citizenry]. ... . [T]hat change in mentality starts with the symbolic yielding of certain types of weapons. The real steps, like the banning of handguns, will never occur unless this one is taken first. ..."—Charles Krauthammer[3]

"The ['assault'] weapons' menacing looks, coupled with the public's confusion over fully automatic machine guns versus semi-automatic assault weapons— anything that looks like a machine gun is assumed to be a machine gun—can only increase the chance of public support for restrictions on these weapons."—Josh Sugarmann, Founder, Violence Policy Center[4]

THE POLITICAL ATTACK ON FIREARMS OWNERSHIP

On December 14, 2012, a deranged and hate-filled mass-murderer first killed his own mother and then snuffed out 26 additional lives at Sandy Hook Elementary School in Newtown, Connecticut. It was one of the worst mass murders at school since 1927, when a defeated school board candidate set off explosives at an elementary school in Bath Township, Michigan, killing 38 children and five adults. The horrific crime at Sandy Hook tore the heart out of the nation. It filled every life-loving American—every parent, grandparent, aunt, and uncle—with anger, dread, and anguish.

In the aftermath of this crime, many Americans are exploring ways to responsibly and realistically reduce the possibility of another such attack, such as by better-addressing mental

* This is an edited, reformatted and augmented version of testimony given on January 30, 2013 before the Senate Judiciary Committee.

illness,[5] training people how to more-effectively respond to "active shooters,"[6] and allowing teachers and other responsible adults to carry concealed handguns in schools—something already successfully implemented in Utah and parts of Texas, Ohio, and Colorado.[7]

Unfortunately, others are promoting repressive laws which would have done nothing to prevent Sandy Hook, and would do nothing to prevent the inevitable copycat crimes that may take place in the near future. The demands for symbolic but useless anti-gun laws are accompanied by an aggressive culture war against dissenters. A *Des Moines Register* journalist declared that well-known defenders of gun rights should be dragged behind pickup trucks, that the Second Amendment should be repealed, that the National Rifle Association (NRA) should be declared a "terrorist organization," and that membership in the NRA should be outlawed.[8] A writer for the *Huffington Post* declared that anyone who believes guns may legitimately be owned for self-defense—or that the Second Amendment protects that right—is a "menace" and "a danger to your children."[9]

Unfortunately, such mean-spirited and unjust demonization and scapegoating of law-abiding American gun owners has become a central feature of the political campaign to ban or restrict semi-automatic guns and the magazines that go with them. Even worse, the Newtown murders are being politically exploited.

Prohibitionists use the false and inflammatory labels of "assault weapon" and "high-capacity magazine" to mischaracterize ordinary firearms and their standard accessories.

The AR-15 rifle has for years been the most popular, best-selling firearm in the United States. Millions of law-abiding Americans own AR-15s and similar guns. In an article for *Slate*, Justin Peters estimates that there may be nearly four million AR-15 rifles in the country—and that's just one brand of rifle.[10] Contrary to media claims, these ordinary citizens are not psychopaths intent on mass murder. Rather, Americans own so-called "assault weapons" for all the legitimate reasons that they own any type of firearm: lawful defense of self and others, hunting, and target practice. They do not own these firearms to "assault" anyone. To the contrary, rifles such as the AR-15, and standard capacity magazines of 11-19 rounds (for handguns) and up to 30 rounds (for rifles) are commonly used by rank and file police officers, because such firearms and magazines are often the best choice for the lawful protection of self and others.

That is why the police choose them so often. At Sen. Feinstein's press conference introducing her new prohibition bill, Rev. Hale, of the National Cathedral, asserted that the guns and magazines are useful only for mass murder. This is a mean-spirited insult to the many police officers who have chosen these very same guns and magazines as the best tools for the most noble purpose of all: the defense of innocent life.

What Is an "Assault Weapon?"

Gun prohibition advocates have been pushing the "assault weapon" issue for a quarter century. Their political successes on the matter have always depended on public confusion. The guns are *not* machine guns. They do *not* fire automatically. They fire only one bullet each time the trigger is pressed, just like every other ordinary firearm. They are *not* more powerful than other firearms; to the contrary, their ammunition is typically intermediate in power, less powerful than guns and ammunition made for big game hunting.

The Difference between Automatic and Semi-Automatic

For an automatic firearm (commonly called a "machine gun"), if the shooter presses the trigger and holds it, the gun will fire continuously, automatically, until the ammunition runs out.[11] Ever since the National Firearms Act of 1934, automatics have been very strictly regulated by federal law: Every person who wishes to possess one must pay a $200 federal transfer tax, must be fingerprinted and photographed, and must complete a months-long registration process with the federal Bureau of Alcohol, Tobacco, Firearms, and Explosives (BATFE). In addition, the transferee must be granted written permission by local law enforcement, via ATF Form 4. Once registered, the gun may not be taken out of state without advance written permission from BATFE.

Since 1986, the manufacture of new automatics for sale to persons other than government agents has been forbidden by federal law.[12] As a result, automatics in U.S. are rare (there are about a hundred thousand legally registered ones), and expensive, with the least expensive ones costing nearly ten thousand dollars.

The automatic firearm was invented in 1883 by Hiram Maxim. The early Maxim Guns were heavy and bulky, and required a two-man crew to operate. In 1943, a new type of automatic was invented, the "assault rifle." The assault rifle is light enough for a soldier to carry for long periods of time. Soon, the assault rifle became the ubiquitous infantry weapon. Examples include the U.S. Army M-16, the Soviet AK-47, and the Swiss militia SIG SG 550. The AK-47 (and its various updates, such as the AK-74 and AKM) can be found all over the Third World, but there are only a few hundred in the United States, mostly belonging to firearms museums and wealthy collectors.

The precise definition of "assault rifle" is supplied by the Defense Intelligence Agency.[13] If you use the term "assault rifle," persons who are knowledgeable about firearms will know precisely what kinds of guns you are talking about. The definition of "assault rifle" has never changed, because the definition describes a particular type of thing in the real world—just like the definitions of "apricot" or "Minnesota."

In contrast, the definition of "assault weapon" has never been stable. The phrase is merely an epithet. It has been applied to things which are not even firearms (namely, air guns). It has been applied to double-barreled shotguns, to single-shot guns (guns whose ammunition capacity is only a single round), and to many other sorts of ordinary handguns, shotguns, and rifles.

The first "assault weapon" ban in the United States, in California in 1989, was created by legislative staffers thumbing through a picture book of guns, and deciding which guns looked bad. The result was an incoherent law which, among other things, outlawed certain firearms that do not exist, since the staffers just copied the typographical errors from the book, or associated a model by one manufacturer with another manufacturer whose name appeared on the same page.

Over the last quarter century, the definition has always kept shifting. One recent version is Sen. Dianne Feinstein's new bill. Another is the pair of bills defeated in the January 2013 lame duck session of the Illinois legislature which would have outlawed most handguns (and many long guns as well) by dubbing them "assault weapons."

While the definitions of what to ban keep changing, a few things remain consistent: The definitions do *not* cover automatic firearms, such as assault rifles. The definitions do *not* ban guns based on how fast they fire, or how powerful they are. Instead, the definitions are based on the name of a gun, or on whether a firearm has certain superficial accessories (such as a bayonet lug, or a grip in the "wrong" place).

Most, but not all, of the guns which have been labeled "assault weapons" are semi-automatics. Many people think that a gun which is "semiautomatic" must be essentially the same as an automatic. This is incorrect.

Semi-automatic firearms were invented in the 1890s, and have been common in the United States ever since. Today, about three-quarters of new handguns are semi-automatics. A large share of rifles and shotguns are also semi-automatics. Among the most popular semi-automatic firearms in the United States today are the Colt 1911 pistol (named for the year it was invented, and still considered one of the best self-defense handguns), the Ruger 10/22 rifle (which fires the low-powered .22 Long Rifle cartridge, popular for small game hunting or for target shooting at distances less than a hundred yards), the Remington 1100 shotgun (very popular for bird hunting and home defense), and the AR-15 rifle (popular for hunting game no larger than deer, for target shooting, and for defense). All of these guns were invented in the mid-1960s or earlier. All of them have, at various times, been characterized as "assault weapons."

Unlike an automatic firearm, a semi-automatic fires only one round of ammunition when the trigger is pressed. (A "round" is one unit of ammunition. For a rifle or handgun, a round has one bullet. For a shotgun, a single round contains several pellets).

In some other countries, a semi-automatic is usually called a "self-loading" gun. This accurately describes what makes the gun "semi"-automatic. When the gun is fired, the bullet (or shot pellets) travel from the firing chamber, down the barrel, and out the muzzle. Left behind in the firing chamber is the now empty case or shell that contained the bullets (or pellets) and the gunpowder.

In a semi-automatic, some of the energy from firing is used to eject the empty shell from the firing chamber, and then load a fresh round of ammunition into the firing chamber. Then, the gun is ready to shoot again, when the user is ready to press the trigger.

In some other types of firearms, the user must perform some action in order to eject the empty shell and load the next round. This could be moving a bolt back and forth (bolt action rifles), moving a lever down and then up (lever action rifles), or pulling and then pushing a pump or slide (pump action and slide action rifles and shotguns). A revolver (the second-most popular type of handgun) does not require the user to take any additional action in order to fire the next round.[14]

The semi-automatic has two principle advantages over lever action, bolt action, slide action, and pump action guns. First, many hunters prefer it because the semi-automatic mechanism allows a faster second shot. The difference may be less than a second, but for a hunter, this can make all the difference.

Second, and more importantly, the semi-automatic's use of gunpowder energy to eject the empty case and then to load the next round substantially reduces how much recoil is felt by the shooter. This makes the gun much more comfortable to shoot, especially for beginners, or for persons without substantial upper body strength and bulk.

The reduced recoil also make the gun easier to keep on target for the next shot, which is important for hunting and target shooting, and extremely important for self-defense.

Semi-automatics also have their disadvantages. They are much more prone to misfeeds and jams than are simpler, older types of firearms, such as revolvers or lever action.

Contrary to the hype of anti-gun advocates and less-responsible journalists, there is no rate of fire difference between a so-called "assault" semi-automatic gun and any other semi-automatic gun.

How Fast Does a Semi-Automatic Fire?

Here is a report on the test-firing of a new rifle:

> 187 shots were fired in three minutes and thirty seconds and one full fifteen shot magazine was fired in only 10.8 seconds.

Does that sound like a machine gun? A "semi-automatic assault weapon"? Actually it is an 1862 test report of the then-new lever-action Henry rifle, manufactured by Winchester. If you have ever seen a Henry rifle, it was probably in the hands of someone at a cowboy re-enactment, using historic firearms from 150 years ago.

The Winchester Henry is a lever-action, meaning that after each shot, the user must pull out a lever, and then push it back in, in order to eject the empty shell casing, and then load a new round into the firing chamber.

The lever-action Winchester is not an automatic. It is not a semiautomatic. It was invented decades before either of those types of firearms. And yet that old-fashioned Henry lever action rifle can fire one bullet per second.

By comparison, the murderer at Sandy Hook fired 150 shots over a 20 minute period, before the police arrived. In other words, a rate of fewer than 8 shots per minute. This is a rate of fire far slower than the capabilities of a lever-action Henry Rifle from 1862, or a semi-automatic AR-15 rifle from 2010. Indeed, his rate of fire could have been far exceeded by a competent person using very old technology, such as a break-open double-barreled shotgun.

Are Semi-Automatics More Powerful Than Other Guns?

The power of a firearm is measured by the kinetic energy it delivers. Kinetic energy is based on the mass (the weight) of the projectile, and its velocity.[15] So a heavier bullet will deliver more kinetic energy than a lighter one. A faster bullet will deliver more kinetic energy than a slower bullet.[16]

How much kinetic energy a gun will deliver has nothing to do with whether it is a semi-automatic, a lever action, a bolt action, a revolver, or whatever. What matter is, first of all, the weight of the bullet, how much gunpowder is in the particular round of ammunition, and the length of the barrel.[17]

None of this has anything to do with whether the gun is or is not a semiautomatic. Manufacturers typically produce the same gun in several different calibers, sometimes in more than a dozen calibers.

Regarding the rifles which some people call "assault weapons," they tend to be intermediate in power, as far as rifles go. Consider the AR-15 rifle in its most common caliber, the .223. The bullet is only a little bit wider than the puny .22 bullet, but it is longer, and thus heavier.

Using typical ammunition, an AR-15 in .223 would have 1,395 foot-pounds of kinetic energy.[18] That's more than a tiny rifle cartridge like the .17 Remington, which might carry 801 foot-pounds of kinetic energy. In contrast, a big-game cartridge, like the .444 Marlin, might have 3,040.[19] This is why rifles like the AR-15 are suitable and often used for hunting small to medium animals (such as rabbits or deer), but are not suitable for the largest animals, such as elk or moose.[20]

Many (but not all) of the ever-changing group of guns which are labeled "assault weapons" use detachable magazines (a box with an internal spring) to hold their ammunition. But this is a characteristic shared by many other firearms, including many non-semiautomatic rifles (particularly, bolt-actions), and by the large majority of handguns. Whatever the merits of restricting magazine size (and we will discuss this below), the size of the magazine depends on the size the magazine. If you want to control magazine size, there is no point in banning certain guns which can take detachable magazines, while not banning other guns which also take detachable magazines.

Bans by Name

Rather than banning guns on rate of fire, or firepower, the various legislative attempts to define an "assault weapon" have taken two approaches: banning guns by name, and banning guns by whether they have certain superficial features.

After a quarter century of legislative attempts to define "assault weapon," the flagship bill for prohibitionists, by Senator Dianne Feinstein, still relies on banning 157 guns by name. This in itself demonstrates that "assault weapons" prohibitions are not about guns which are actually more dangerous than other guns.

After all, if a named gun really has physical characteristics which make it more dangerous than other guns, then legislators ought to be able to describe those characteristics, and ban guns (regardless of name) which have the supposedly dangerous characteristics.

Banning guns by name violates the Constitution's prohibition on Bills of Attainder. It is a form of legislative punishment, singling out certain politically disfavored companies for a prohibition on their products.

Bans by Features

An alternative approach to defining "assault weapon" has been to prohibit guns which have one or more items from a list of external features. These features have nothing to do with a gun's rate of fire, its ammunition capacity, or its firepower. Below are various items from Senator Feinstein's 1994 and/or 2013 bills.

Bayonet Lugs

A bayonet lug gives a gun a military appearance. But to say the least, it has nothing to do with any real-world issue. Drive-by bayonetings are not a problem in this country.

Attachments for Rocket Launchers and Grenade Launchers

Since nobody makes guns for the civilian market that have such features, these bans would affect nothing. Putting the words "grenade launcher" and "rocket launcher" into the bill gives readily-gulled media the opportunity to ask indignantly "How can anyone support guns made to shoot grenades!?!" Besides that, grenades and rockets are subject to extremely severe controls, and essentially impossible for civilians to acquire.

Folding or Telescoping Stocks

Telescoping stocks are extremely popular because they allow shooters to adjust the gun to their own size and build, to the clothing they're wearing, or to their shooting position. Folding stocks make a rifle or shotgun much easier to carry in a backpack while hunting or camping. Even with a folding stock, the gun is still far larger, and less concealable, than a handgun.

Grips

The Feinstein bills outlaw any long gun that has a grip, or anything which can function as a grip. Of course, all guns have grips—or they couldn't be held in the hand to fire at all. While this means that some bills would presumptively ban nearly all semi-autos, the likely intent is to ban pistol-style grips. This reflects the fact that gun prohibitionists learn much of what they know about guns by watching movies made by other gun prohibitionists, such as the "Rambo" series by Sylvester Stallone. So they think that the purpose of a "pistol grip" is to enable somebody to "spray fire" a gun. And, of course, the prohibitionists imagine that semiautomatic rifles *are* exactly the same as the machine guns in the Rambo movies.

In truth, a grip helps a responsible shooter stabilize the rifle while holding the stock against his shoulder. It is particularly useful in hunting, where the shooter will not have sandbags or a benchrest, or perhaps anything else on which to rest the forward part of the rifle. Accurate hunting is humane hunting. And should a long gun be needed for self-defense, accuracy can save the victim's life.

The gun prohibition lobbies, though, oppose firearms accuracy. On the January 16, 2013, PBS Newshour, Josh Horwitz (an employee of the Coalition to Stop Gun Violence) said that grips should be banned because they prevent "muzzle rise" and thereby allow the shooter to stay on target.

Well, yes, a grip helps stabilize the gun so that a second shot (whether at a deer or a violent attacker) will go where the first shot went. Horowitz was essentially saying that guns which are easy to fire accurately should be banned.

This is backwards. It is like claiming that history books which are especially accurate should be banned, while less-accurate books could still be allowed.

Guns which are more accurate are better for all the constitutionally-protected uses of firearms, including self-defense, hunting, and target shooting. To single them out for prohibition is flagrantly unconstitutional.

Barrel Covers

For long guns that do not have a forward grip, the user may stabilize the by holding the barrel with her non-dominant hand. A barrel cover or shroud protects the user's hand. When a gun is fired repeatedly, the barrel can get very hot. This is not an issue in deer hunting (where no more than a few shots will be fired in a day), but it is a problem in some other kinds of hunting, and it is a particular problem in target shooting, where dozens of shots will be fired in a single session.

Threaded Barrel for Safety Attachments

Threading at the end of a gun barrel can be used to attach muzzle brakes or sound suppressors.

When a round is fired though a gun barrel, the recoil from the shot will move the barrel off target, especially for a second, follow-up shot. Muzzle brakes reduce recoil and keep the gun on target. It is very difficult to see how something which makes a gun more accurate makes it so "bad" that it must be banned.

A threaded barrel can also be used to attach as sound suppressor. Suppressors are legal in the United States; buying one requires the same very severe process as buying a machine gun. They are sometimes, inaccurately, called "silencers." They typically reduce a gunshot's noise by about 15-20 decibels, which still leaves the gun four times louder than a chainsaw.

But people who only know about firearms by watching movies imagine that a gun with a "silencer" is nearly silent, and is only used by professional assassins. In real life, sound suppressors are used by lots of people who want to protect their hearing, or to reduce the noise heard by neighbors of a shooting range. Many firearms instructors choose suppressors in order to help new shooters avoid the "flinch" that many novices display because of a gun's loudness.

The bans on guns with grips, folding stocks, barrel covers, or threads focus exclusively on the relatively minor ways in which a feature might help a criminal, and completely ignore the feature's utility for legitimate sports and self-defense. The reason that manufacturers include these features on firearms is because millions of law-abiding firearms owners choose them for entirely legitimate purposes.

Sen. Dianne Feinstein's 2013 Legislation

Sen

Feinstein attempts to reassure gun owners by also including an appendix of guns which she is not banning. In 1994, she exempted 670 "recreational" firearms. In 2013, the exempted guns list grows to over 2,200. Notably, not a single handgun appears on either of Sen. Feinstein's lists. The basis for a gun being exempted is because it is, supposedly, suitable for recreational uses. This ignores the holding of *District of Columbia v. Heller* that self-defense is the core of the Second Amendment.

The exemption list is meaningless. It is inflated by naming certain models repeatedly. For example, the Remington 870 pump action shotgun appears 16 different times, in its various configurations. Besides that, none of the exempted guns are covered by the bill's ban on guns by name or by feature.

Regarding grandfathered guns, Sen. Feinstein makes them nontransferable, thus imposing a slow-motion form of uncompensated confiscation.

Grandfathering with slow-motion confiscation may be a way-station to immediate confiscation, when political circumstances allow. As Sen. Feinstein told CBS 60 Minutes in 1995, "If it were up to me, I would tell Mr. and Mrs. America to turn them in—turn them all in."[21]

Would a Ban Do Any Good?

Connecticut banned so-called "assault weapons" in 1993, and the ban is still on the books. The Bushmaster rifle used by the Sandy Hook murderer was not an "assault weapon" under Connecticut law. Nor was it an "assault weapon" under the 1994-2004 Feinstein ban.[22] The new Feinstein ban would cover that particular model of Bushmaster. But it would allow Bushmaster (or any other company) to manufacture other semi-automatic rifles, using a different name, which fire just as fast, and which fire equally powerful bullets.

To reiterate, the Sandy Hook murderer's rate of fire (150 shots in 20 minutes) could be duplicated by any firearm produced in the last century and a half.

We do not have to speculate about whether "assault weapon" bans do any good. A Department of Justice study commissioned by the Clinton administration found that they do not.

In order to pass the 1994 federal ban, proponents had to accept two related provisions. First, the ban would sunset after 10 years. Second, the Department of Justice would have to commission a study of the ban's effectiveness. The study would then provide Congress with information to help decide whether to renew the ban.

The Justice Department of Attorney General Janet Reno chose the Urban Institute to conduct the required study. The Urban Institute is well-respected and long-established progressive think tank in Washington. The study found the Feinstein ban to be a complete failure. There was no evidence that lives were saved, no evidence that criminals fired fewer shots during gun fights, no evidence of any good accomplished. Given the evidence from the researchers selected by the Clinton-Reno Department of Justice, it was not surprising that Congress chose not to renew the 1994 ban.

The final report was published by the U.S. Department of Justice's research arm, the National Institute of Justice, in 2004, based on data through 2003. The authors were Christopher S. Koper, Daniel J. Woods, and Jeffrey A. Roth.[23] The 2004 final report replaced two preliminary papers by Roth and Koper, one of which was published in 1997, and the other in 1999.[24]

The 2004 final report concludes: "we cannot clearly credit the ban with any of the nation's recent drop in gun violence. ... Should it be renewed, the ban's effects on gun violence are likely to be small at best and perhaps too small for reliable measurement."

As the paper noted, "assault weapons" "were used in only a small fraction of gun crimes prior to the ban: about 2% according to most studies and no more than 8%." Most of those that were used in crime were pistols, not rifles.

Recall that "assault weapons" are arbitrarily categorized guns that are functionally equivalent to other guns. Thus, criminals, to the degree that the ban affects them at all, can and did easily substitute other guns for so-called "assault weapons."

Regarding the ban's impacts on crime, the 2004 paper concludes that "the share of crimes involving" so-called "assault weapons" declined, due "primarily to a reduction in the use of assault pistols," but that this decline "was offset throughout at least the late 1990s by steady or rising use of other guns equipped with" magazines holding more than ten rounds. In other words, as anyone with common sense could have predicted, criminals easily substituted some guns for others. (Magazines are discussed in the next section.)

Unfortunately, Senator Feinstein's website is somewhat inaccurate in claiming that the 1994 ban was helpful. The Senator's web page on "assault weapons" lists five sources that allegedly show the “effectiveness” of the 1994 ban. However, four of those sources pertain, not to changes in crime rates, but to changes in weapon and magazine use. Such trends do not show that the 1994 ban was effective. Instead, they show, among other things, that the ban took place in a period of declining crime rates. Crime was declining before the imposition of the ban, and it continued to decline after the ban was lifted. The shift in gun use in crime also shows that criminals can easily replace “assault” semi-automatic guns with other, functionally equivalent semi-automatic guns.[25]

The four cited sources show that if you make it illegal to manufacture a gun with a certain name, then firearms companies will make guns with different names. Then, guns with the “bad” names will become a smaller fraction of the total U.S. gun supply. Some of the guns in the legal pool of guns are eventually acquired by criminals. (The principal means are thefts, and “straw purchases,” in which a confederate who does not have a criminal record purchases a firearm on behalf of a convicted criminal. Straw purchases are federal felonies.) So over time, criminals have fewer guns with the “bad” name, and more guns with other names. Changing the names of the guns that criminals use does not make anyone any safer.

For the fifth source, the website makes the following claim:

> In a Department of Justice study, Jeffrey Roth and Christopher Koper find that the 1994 Assault Weapons Ban was responsible for a 6.7 percent decrease in total gun murders, holding all other factors equal. ...
>
> Original source (page 2): Jeffrey A. Roth & Christopher S. Koper, “Impact Evaluation of the Public Safety and Recreational Firearms Use Protection Act of 1994,” The Urban Institute (March 1997).

Attentive readers will notice that Roth and Koper are two of the authors of the 2004 study discussed above. So why does the website cite the 1997 study by these researchers, but not their 1999 study or (regarding this point) their 2004 study? The later studies repudiated the preliminary guess in the 1997 study.

Here is what the 1997 study actually said:

> Our best estimate is that the ban contributed to a 6.7 percent decrease in total gun murders between 1994 and 1995, beyond what would have been expected in view of ongoing crime, demographic, and economic trends. However, with only one year of post-ban data, we cannot rule out the possibility that this decrease reflects chance year-to-year variation rather than a true effect of the ban.[26]

So initially, the researchers mistook a “year-to-year variation”—actually part of a long-term decline in crime rates—for the effects of the “assault weapons ban.” They corrected this error in their subsequent reports—a fact that Senator Feinstein’s website does not acknowledge.

What about state-level “assault weapons bans?” Remember that Connecticut has had such a ban since 1993. The Newtown murders are a vivid illustration that such bans do not save lives.

Economist John Lott examined data for the five states with “assault weapon” bans in his 2003 book, *The Bias Against Guns*. Controlling for sociological variables, and testing the five states with bans against the other 45 states, he found no evidence of a reduction in crime. To the contrary, the bans were associated with increased crime in some categories.[27] Whether the adverse effect Lott reports is a phantom of statistical analyses or random factors, or whether it is the result of criminals feeling relatively empowered due to state governments cracking down on law-abiding gun owners, the state-level data do not support the claim that "assault weapons" bans reduced crime rates.

It is ridiculous to claim that banning some semi-automatic guns, while leaving other, functionally equivalent semi-automatic guns legal, will reduce violent crime. It is analogous to banning knives with black handles, but not knives with brown handles, and expecting that to reduce knife-related crime.

Regarding mass murders in particular, *Mother Jones* examined 62 mass shootings since 1982, finding that 35 of the total 142 guns used were designated as "assault weapons."[28] To take one example not involving an "assault weapon," in 1991 a man murdered 22 people at a Texas cafeteria using a pair of ordinary semi-automatic pistols, not an "assault weapon." He reloaded the gun multiple times.[29] Tragically, in order to comply with laws against concealed carry, Suzanna Hupp had locked her own handgun in her vehicle before entering the cafeteria, rendering her defenseless as the attacker murdered her parents and many others.[30]

Obviously criminals need not limit themselves to semi-automatic guns. Consider first the potential lethality of shotguns. The Winchester Model 12 pump action shotgun (defined as a "recreational" firearm by the 1994 federal "assault weapons" ban) can fire six 00 buckshot shells, each shell containing twelve .33 caliber pellets, in three seconds. Each of the pellets is larger in diameter than the bullet fired by an AKS (a semiautomatic look-alike of an AK-47 rifle). In other words, the Winchester Model 12 pump action shotgun can in three seconds unleash seventy-two separate projectiles, each single one capable of causing injury or death. The Remington Model 1100 shotgun (a common semiautomatic duck-hunting gun, also defined as a "recreational" firearm under the 1994 ban) can unleash the same seventy-two projectiles in 2.5 seconds. In contrast, an AKS would take about a minute to fire forty aimed shots (or perhaps twice that many without aiming).[31] Notably, a pump-action shotgun is extremely easy to reload without lowering the gun from firing position, and each additionally loaded shell can be fired immediately. When mass murderers target victims in tightly-packed venues, a "recreational" shotgun could be particularly deadly.

The Purpose of Gun Bans Is to Ban Guns

The only true utility of a ban on "assault weapons" is to condition the public to bans on more guns. For example, Douglas Anthony Cooper advocates a ban on "assault" semi-automatics and "high-capacity" magazines, though he grants such legislation makes little or no difference. His solution is to ban all semi-automatic rifles and all pump-action shotguns, writing that pump-action shotguns "are in some ways *more* useful than many often-banned weapons, if you intend to shoot a huge number of people, quickly."[32]

In the 1996 op-ed quoted above, Charles Krauthammer calls for government to "disarm its citizenry," and he sees the "assault weapons ban" as meaningful only as a step in that direction. Krauthammer argues, "The claim of the advocates that banning these 19 types of 'assault weapons' will reduce the crime rate is laughable. There are dozens of other weapons, the functional equivalent of these 'assault weapons,' that were left off the list and are perfect substitutes for anyone bent on mayhem." Nevertheless, Krauthammer sees the ban as useful insofar as it leads to "real steps, like the banning of handguns," down the road.[33]

Although writer Christian Chung does not offer a detailed plan on the legislation he would eventually like to see in place, he refers to Feinstein's newly proposed "assault weapons ban" as "only the start" of much more extensive legislation. One of Chung's complaints is that the "assault weapons ban" arbitrarily outlaws some semi-automatic guns because of some "cosmetic addition" while leaving functionally equivalent guns legal.[34]

Writing for the *Atlantic*, senior editor Robert Wright similarly complains about the "assault weapons ban," arguing that "the assault weapons issue is a red herring." As he points out, "there's no clear and simple definition of an assault weapon, and this fact has in the past led to incoherent regulation." What is Wright's preferred legislation? He advocates legislation to accomplish the following: "It's illegal to sell or possess a firearm—rifle or pistol—that can hold more than six bullets. And it's illegal to sell or possess a firearm with a detachable magazine."[35] In other words, Wright wants to outlaw the overwhelming majority of semi-automatic guns.

MAGAZINES

Nationally, anti-gun advocates are calling for a ban on magazines holding more than 10 rounds. New York Governor Andrew Cuomo has gone even further, with a ban on anything holding more than seven.[36] These bans are unconstitutional, and harmful to public safety.

A magazine is the part of the firearm where ammunition is stored. Sometimes the magazine is part of the firearm itself, as in tube magazines underneath barrels. This is typical for shotguns.

For rifles and handguns, the typical magazine is detachable. A detachable magazine is a rectangular or curved box, made of metal or plastic. At the bottom of the magazine is a spring, which helps push a fresh round of ammunition into the firing chamber, after the empty shell from the previous round has been ejected. Some people use the word "clip," but this is incorrect.

The type or model of gun does not determine what size magazine can be used. Any gun that uses a detachable magazine can accommodate a detachable magazine of any size.

As detailed above, the 1994 Feinstein ban was predicated on the theory that "recreational" firearm use is legitimate, and other firearms use is not. The ban did in fact impede recreational firearms use. More importantly, the ban is plain a violation of *Heller*, which affirms the right of defensive gun ownership.

For target shooting competitions, there are many events which *require* the use of magazines holding more than 10 rounds. For hunting, about half the states limit the magazine size that a hunter can carry in the field, but about half the states do not.

In some scenarios, such as deer hunting, it is quite true that a hunter will rarely get off more than two shots at a particular animal. But in other situations, particularly pest control, the use of 11 to 30 round magazines is quite typical, because the hunter will be firing multiple shots. These include the hunting of packs of feral wild hogs (which are quite strong, and are often difficult to put down with a single shot), prairie dogs, and coyotes.

More generally, the rifle that might shoot only one or two shots at a deer might be needed for self-defense against a bear, or against human attackers. In 2012, Arizona repealed its limitations on magazine capacity for hunters precisely because of the need for self-defense against unexpected encounters with smuggling gangs in the southern part of the state. It is well-established that drug traffickers and human traffickers often use the same wild and lonely lands that hunters do.

For the firearms that are most often chosen for self-defense, asserting that any magazine over 10 (or seven) rounds is "high capacity" is incorrect. The term "high-capacity magazine" might have a legitimate meaning when it refers to a magazine that extends far beyond that intended for the gun's optimal operation. For example, although a semi-automatic handgun can accept a 30-round magazine, such a magazine extends far beneath the gun grip, and it is therefore impractical to use with a concealed-carry permit, to take one example. For a handgun, a 30-round magazine may be a "high-capacity magazine."

The persons who have the most need for actual high-capacity magazines are persons who would have great difficulty changing a magazine—such as elderly persons, persons with handicaps, persons with Parkinson's disease, and so on. For a healthy person, changing a magazine takes only a second or two. How is this accomplished? Typically a gun's magazine-release button is near the trigger. To change a magazine, the person holding the gun presses the magazine-release button with a thumb or finger. The magazine instantly drops to the floor. While pushing the magazine-release button with one hand, the other hand grabs a fresh magazine (which might be carried in a special holster on a belt) and bringing it towards the gun. The moment the old magazine drops out, a fresh one is inserted.[37]

Although changing magazines is quick, persons being attacked by violent criminals will typically prefer not to spend even two seconds in a magazine change. This is why semi-automatic handguns often come factory-standard with a magazine of 11 to 19 rounds. For example, Rep. Gabrielle Giffords has said that she owns a 9mm Glock handgun. The most popular Glocks in this caliber come standard with 15 or 17 round magazines.[38]

For most other manufacturers as well, handgun magazines with a capacity of 11 to 19 rounds are factory standard. A ban on magazines with a capacity of more than 10 rounds means a ban on the most common and most useful magazines purchased for purposes of recreational target practice and self-defense.

One thing that proves the obvious usefulness of standard capacity magazines is the fact that most police officers use them. An officer typically carries a semi-automatic handgun on a belt holster as his primary sidearm. The magazine capacity is typically in the 11-19 range.

Likewise, the long gun that is carried in police patrol cars is quite often an AR-15 rifle with a 30-round magazine.[39]

True, a police officer is much more likely than other civilians to find him- or herself in a confrontation with violent criminals. Nevertheless, every civilian faces some risk of such a confrontation, and every law-abiding citizen has a moral right to own the best tools of self-defense should such a confrontation come to pass. Although different guns work better for different individuals in different circumstances, in many contexts the officer's advice is equally sound for non-police civilians who own a gun for self-defense.

Why might someone "need" a factory-standard fifteen-round magazine for a common 9 mm handgun? Beyond the fact that government should recognize and protect people's rights, not dictate to free Americans what they "need" to own, standard-capacity magazines can be extremely useful for self-defense. This is true in a variety of circumstances, such as if a defender faces multiple attackers, an attacker is wearing heavy clothing or body armor, an attacker is turbo-charged by methamphetamine or cocaine, an attacker poses an active threat from behind cover, or a home invader cuts the lights to the home before entering at night.

Especially because, in stressful circumstances, police as well as non-police civilians often miss when firing a handgun even at close range, having the extra rounds can be crucially important in some defensive contexts.

Consider the advantages a criminal has over his intended victims. The criminal often takes time to carefully prepare an attack; the victim is caught off-guard. The criminal has the element of surprise; the victim is the one surprised. The criminal can adapt his plans, as by selecting different weaponry; the victim must respond with what's at hand at the moment of attack. A criminal can, for instance, substitute a shotgun or a bag full of revolvers for a semi-automatic gun. A criminal can pack multiple magazines if he uses a semi-automatic gun. The intended victim, on the other hand, usually will have on hand at most a single defensive gun, carrying (if it is a semi-automatic) a single magazine. Thus, what legislation such as a ban on "high-capacity" magazines does is give the criminal a greater advantage over his intended victims.

Would a Magazine Ban Do Any Good?

Recall that in 2004 the National Institute of Justice study found that the 1994-2004 ban on the manufacture or import of such magazines had no discernible benefit. As the authors noted, the existing supply of such magazines was so vast that criminals apparently had no trouble obtaining magazines of whatever size they wished.[40]

Since the September 2004 expiration of the ban on new magazines, the supply has grown vaster still. In other words, we know that the pre-1994 supply of magazines was so large that nine years of prohibition had no effect. The much larger supply of magazines as of 2013 means that the already-demonstrated period of nine years of futility would be far longer.

No one can say if a ban on new magazines would ever do any good. But we can be rather certain that a ban would be ineffectual for at least fifteen years, and perhaps many more. Preventing the next Newtown is something that requires solutions which will start working this year—and not futile laws which, in the best case scenario, might possibly begin to have their first benefits around 2030.

It is entirely possible to speculate what might happen if criminals did not have magazines with 11 or more rounds, just as one can speculate about what might happen if all criminals could not obtain stolen cars, or if criminals could not obtain guns, or if all criminals were left-handed. But there is no particular reason to think that any of these scenarios might ever come true.[41]

A national ban on the millions of currently owned "high capacity" magazines would require a heavy-handed police state to enforce. The new Cuomo ban in New York will be enforceable only if the state's motto of "The Empire State" is changed to "The Police State."

It would be possible to outlaw the legal transfer of grandfathered magazines, but this would not remove "high-capacity" magazines from the black market.

Regarding "shootout" scenarios, the types of criminals most likely to get into shootouts with the police or with other criminals are precisely the types of criminals expert at acting on the black market. Although gun prohibitionists often link "assault weapons" to gang violence associated with the illegal drug trade,[42] they miss the irony of their argument. They are, in effect, claiming that gangs operating the black market in drugs will somehow be restricted from acquiring "high capacity" magazines by legislation limiting the manufacture and sale of such magazines. In short, their argument—at least as it pertains to career criminals—is ludicrous. If gangsters can obtain all the cocaine they want, despite a century of severely-enforced prohibition, they are going to be able to get 15 round magazines.

Besides that, magazines are not very difficult to build. Anyone with moderate machine shop skills can build a small metal box and put a spring in it. Building magazines is vastly easier than building guns, and we know that tribespeople in Ghana (who do not have access to high-quality machine shops) produce a hundred thousand working copies of the AK-47 per year.[43]

Moreover, 3-D printing technology has *already* produced "printed" plastic magazines.[44] It's not very hard—just a box in a particular shape, along with a spring. For manufacturing actual firearms, 3-D printing is currently just a hypothetical; a firearm needs to be strong enough to withstand (over the course of its use) many thousands of gunpowder explosions in the firing chamber. But for a mere magazine, the current strength of printed plastics is sufficient.

We can limit the discussion, then, to mass murders in which the perpetrator targets victims randomly, often seeking the global infamy the mass media so readily provide them. Of course some such people could still illegally purchase a "high capacity magazine" on the black market. Given that 36 percent of American high school seniors illegally acquire and consume marijuana,[45] it is unrealistic to think that someone intent on mass mayhem would be unable to find his magazine of choice on the black market.

Besides that, the truly high-capacity magazines (e.g., a 100 round drum), are very prone to malfunction. For example, during the mass murder at the movie theater in Aurora, the murderer's 100-round magazine malfunctioned, causing the killer to cease using the gun with the magazine.[46] Had the killer had numerous, smaller magazines, he would have been able to fire more rounds from that particular gun. Hundred round magazines are novelty items, and are not standard for self-defense by civilians or police.

Advocates of the ban on standard capacity magazines assert that while the attacker is changing the magazine, one of the victims can tackle him.

There are three known instances where something this may have happened: in Springfield, Oregon, in 1998; in Tucson, Arizona, in 2011;[47] and the Long Island Railroad in 1991.

Far more commonly, however, the victims are fleeing, and are not close enough to the shooter to tackle him during a two-second interval. At Newtown, the murderer changed magazines many times, firing only a portion of the rounds in each magazine.[48] At the 1991 murders at the Luby's Texas cafeteria (24 dead), the perpetrator changed magazines multiple times. In the Virginia Tech murders, the perpetrator changed magazines 17 times.[49]

The *Heller* decision teaches us that one does not decide on the constitutionality of banning something simply by looking at instances of misuse. Handguns are used in thousands of homicides annually, and in several hundred thousand other gun crimes. A ban on handguns (imagining it would be effective) would have orders of magnitude greater benefits than a ban on magazines holding more than 10 rounds (imagining that too to be effective).

Heller, however, reminds us that the Second Amendment has already done the cost-benefit analysis. The Framers were quite familiar with gun crime, and with lawful defensive gun use. The arms and accessories protected by the Second Amendment are those which are commonly used by law-abiding citizens for legitimate purposes, especially self-defense. In today's America, this certainly includes handguns and rifles with magazines that prohibitionists would consider "large."

International Comparisons

Some Americans, including Howard Dean, the former chair of the Democratic National Committee, have advocated the mass confiscation of firearms. Their model is the confiscations that took place in the past quarter-century in Great Britain.

This dystopian situation in Great Britain actually shows the perils of repressive anti-gun laws:

- A woman in Great Britain is three times more likely to be raped than an American woman.
- In the United States, only about 13% of home burglaries take place when the occupants are home, but in Great Britain, about 59% do. American burglars report that they avoid occupied homes because of the risk of getting shot. English burglars prefer occupied homes, because there will be wallets and purses with cash, which does not have to be fenced at a discount. British criminals have little risk of confronting a victim who possesses a firearm. Even the small percentage of British homes which have a lawfully-owned gun would not be able to unlock the gun from one safe, and then unlock the ammunition from another safe, in time to use the gun against a home invader. It should hardly be surprising, then, that Britain has a much higher rate of home invasion burglaries than does the United States.[50]
- Overall, the violent crime rate in England and Wales is far above the American rate. (Using the standard definition for the four most common major violent crimes: homicide, rape, robbery, and aggravated assault.)
- According to the United Nations (not exactly a "pro-gun" organization), Scotland is the most violent nation in the developed world.[51]

In the early 20th century, the Great Britain had virtually no gun control, virtually no gun control. Today, it has a plethora of both.

What went wrong? Various minor and ineffectual gun controls were enacted in the late nineteenth and early twentieth centuries; proposals for more extensive controls ran into strenuous opposition in Parliament from MPs who still believed in natural rights. The advocacy for gun control was almost always accompanied by a bodyguard of lies, such as when the government, fearful of a workers rebellion, pushed through the Firearms Act of 1920. The government falsely told the public that gun crimes were rapidly increasing, and hid the law's true motive (political control) from the public, presenting the law as a mere anti-crime measure.[52] In practice, the law eliminated the right of British subjects to be armed, and turned it into a privilege. The Firearms Act also began a decades-long process of eliminating the public's duty to protect their society and right to protect themselves. By the late 20th century, Great Britain had one of the lowest rates of gun ownership in the Western World. Only 4% of British households would admit gun ownership to a telephone pollster.[53]

In 1998, after a known pedophile used a handgun to murder kindergarten children in Dunblane, Scotland, the Parliament banned non-government possession of handguns. As a result the Gun Control Network (a prohibition advocacy group) enthused that "present British controls over firearms are regarded as 'the gold standard' in many countries." According to GCN spokesperson Mrs. Gill Marshall-Andrews, "the fact that we have a gold standard is something to be proud of...."[54]

A July 2001 study from King's College London's Centre for Defence Studies found that handgun-related crime increased by nearly 40% in the two years following implementation of the handgun ban. The study also found that there had been "no direct link" between lawful possession of guns by licensed citizens and misuse of guns by criminals. According to the King's College report, although the 1998 handgun ban resulted in over 160,000 licensed handguns being withdrawn from personal possession, "the UK appears not to have succeeded in creating the gun free society for which many have wished. Gun related violence continues to rise and the streets of Britain...seem no more safe."[55]

A few weeks before the King's College study was released, Home Office figures showed that violent crime in Great Britain was rising at the second fastest rate in the world, well above the U.S. rate, and on par with crime-ridden South Africa.[56] In February 2001, it was reported that 26 percent of persons living in England and Wales had been victims of crime in 1999.[57] Home Secretary Jack Straw admitted, "levels of victimisation are higher than in most comparable countries for most categories of crime." On May 4, 2001, *The Telegraph* disclosed that the risk of a citizen being assaulted was "higher in Britain than almost anywhere else in the industrialized world, including America."[58]

As King's College observed, with passage of the Firearms Act of 1997, "it was confidently assumed that the new legislation effectively banning handguns would have the direct effect of reducing certain types of violent crime by reducing access to weapons."[59] The news media promised that the "world's toughest laws will help to keep weapons off the streets."[60]

Yet faster than British gun-owners could surrender their previously-registered handguns for destruction, guns began flooding into Great Britain from the international black market (especially from eastern Europe and China), driven by the demands of the country's rapidly developing criminal gun culture.[61]

It is true that there are far fewer gun deaths in Great Britain than in the United States. Most of the difference is due to different methods of suicide; guns being scarce in Great Britain, suicides are perpetrated with other methods.

The one major criminal justice statistic in which Great Britain appears to be doing better than the U.S. is the homicide rate, with the U.S. rate at a little more than 4, and the England and Wales rate at 1.4. However, the U.S. rate is based on initial reports of homicides, and includes lawful self-defense killings (about 10-15% of the total); the England and Wales rate is based only on final dispositions, so that an unsolved murder, or a murder which is pleaded down to a lesser offense, is not counted a homicide. In addition, multiple murders are counted as only a single homicide for Scottish statistics.[62]

But let's assume that the entire difference is the homicide rates between the U.S. and Great Britain is due to gun control. The advocates of British-style controls in America ought to acknowledge the fearsome price that gun control has exacted on the British people: an astronomical rate of rape, of home invasions, and of violent crime in general.

Registration

An important difference between Great Britain and the United States is that in Great Britain, many people complied with gun confiscation because their guns were already registered.

The evidence is overwhelming that Americans will not comply with gun confiscation programs; a recent Rasmussen poll showed that 65 percent of American gun owners would not obey government orders to surrender their guns.

Nor will Americans obey laws which retroactively require them to register their guns. During the first phase of the "assault weapon" hoax, several states and cities passed bans, and allowed grandfathered owners to keep the guns legally by registering the guns. The non-compliance rates for retroactive registration were always at least 90%, and frequently much higher than that.[63] Americans are quite aware that gun registration can be a tool for gun confiscation. That is why Congress has enacted three separate laws (1941, 1986, and 1993) to prohibit federal gun registration. Congress first acted in 1941 because Congress saw how Hitler and Stalin had been using gun registration for confiscation.[64] Since then, registration lists have been used in many countries, and in New York City, for confiscation. Indeed, even if we look only at registration laws enacted by democratic nations, in most countries gun registration lists have eventually been used for the confiscation of many firearms.

Congress cannot expand or contract the judicially-declared scope of a constitutional right;[65] but Congress can, under section 5 of the Fourteenth Amendment, enact "prophylactic" measures to prevent state and local governments from endangering civil rights,[66] provided that these laws are "congruent and proportional" to the problem that Congress is addressing.[67] Congress should use this power to prohibit all state and local registration of guns and gun owners, and to require the destruction of any existing records. Persons who are advocating gun confiscation are irresponsible in the extreme. Confiscation would endanger the lives of law enforcement officers who were ordered to carry it out. We should remember that the political dispute between the American Colonies and Great Britain turned into a shooting war precisely at the moment when the British attempted house-tohouse gun confiscation.[68]

Mass prohibitions of guns or gun accessories invite a repetition of the catastrophe of alcohol prohibition. Just as alcohol prohibition in the 1920s and drug prohibition in modern times have spawned vast increases in state power, and vast infringements on the Bill of Rights, another national war against the millions of Americans who are determined to possess a product which is very important to them is almost certain to cause tremendous additional erosion of constitutional freedom and traditional liberty. Legal and customary protections unreasonable search and seizure, against invasion of privacy, against selective enforcement, and against harsh and punitive statutes would all suffer.[69]

WHAT CAN BE DONE?

Acknowledging Success

Regarding firearms crime in general (and not just the highly-publicized mass homicides), we should start by acknowledging the success of policies of the last three decades. Since

1980, the U.S. homicide rate has fallen by over half, from more than 10 victims per 100,000 population annually, to under 5 today.[70]

Homicide, as horrifying as it is, did not make the top fifteen causes of death for 2011, according to preliminary data published by the Centers for Disease Control.[71] Of the 2,512,873 total deaths for that year, the large majority were caused by health-related problems. The fifth leading cause of death was accidents, at 122,777 deaths. Suicide made the top ten with 38,285 deaths.

Appropriately, the media tend to report homicides much more frequently and emphatically than they report deaths from other causes. The problem is that the uncritical consumer of media might develop a skewed perspective of the actual risks he or she faces.

In 2011, homicides numbered 15,953, or 0.63 percent of all deaths. Of those, 11,101 were caused by "discharge of firearms"—or nearly 70 percent of all homicides.

The vast majority of these were from handguns, which shotguns in second place. The FBI reports that in 2011, 13 percent of homicides were committed with "knives or cutting instruments," while nearly 6 percent were committed with "personal weapons" such "hands, fists, feet, etc."[72]

Most of the guns which are inaccurately called "assault weapons" are rifles. All types of rifles combined comprise only about two percent of homicide weapons—far less than "blunt instruments" such as hammers, clubs, and so on.

As for accidents in 2011, 34,676 deaths were caused by "motor vehicle accidents"; 33,554 deaths by "accidental poisoning and exposure to noxious substances"; 26,631 deaths by falls; 3,555 deaths by "accidental drowning and submersion"; and 851 deaths by "accidental discharge of firearms."[73]

Regarding violent crime in general, violent crime has been on a 20-year decline, so that today Americans are safer from violent crime than at any time since the early 1960s.[74]

The news is even better for young people. According to Bureau of Justice Statistics (part of the U.S. Department of Justice), "From 1994 to 2010, the overall rate of serious violent crime against youth declined by 77%."[75]

These successes have taken place during a period when American gun ownership has soared. In 1964, when crime was about the same as it is now, per capita gun ownership was only .45, less than 1 gun per 2 Americans. In 1982, there were about .77 guns per capita. (About 3 guns per 4 Americans). By 1994, that had risen to .91 (9 guns per 10 Americans). Today, there are slightly more guns in America than Americans. We have increased from 232 million guns in 1982 to over 308 million in 2010.[76]

The causes of crime fluctuations are many. They include (among other things) changes in illegal drug activity and government enforcement thereof, changes in police tactics, changes in incarceration rates, changes in the average age of the population (which in the U.S. has been increasing), and changes in reporting (which can mask real changes in underlying crime trends).

It would not be accurate to say that increased gun ownership, and the spread of laws allowing the licensed carry of handguns is the only cause of progress that has been made in recent decades. We can say with certainty that "more guns" is not associated with "more crime." If anything, just the opposite is true.

ARMED DEFENDERS

Sandy Hook Elementary School was a pretend "gun free zone": responsible adults were legally prohibited from effectively protecting the children in their care, while an armed criminal was could not be prevented from entering.

What did finally stop the murderer? He killed himself just before being confronted by men carrying guns, guns that no doubt included "assault weapons" with "high-capacity magazines." As the Associated Press reports, the murderer "shot himself in the head just as he heard police drawing near to the classroom where he was slaughtering helpless children."[77]

The Newtown murders took place in a state with a ban on "assault weapons," and with a strict system of gun owner licensing and registration— one of the most restrictive in the nation. Not even the most restrictive laws (short of complete prohibition of all legal gun ownership) can remedy the problems of an absent, divorced, and detached father, and a custodial mother who is so recklessly irresponsible that even while she tells people in town about her plans to have her son committed to a mental institution, she leaves her registered guns readily accessible to him.

Armed guards are generally successfully at deterring the robbery of diamond stores and banks, and they equally legitimate for preventing the murder of children, who are far more valuable than diamonds or greenbacks.

There are at least 10 cases in which armed persons have stopped incipient mass murder: Pearl High School in Mississippi; Sullivan Central High School in Tennessee; Appalachian School of Law in Virginia; a middle school dance in Edinboro, Pa.; Players Bar and Grill in Nevada; a Shoney's restaurant in Alabama; Trolley Square Mall in Salt Lake City; New Life Church in Colorado; Clackamas Mall in Oregon (three days before Sandy Hook); Mayan Palace Theater in San Antonio (three days after Sandy Hook).

Sometimes the hero was an armed school guard (Sullivan Central High). Sometimes it was an off-duty police officer or mall security guard (Trolley Square, Mayan Theater, Clackamas Mall and the Appalachian Law School, where two law students, one of them a police officer and the other a former sheriff's deputy, had guns in their cars). Or a restaurant owner (Edinboro). Or a church volunteer guard with a concealed carry permit (Colorado). Or a diner with a concealed carry permit (Alabama and Nevada). At Pearl High School, it was the vice principal who had a gun in his car and stopped a 16- year-old, who had killed his mother and two students, before he could drive away, perhaps headed for the junior high.

For schools, Utah provides a model. In Utah, if a law-abiding adult passes a fingerprint-based check and a safety training class, then he or she is issued a permit to carry a concealed handgun throughout the state. Thus, teachers may carry at school. Several Texas school districts also encourage armed teachers. Connecticut, however, is similar to most of the other 40 other states that generally allow law-abiding adults to carry in public places: It limits where guns may be carried, and no civilian, not even teachers and principals, may carry at school.

Anti-gun ideologues invent all sorts of fantasy scenarios about the harms that could be caused by armed teachers. But the Utah law has been in effect since 1995, and Texas since 2008, with not a single problem.

Gun prohibitionists also insist that armed teachers or even armed school guards won't make a difference. But in the real world, they have — even at Columbine, where the armed "school resource officer" (a sheriff's deputy, in this case) was in the parking lot when the first shots were fired. The officer twice fired long-distance shots and drove the killers off the school patio, saving the lives of wounded students there. Unfortunately, however, the officer failed to pursue the killers into the building—perhaps due to a now-abandoned law enforcement doctrine of waiting for the SWAT team to solve serious problems.

Whatever should be done in the long run, the long gun will be much too late to stop the next copycat sociopath who attacks a school (or a mall or movie theater). More concealed carry laws like the ones in Utah and Texas are the best way to save lives right now. Teachers who are already licensed to carry a gun everywhere else in the state should not be prevented from protecting the children in their care.

Doing Something Effective

While armed defense is a necessity, in the short run, to thwart copycat killers, long-term solutions are also necessary.

A very large proportion of mass murders—and about one-sixth of "ordinary" murderers—are mentally ill. Better care, treatment, and stronger laws for civil commitment could prevent many of these crimes. Of course any involuntary commitment must respect the Constitution which, as applied by the U.S. Supreme Court, requires proof by "clear and convincing evidence" that the individual is a danger to himself or others in order for the person to be committed. Better mental health treatment is expensive in the short run, but pays for itself in the long run, through reduced criminal justice and imprisonment costs, not to mention reduced costs to victims.[78]

Although "universal background checks" are, at the highest level of generality, a popular idea, one should pay attention to the details. Every "background check" bill introduced in Congress in the last several years has come from Michael Bloomberg's gun prohibition lobby, and has included a gun registration component. For the reasons detailed above, gun registration is anathema to the Second Amendment.

Consider, for example, the misnamed "Fix Gun Checks Act," from the previous Congress, S. 436 (sponsored by Sen. Schumer). Here is what the bill actually would have done:

- Create a national firearms registry.
- Make it a federal felony to temporarily allow someone to use or hold's one's firearm in the following circumstances:
  - While a friend visits your home.
  - While taking a friend target shooting on your property, or on public lands where target shooting is allowed.
  - While instructing students in a firearms safety class.
- Current law bans gun possession if there has been a formal determination that a person's mental illness makes him a danger to himself or others. S. 436 would abolish the requirement for a fair determination and a finding of dangerousness Instead, S. 436 would ban gun possession by anyone who has ever been ordered to receive counseling for any mental problem. This would include:

- A college student who was ordered to get counseling because the school administration was retaliating against him for criticizing the administration.
- An adult who when in fifth grade was ordered to receive counseling for stuttering, for attention deficit disorder, or for mathematics disorder.
- A person who was once ordered to receive counseling for homosexuality, cross-dressing, or for belonging to some other sexual minority.
- A women who was raped in an elevator, and who has therefore developed a phobia about elevators.

- S. 436 rejects the constitutional standards of due process and fair trial. S. 436 allows for the prohibition of gun ownership based on an arrest, rather than a conviction. Thus, S. 436 would make it gun possession a felony for a person who was once arrested for marijuana possession, and was later found innocent because a police officer mistook tobacco for marijuana.
- Among the reasons that S. 436 was unconstitutional was because it:
    - Strips a person of a fundamental constitutional right because of an arrest, rather than a conviction.
    - Is purportedly based on the congressional power "to regulate Commerce ... among the several States"—but its transfer bans apply solely to transfers that are not commerce, and are not interstate.
    - Violates the scope of gun control laws approved by the Supreme Court in *District of Columbia v. Heller*. The Heller Court approved of some "laws imposing conditions and qualifications on the commercial sale of arms." Yet S. 436 attempted to control non-retail "transfers" that are not even "commercial" or "sales"— such as letting a friend use a gun while target shooting.
    - Is unconstitutionally "overbroad" because rather than banning gun possession by persons who have been determined to pose a threat to themselves or others (current laws) bans gun possession by anyone who has been ordered to get counseling even for non-dangerous mental problems (such as nicotine dependence, or lack of interest in sex).
    - Violates the Fifth Amendment requirement of due process of law, because it imposes gun bans without due process—such as a mere arrest, or the mere order by a school employee or work supervisor that a person receive counseling. Regardless of whether that employee or supervisor offered the person a fair hearing, and regardless of whether the counselor eventually determined that the person had no mental problem at all.
    - Violates the equal protection of the laws guarantee which is implicit in the Fifth Amendment, because it bans possession for categories of persons who cannot rationally be classified as more dangerous than other persons. The victims of S. 436's unfair gun bans would include homosexuals and other sexual minorities, persons who have a phobia about elevators or diseases, and many other persons who are ordered into counseling for reasons that have nothing to do with dangerousness.

Today, the media are reporting that a backroom deal is being worked out in the Senate on "universal background checks." Senators who sincerely follow their oath to protect the United States Constitution would not support a bill which has a title of "Universal Background

Checks," but which contains any of the poisonous anti-constitutional provisions of last session's Bloomberg "background checks" bill.

Moreover, without universal gun registration, mandated background checks on purely private sales (e.g., friends in a hunting club selling guns to each other) are impossible to enforce. Universal gun registration is impossible in practice, and would lead to massive resistance. When Canada tried to impose universal gun registration, the result was a complete fiasco. The registration system cost a hundred times more than promised. Noncompliance (by Canadians, who are much more compliant with government than Americans) was at least fifty percent. And the registration system proved almost entirely useless in crime solving or crime prevention. In 2012, the Canadian government repealed the registration law, and ordered all the registration records destroyed.

Obviously, criminals who are selling guns to each (which is completely illegal, and already subject to severe mandatory sentences) are not going to comply with a background check mandate. It will be irrelevant to them.

Ordinary law-abiding citizens who selling guns to each other might be happy to take the gun into a firearm store for a voluntary check, provided that the check is not subject to a special fee, that there is no registration, and that the check is convenient and expeditious. Changing statutes and regulations so that gun stores can carry out voluntary checks for private sellers is the most that can be expected, realistically. President Obama's order that the Bureau of Alcohol, Tobacco, Firearms and Explosives provide instructions to dealers on how to facilitate voluntary checks is a good idea. In light of this order, there is no need for Congress to enact additional legislation to impose a futile and unenforceable mandate.

"Doing something" is the slogan for politicians who seek merely to exploit terrible crimes for self-serving purposes. "Doing something effective" is the approach of people who want to save lives and protect the public, especially children.

The lives of Americans, especially schoolchildren, depend on the choice that elected officials make between these two alternatives.

End Notes

[1] Some of this testimony is based on a Policy Analysis which Kopel and co-author Ari Armstrong are writing for the Cato Institute. The published Cato version will include more complete endnotes, which were impossible to provide for this testimony, given the very short time available.

[2] Christopher S. Koper, Daniel J. Woods, and Jeffrey A. Roth, "An Updated Assessment of the Federal Assault Weapons Ban: Impacts on Gun Markets and Gun Violence, 1994-2003: Report to the National Institute of Justice, United States Department of Justice," University of Pennsylvania, June 2004, http://www.sas.upenn.edu/jerrylee/research/aw final2004.pdf.

[3] Charles Krauthammer, "Disingenuous Debate on Repeal of Assault Weapons Ban," *Chicago Tribune*, April 8, 1996, http://articles.chicagotribune.com/1996-04- 08/news/9604080024 1 assault-weapons-ban-gun-control-crime-rate.

[4] Josh Sugarmann, "Conclusion," *Assault Weapons and Accessories in America*, Violence Policy Center, 1988, http://www.vpc.org/studies/awaconc.htm.

[5] See, for example, David Kopel, "Guns, Mental Illness and Newtown," *Wall Street Journal*, December 17, 2012, http://online.wsj.com/article/SB10001424127887323723104578185271857424036.html.

[6] See Ari Armstrong, "Civilian Responses to Active Shooters," *Free Colorado*, July 21, 2012, http://ariarmstrong.com/2012/07/civilian-responses-to-active-attackers; *Active Shooter Survival* (Direct Measures, 2012), Survival Edge Series, Disc 1, http://www. directmeasures.com/buy-ACT-LastResort.htm.

7 Alexander Abad-Santos, "This Is What Teachers Learning to Shoot Guns Look Like," *Atlantic Wire*, December 28, 2012, http://www.theatlanticwire.com/national/2012/12/postnewtown-teacher-gun-training-classes/60409; Angela K. Brown, "Texas Town Allows Teachers to Carry Concealed Guns," Associated Press, December 20, 2012, http://www.usatoday.com /story /news/nation/2012/12/20/texas-town-teachers-guns/1781663; Cathy Lynn Grossman and Greg Toppo, "Trainer for Gun-Toting Teachers: 'Make it Hard to Kill a Kid,'" *USA Today*, December 28, 2012, http://www.usatoday.com/story/news/nation/2012/12/27/gun-classes-teachers-utah-ohioshooting/1793773; Michelle Malkin, "The Gift of Self-Empowerment," December 26, 2012, http://michellemalkin.com/2012/12/26/the-gift-of-self-empowerment.

8 Tim Graham, "Des Moines Register Publishes Gun-Ban Column Advocating Deadly Violence Against NRA, GOP Leaders," *Fox News*, January 2, 2013, http://www.foxnews.com /opinion/2013/01/02/liberal-ex-columnist-death-threats-published-indes-moines-register.

9 Douglas Anthony Cooper, "A Proven Way to End the Gun Slaughter: Will We Fight for It?", *Huff Post Politics*, December 26, 2012, http://www.huffingtonpost.com/douglas-anthonycooper/proven-way-end-slaughter b 2341815.html.

10 Justin Peters, "How Many Assault Weapons Are There In America? How Much Would It Cost the Government To Buy Them Back?", *Slate*, December 20, 2012, http://www.slate.com /blogs/crime/2012/12/20/assault rifle stats how many assault rifles are there in america.html.

11 Some machine guns are or may be set to fire a certain number of rounds with one pull of the trigger.

12 "Fully-Automatic Firearms," NRA–ILA, July 29, 1999, http://www.nraila.org/newsissues/fact-sheets/1999/fully-automatic-firearms.aspx; "National Firearms Act (NFA)— Machine Guns," http://www.atf.gov/firearms/faq /national-firearms-act-machine-guns.html, accessed January 3, 2013.

13 See David B. Kopel, *Guns: Who Should Have Them* (New York: Prometheus Books, 1995), p. 162; *Defense Intelligence Agency, Small Arms Identification and Operation Guide— Eurasian Communist Countries* (Washington, D.C.: Government Printing Office, 1988), p. 105.

14 However, the energy which is used to turn the cylinder of the revolver (bringing the next round into place, ready to fire) comes from the user pulling the trigger. (The trigger is mechanically linked to the cylinder, and a trigger pull performs the "double action" of cocking the hammer and firing a round.) Thus, the revolver does not use gunpowder energy in order to load the next round. So even though a revolver is comparable to a semi-automatic handgun in that each pull of the trigger chambers and fires one round, a revolver is a not a semi-automatic.

15 The formula is: $KE= 1/2\ MV^2$. Or in words: one-half of mass times the square of the velocity.

16 Rifles have longer barrels than handguns, and rifle cartridges generally burn more gunpowder. Thus, a bullet shot from a rifle spends more time traveling through the barrel than does a bullet shot from a handgun. As a result, the rifle bullet receives a longer, more powerful push from the expanding cloud of gunpowder in the barrel. So rifles generally deliver more kinetic energy than do handguns. (As for shotguns, the mass of shot pellets is much heavier than any single rifle or handgun bullet, so shotguns have very high kinetic energy at short ranges. But their kinetic energy drops rapidly, because the round pellets rapidly lose speed due to air friction. Rifle and handgun bullets are far more aerodynamic than are shotgun pellets.)

17 If the gun's caliber is .17, that means the gun's barrel is 17/100 of an inch wide, and can accommodate a bullet which is very slightly smaller than that. So a .38 caliber bullet is bigger than a .17 caliber bullet, and a .45 caliber bullet is bigger than either of them. (Calibers can also be expressed metrically. 9mm is nearly the same as .357, which is slightly smaller than .38).

The bullet's size depends on its width (caliber) and on its length. So one .45 caliber bullet might be longer, and hence heavier, than another .45 caliber bullet.

For any particular gun in any particular caliber, there are a variety of rounds available, some of which have more gunpowder than others. More gunpowder makes the bullet fly straighter for longer distances (especially important in many types of hunting or target shooting); less gunpowder reduces recoil, and makes the gun more comfortable to shoot and more controllable for many people.

18 Measured at the muzzle. Kinetic energy begins declining as soon as the bullet leaves the barrel, because air friction progressively reduces velocity.

19 For details, see David B. Kopel, *Guns: Who Should Have Them* (New York: Prometheus Books, 1995), pp. 168–70.

20 The assertion that so-called "assault weapons" are "high-velocity" is true only in the trivial sense that most guns which are called "assault weapons" are rifles, and rifles are generally higher velocity than handguns or shotguns.

As for the handguns which are sometimes dubbed "assault weapons," they are necessarily lower velocity, with less powerful bullets, than the most powerful handguns. The most powerful handgun calibers, such as .44 magnum or .454 Casull (often carried by hikers for self-defense against bears) have so much gunpowder that the relatively delicate mechanisms of a semi-automatic handgun cannot handle them. These heavy-duty calibers are available only for revolvers.

[21] Quoted in Randy E. Barnett and Don B. Kates, "Under Fire: The New Consensus on the Second Amendment," *Emory Law Journal*, vol. 45, 1996, reproduced at http://www.bu.edu/rbarnett/underfire.htm#Document0zzFN B535. Feinstein's quote is from an interview with Lesley Stahl on *60 Minutes* in February 1995.

[22] Jacob Sullum, "How Do We Know an 'Assault Weapon' Ban Would Not Have Stopped Adam Lanza? Because It Didn't," *Reason*, December 17, 2012, http://reason.com/blog/2012 /12/17/how-do-we-know-an-assault-weapon-ban-wou.

[23] Christopher S. Koper, Daniel J. Woods & Jeffrey A. Roth, "An Updated Assessment of the Federal Assault Weapons Ban: Impacts on Gun Markets and Gun Violence, 1994-2003: Report to the National Institute of Justice, United States Department of Justice," University of Pennsylvania, June 2004, http://www.sas.upenn.edu/jerrylee/research/aw final2004.pdf.

[24] Jeffrey A. Roth & Christopher S. Koper, "Impacts of the 1994 Assault Weapons Ban: 1994– 96," National Institute of Justice Research in Brief, U.S. Department of Justice, March 1999, https://www.ncjrs.gov /pdffiles1/173405.pdf.

[25] "Stopping the Spread of Deadly Assault Weapons," http://www.feinstein.senate.gov/public /index.cfm/assault-weapons, accessed January 2, 2013. For another reply to Feinstein's claims, see Gregory J. Markle, "A Short Analysis of Senator Feinstein's 'Proof' of the Efficacy of the 1994 Assault Weapons Ban," December 29, 2012, http://pc3c.org /files/feinstein fisking.pdf.

[26] Jeffrey A. Roth & Christopher S. Koper, "Impact Evaluation of the Public Safety and Recreational Firearms Use Protection Act of 1994: Final Report," Urban Institute, March 13, 1997, http://www.sas.upenn.edu/jerrylee /research/aw final1997.pdf.

[27] John Lott, *The Bias Against Guns: Why Almost Everything You've Heard About Gun Control Is Wrong* (Washington, D.C.: Regnery Publishing, 2003), p. 214.

Looking at the raw crime data, Lott observes:

> The comparison group here is the forty-five states that did not adopt a ban. For both murder and robbery rates, the states adopting assault weapons bans were experiencing a relatively faster drop in violent crimes prior to the ban and a relatively faster increase in violent crimes after it. For rapes and aggravated assaults, the trends before and after the law seem essentially unchanged.

Based on the crime data, Lott concludes that it is "hard to argue that ... banning assault weapons produced any noticeable benefit in terms of lower crime rates." In statistical analyses that seek to control for other possible factors in the fluctuations of crime rates, Lott finds that, if anything, the state-level "assault weapons" bans had an adverse effect on crime rates:

> Presumably if assault weapons are to be used in any particular crimes, they will be used for murder and robbery, but the data appears more supportive of an adverse effect of an assault weapons ban on murder and robbery rates ... , with both crime rates rising after the passage of the bans. ... Murder and robbery rates started off relatively high in the states that eventually adopted a ban, but the gap disappears by the time the ban is adopted. Only after instituting the ban do crime rates head back up. There is a very statistically significant change in murder and rape rate trends before and after the adoption of the ban. ... It is very difficult to observe any systematic impact of the ban on rape and aggravated assault rates.

[28] Mark Follman, Gavin Aronsen, and Deanna Pan, "A Guide to Mass Shootings in America," *Mother Jones*, December 15, 2012, http://www.motherjones.com/politics/2012/07/massshootings-map; see also Mark Follman, Gavin Aronsen, and Deanna Pan, "US Mass Shootings, 1982–2012: Data from Mother Jones' Investigation," *Mother Jones*, December 28, 2012, http://www.motherjones.com/politics/2012/12/mass-shootings-mother-jones-full-data.

[29] Thomas C. Hayes, "Gunman Kills 22 and Himself in Texas Cafeteria," *New York Times*, October 17, 1991, http://www.nytimes.com/1991/10/17/us/gunman-kills-22-and-himself-intexas-cafeteria.html.

[30] "About Suzanna," http://www.suzannahupp.com/?pageid=2, accessed January 13, 2013.

[31] Most of the text in this paragraph is adapted from David B. Kopel, *Guns: Who Should Have Them* (New York: Prometheus Books, 1995), p. 164. That book in turn cites William R. Magrath, "An Open Letter to American Politicians," *Police Marksman*, May–June 1989, p. 19; Edward Ezell, *The AK-47 Story* (Mechanicsburg, PA: Stackpole Books, 1986); Kent Jenkins Jr., "Calls for Ban Boost Assault Rifle Sales," *Washington Post*, March

6, 1989, p. B1; and "Assault Weapon Import Control Act of 1989," 1989: Hearings on H.R. 1154 before Subcommittee on Trade of the House Committee on Ways and Means, 101st Cong., 1st Sess. (1989).

[32] Douglas Anthony Cooper, "A Proven Way to End the Gun Slaughter: Will We Fight for It?", *Huff Post Politics*, December 26, 2012, http://www.huffingtonpost.com/douglas-anthonycooper/proven-way-end-slaughter b 2341815.html.

[33] Charles Krauthammer, "Disingenuous Debate on Repeal of Assault Weapons Ban," *Chicago Tribune*, April 8, 1996, http://articles.chicagotribune.com/1996-04- 08/news/9604080024 1 assault-weapons-ban-gun-control-crime-rate.

[34] Christian Chung, "Dianne Feinstein New Assault Weapons Ban Doesn't Go Far Enough: It's Only the Start," *Policymic*, December 29, 2012, http://www.policymic.com/articles /21639/dianne-feinstein-new-assault-weapons-ban-doesn-tgo-far-enough-it-s-only-the-start.

[35] Robert Wright, "A Gun Control Law That Would Actually Work," *Atlantic*, December 17, 2012, http://www.theatlantic.com/national/archive/2012/12/a-gun-control-law-that-would- actually-work/266342.

[36] The "features" on semi-automatic shotguns under the ban are similar to the features list for rifles, with one important addition. Feinstein outlaws any semi-auto shotgun that has "A fixed magazine with the capacity to accept more than 5 rounds." This bans a wide variety of home defense shotguns. It also means that if you use a magazine extender to turn your 5- round Remington 1100 into a 7-round gun, you are now an instant felon.

[37] See Clayton E. Cramer, "High-Capacity-Magazine Bans," *National Review*, December 19, 2012, http://www.nationalreview.com/articles/336006/high-capacity-magazine-bans-clayton-ecramer. (If the final round from the last magazine has been fired, the first round from the new magazine must be chambered before the gun will fire. Chambering a round involves "racking" the gun by manually operating the gun's slide mechanism, a process that typically takes fractions of a second.)

[38] The G17 (standard), G19 (compact), and G34 (competition). Optional magazines of 19 or 33 rounds are available. The subcompact G26 comes with a 10 round magazine, with 12, 15, 17, 19, and 33 round magazines available. For a 9mm handgun standard-sized handgun, the 15 or 17 round magazine is "normal capacity," not "high capacity," whereas a 10-round magazine is "restricted capacity." The Glock 30 SF, a larger .45 caliber, comes standard with a 10-round magazine, with factory options of 9 and 13 rounds. Because the bullets are larger (.45 inch vs. 9 mm, which is about .35 inch), fewer can fit in a given space—hence, the smaller magazine capacity. Other Glock .45 handguns come standard with larger or smaller magazines, depending on the size of the gun. "Glock 19 Gen4," http://us.glock.com/products/model/g19gen4; "Glock 30 SF," http://us.glock.com/products/model/g30sf; "Glock 21 Gen4," http://us.glock.com/products/model/g21gen4; "Glock 36," http://us.glock.com/products/model/g36; each accessed January 3, 2013.

[39] A "high-capacity" magazine on his hip, and often he carries a pump-action shotgun or "assault" rifle (or both) in his trunk. A look at a forum thread at Officer.com, "What Gun Does Your Department Use" (see http://forums.officer.com/t138759), offers an insightful look at typical police weaponry—the list includes Glocks with 17-round magazines and AR-15 semi-automatic rifles.

Regarding magazine capacity, one veteran from a municipal police department in Texas advises:

> I would not carry a duty gun that carries fewer than 12 rounds in the magazine. One of the great advantages offered by semi-automatic handguns is the increased carrying capacity. Most manufacturers have increased the capacity of .45 pistols to at least 12 rounds, so this would be the minimum I would be comfortable with "What is the Best Pistol for Police Officers?", *Spartan Cops*, March 30, 2009, http://www.spartancops.com/pistol-police-officers; "About," Spartan Cops, http://www.spartancops.com/about. Nashville Police can now carry their personal AR-15s in their vehicles while on duty. http://tnne.ws/ULB0HY.

[40] What about magazines? "The failure to reduce LCM use has likely been due to the immense stock of exempted pre-ban magazines, which has been enhanced by recent imports," the 2004 paper speculates. The paper notes that "millions" of "assault weapons" and "large-capacity magazines" were "manufactured prior to the ban's effective date."

[41] Still, if one wants to speculate, Koper, Woods, and Roth do so in an articulate fashion. Their 2004 report states:

> [S]emiautomatic weapons with LCMs [large-capacity magazines] enable offenders to fire high numbers of shots rapidly, thereby potentially increasing both the number of persons wounded per gunfire incident (including both intended targets and innocent bystanders) and the number of gunshot victims suffering multiple wounds, both of which would increase deaths and injuries from gun violence.

Because of this, the paper's writers speculate, "the LCM ban has greater potential for reducing gun deaths and injuries than does the AW [assault weapons] ban." They continue:

> [A] ban's impact on gun violence is likely to be small at best, and perhaps too small for reliable measurement. . . . Guns with LCMs are used in up to a quarter of gun crimes, but it is not clear how often the outcomes of gun attacks depend on the ability to fire more than 10 shots (the current limit on magazine capacity) without reloading.
> Nonetheless, reducing crimes with . . . LCMs could have non-trivial effects on gunshot victimizations. As a general matter, hit rates tend to be low in gunfire incidents, so having more shots to fire rapidly can increase the likelihood that offenders hit their targets, and perhaps bystanders as well. While not entirely consistent, the few available studies contrasting attacks with different types of guns and magazines generally suggest that attacks with semiautomatics—including AWs and other semiautomatics with LCMs—result in more shots fired, persons wounded, and wounds per victim than do other gun attacks.

The authors of the 2004 report, then, believe that a ban on magazines holding more than ten rounds likely would not reduce the number of crimes committed, but that such a ban might reduce the harm of certain types of rare crimes (presumably mass murders with many rounds fired and "shootouts"). The authors do not (and do not claim to) present convincing evidence that their hypothesis is correct; they present their claim as reasonable speculation.

However, a careful reading of the paragraphs cited above reveals one of the major flaws of the writers' argument. The writers claim that "attacks with semiautomatics"—whether or not they are used with "large capacity" magazines—result in greater harm. There are good reasons to think that, even if criminals could somehow be restricted to using ten-round magazines—and obviously they cannot—they could typically cause the same level of harm, and sometimes more harm.

The general problem with the claims of those who wish to ban magazines holding more than ten rounds is that such advocates fail to account for the adaptability of criminals. Such advocates assume they can hold "all other things equal," when clearly criminals thrive on adapting their plans in order to surprise and overwhelm their intended victims.

[42] Josh Sugarmann, "Drug Traffickers, Paramilitary Groups... ," *Assault Weapons and Accessories in America*, Violence Policy Center, 1988, http://www.vpc.org/studies /awadrug.htm.

[43] David B. Kopel, Paul Gallant & Joanne D. Eisen, "The Arms Trade Treaty: Zimbabwe, the Democratic Republic of the Congo, and the Prospects for Arms Embargoes on Human Rights Violators," 114 *Penn State Law Review* 891, at note 46 (2010).

[44] http://defcad.org/

45 "Third of High School Seniors Take Marijuana," *News Medical*, December, 22, 2012, http://www.news-medical.net/news/20121222/Third-of-high-school-seniors-takemarijuana.aspx.

[46] Alicia A. Caldwell, "James Holmes' Gun Jammed During Aurora Attack, Official Says," *Associated Press*, July 22, 2012, http://www.huffingtonpost.com/2012/07/22/james-holmesgun-jammed-aurora-colorado-dark-knight-shooting n 1692690.html.

[47] An additional fact about this case is that, had the Arizona murderer not been tackled by bystanders, he would have faced armed opposition moments later. Joe Zamudio, another man who helped restrain the murderer, said the following during an MSNBC interview:

> I carry a gun, so I felt like I was a little bit more prepared to do some good than maybe somebody else would have been. . . . As I came out of the door of the Walgreens . . . I saw several individuals wrestling with him, and I came running. . . . I saw another individual holding the firearm, and I kind of assumed he was the shooter, so I grabbed his wrists, and . . . told him to drop it, and forced him to drop the gun on the ground. When he did that, everybody said, no, it's this guy . . . and I proceeded to help hold that man down. . . . When I came through the door, I had my hand on the butt of my pistol, and I clicked the safety off. I was ready to kill him. But I didn't have to do that, and I was very blessed I didn't have to go to that place. Luckily, they'd already begun the solution, so all I had to do is help. If they hadn't grabbed him, and he'd have been still moving, I would have shot him.

We were unable to locate the video on the MSNBC web page. It is reproduced at http://youtu.be/y-3GTwalrGY.

In return for this profoundly courageous act of heroism in which Zamudio ran toward gunfire, William Saletan libeled Zamudio in an article for Slate, wrongly claiming he "nearly shot the wrong man." William Saletan, "Friendly Firearms," *Slate*, January 11, 2011, http://www.slate.com/articles/health and science/human nature/2011/01/friendly firearms.h tml.

Obviously in the brief seconds of the incident, Zamudio considered the possibility that the man holding the gun might be the perpetrator of the crime—and then Zamudio acted with restraint, appropriately disarmed the man holding the gun, and helped restrain the perpetrator. Although police in Arizona likely are more responsible with their firearms than are police in New York, the recent incident in which New York police shot nine bystanders illustrates that Zamudio did the other man holding the gun—and everyone else in the crowd—a profound favor by forcing him to drop it.) "NYPD: 9 Shooting Bystander Victims Hit By Police Gunfire," *Associated Press*, August 25, 2012, http://www.foxnews.com /us/2012/08/25/nypd-shooting-bystander-victims-hit-by-policegunfire.

[48] Philip Caulfield, "Sandy Hook Elementary School Shooter Adam Lanza Wore Earplugs, Rapidly Changed Clips, Shot Up Cars in Parking Lot: Report," New York *Daily News*, January 7, 2013, http://www. nydailynews.com/ news/national/lanza-wore-earplugs-shot-carsarticle-1.1234747.

[49] Will Grant, "Active Shooter Response: Lessons for Experts," *Blackwater*, January 6, 2013, http://blackwaterusa. com/active-shooter-response-lessons-from-experts.

Even if they resorted to revolvers, criminals could impose mass casualties. Recall that Robert Wright, a senior editor at the Atlantic, wants to ban all detachable magazines and all guns "that can hold more than six bullets." In other words, he wants to ban the large majority of guns in existence. (Like Cooper, Wright totally ignores the use of guns in self-defense.) Even if we assume that criminals could not still purchase their weapons of choice on the black market—an assumption that is obviously false—Wright's analysis of the likely results is faulty.

Wright tries to hold "other things equal" that cannot be held equal. Wright uses the example of the Newtown murders, noting that the criminal carried a rifle and two handguns and that he shot about twelve rounds before reaching the students. Wright supposes, "At that point, as he headed for the classrooms, he'd have six more rapid-fire bullets left, after which he'd have to reload his guns bullet by bullet." Robert Wright, "A Gun Control Law That Would Actually Work," *Atlantic*, December 17, 2012, http://www.theatlantic.com /national /archive/2012/12/a-gun-control-law-that-would-actuallywork/266342.

Wright ignores several obvious facts here. A criminal limited to six-round guns likely would choose larger-caliber guns and target each round more carefully. More significantly in a mass-murder scenario, a criminal would by no means be limited to three guns; he could easily carry many revolvers (or six-round semiautomatics). Like semi-automatics, double-action revolvers fire one round with each pull of the trigger.

For more on the effective firing rates of revolvers and other types of guns, see David B. Kopel, *Guns: Who Should Have Them* (New York: Prometheus Books, 1995), pp. 164–165 (The finger must accomplish more of the mechanical work with a double-action revolver.) Revolvers typically are extremely reliable, and often they are less expensive than other types of guns. Even a gun ban that banned most guns in existence—a far more ambitious proposal than legislation pertaining to the manufacture and sale of new "high capacity" magazines— would do nothing to curb black market sales, and it would have little or no impact on criminals' ability to commit violent atrocities.)

[50] David B. Kopel, "Lawyers, Guns, and Burglars," 43 *Arizona Law Review* 345 (2001).

[51] "Scotland Worst for Violence – UN," *BBC News*, Sept. 18, 2005 ("Scotland has been named the most violent country in the developed world by a United Nations Report.").

[52] Joyce Malcolm, *Guns and Violence: The English Experience* 141-142 (2002); Joseph Edward Olson & Clayton Cramer, "Gun Control: Political Fears Trump Crime Control," 61 *Maine Law Review* 57-81 (2009), http://ssrn.com/abstract=1083528.

[53] David B. Kopel & Joseph P. Olson, "All the Way Down the Slippery Slope: Gun Prohibition in England, and Some Lessons for America," 22 Hamline Law Review 399 (1999).

[54] House of Commons, Home Affairs – Second Report – Controls over Firearms, Session 1999- 2000, Apr. 6, 2000, at 22, http://www.publications.parliament.uk/pa/cm199900/cmselect /cmhaff/95/9502.htm.

[55] Illegal Firearms in the United Kingdom, Centre for Defence Studies, King's College London, Jul. 2, 2001, Working Paper 4.

[56] Nick Paton Walsh, "UK Matches Africa in Crime Surge," *The Guardian*, Jun. 3, 2001.

[57] Sean O'Neill, "A Quarter of English are Victims of Crime," *The Telegraph*, Feb. 23, 2001.

[58] Philip Johnston, "Britain Leads the World on Risk of Being Assaulted," *The Telegraph*, May 4, 2001

[59] Illegal Firearms, Working Paper 1, at 7.

[60] Philip Johnston, "World's Toughest Laws Will Help to Keep Weapons off the Streets," *The Telegraph*, Nov. 2, 1996.

[61] *Illegal Firearms*, Working Paper 4, at 15.

[62] See Joyce Malcolm, *Guns and Violence: The English Experience* 228-31 (2002); Patsy Richards, Homicide Statistics, Research Paper 99/56, House of Commons Library Social and General Statistics Section, May 27, 1999, at 9. See also Statistics Release, Homicides in Scotland in 2001 – Statistics Published: A Scottish Executive National Statistics Publication, Nov. 28, 2002, http://www.scotland.gov.uk/stats/bulletins/00205-

00.asp (visited May 16, 2006), at Note 2 ("A single case of homicide is counted for each act of murder or culpable homicide irrespective of the number of perpetrators or victims.")

[63] David B. Kopel, *Guns: Who Should Have Them?* (Prometheus Books, 1995).

[64] Stephen P. Halbrook, "Congress Interprets the Second Amendment: Declarations by a Co-Equal Branch on the Individual Right to Keep and Bear Arms," 61 Tenn. L. Rev. 597 (1994).

[65] City of Boerne v. Flores, 521 U.S. 507 (1997).

[66] Katzenbach v. Morgan, 384 U.S. 641 (1966).

[67] *E.g.*, Board of Trustees of Univ. of Alabama v. Garrett (2001); Nevada Dept. of Human Resources v. Hibbs (2003),

[68] David B. Kopel, "How the British Gun Control Program Precipitated the American Revolution," 38 *Charleston Law Review* 283 (2012), http://ssrn.com/abstract=1967702.

[69] For more detailed analysis of the civil rights implications of gun prohibition laws, *see, e.g.*, David B. Kopel, *Peril or Protection? The Risks and Benefits of Handgun Prohibition*, 12 ST. LOUIS U. PUB. L. REV. 285, 319-23 (1993).

[70] "Estimated Crime in United States—Total," U.S. Department of Justice, Uniform Crime Reporting Statistics, http://www.ucrdatatool.gov/Search/Crime/State/RunCrime Stateby State.cfm,accessed January 4, 2013.

[71] Donna L. Hoyert and Jiaquan Xu, "Deaths: Preliminary Data for 2011," *National Vital Statistics Reports*, vol. 61, no. 6, October 10, 2012, p. 28, http://www.cdc.gov/nchs /data/nvsr/nvsr61/nvsr61_06.pdf.

[72] "Murder, by State, Types of Weapons, 2011," *Crime in the United States 2011*, Table 7, http://www.fbi.gov/ about-us/cjis/ucr/crime-in-the-u.s/2011/crime-in-the-u.s.- 2011/tables/expanded-homicide-data-table-7.

[73] Donna L. Hoyert and Jiaquan Xu, "Deaths: Preliminary Data for 2011," *National Vital Statistics Reports*, vol. 61, no. 6, October 10, 2012, pp. 41–42, http://www.cdc.gov /nchs/data/nvsr/nvsr61/nvsr61 06.pdf.

[74] For example, the homicide rate in 1962 and 1963 was 4.6 deaths per 100,000 population. In 1964 it was 4.8

[75] Nicole White & Janet L. Lauritsen, Violent Crime Against Youth, 1994–2010, Bureau of Justice Statistics, NCJ 240106 (Dec. 2012), http://www.bjs.gov /content/pub/pdf /vcay9410.pdf.

[76] Nicholas J. Johnson, David B. Kopel, Michael P. O'Shea & George Moscary, *Firearms Law and the Second Amendment: Regulation, Rights, and Policy* (Aspen Publishers 2012), online chapter 12, forthcoming at http://firearmsregulation.org.

[77] Matt Apuzzo and Pat Eaton-Robb, "Conn. Gunman Had Hundreds of Rounds of Ammunition," Associated Press, December 17, 2012, http://bigstory.ap.org/article/agentsvisit-conn-gun-shops-after-school-massacre.

[78] Clayton E. Cramer, *My Brother Ron: A Personal and Social History of the Deinstitutionalization of the Mentally Ill* (2012).

In: Mass Shootings and Gun Violence in America
Editor: John C. Zandler
ISBN: 978-1-62618-893-8

Chapter 8

TESTIMONY OF CHIEF JIM JOHNSON, BALTIMORE COUNTY POLICE DEPARTMENT. HEARING ON "WHAT SHOULD AMERICA DO ABOUT GUN VIOLENCE?"*

Mr. Chairman, Ranking Member, and Members of the Committee, I want to thank you for the opportunity to testify today. I am here on behalf of the National Law Enforcement Partnership to Prevent Gun Violence, an alliance of the nation's law enforcement leadership organizations concerned about the unacceptable level of gun violence in the United States.

The Partnership, founded in 2010, includes: the Commission on Accreditation of Law Enforcement Agencies; Hispanic American Police Command Officers Association; International Association of Campus Law Enforcement Administrators; International Association of Chiefs of Police; Major Cities Chiefs Association; National Association of Women Law Enforcement Executives; National Organization of Black Law Enforcement Executives; Police Executive Research Forum; and the Police Foundation.

We mourn those lost to gun violence, including the 20 children in Newtown, along with the six brave adults whose lives were cut short by a deranged individual armed with firepower originally designed for combat, not for gunning down innocent members of our communities.

More than 30 homicides occur in America each day. Two-thousand children, ages 18 and under, die of firearm-related deaths in the U.S. every year. In 2011, for the first time in 14 years, firearms were the leading cause of death for police officers killed in the line of duty. In just the two-week period after the Newtown massacre, six police officers were killed and 10 injured in 12 separate shootings.

In a one-week period in 2011, the Police Executive Research Forum (PERF) found that gun crime in six cities cost more than $38 million, and in the year 2010 cost the entire country more than $57 billion.

We urgently need Congress to address the rising epidemic of gun violence. Law enforcement leaders support the President's comprehensive approach, which includes enhancing safety at educational institutions and addressing mental health issues. But on

* This is an edited, reformatted and augmented version of a testimony presented January 30, 2013 before the Senate Judiciary Committee.

behalf of my colleagues across the nation, I am here today to tell you that we are long overdue in strengthening our nation's gun laws. Doing so must be a priority for Congress.

The organizations in the National Law Enforcement Partnership to Prevent Gun Violence are united in urgently calling on Congress to:

- Require background checks for all firearm purchasers;
- Ensure that prohibited purchaser records in the National Instant Criminal Background Check System (NICS), are up-to-date and accurate; and
- Limit high capacity ammunition feeding devices to ten rounds.

Seven of our nine groups, including the largest organizations among us, also support a ban on assault weapons and Senator Feinstein's legislation.

Federal law prohibits dangerous individuals, such as convicted felons and those with mental health disqualifiers, from possessing firearms. While background checks are required for purchases through federally licensed gun dealers, no check is required for private sales, such as those through Internet postings, print ads or gun shows.

From November 2011 to November 2012, an estimated 6.6 million firearm transactions occurred without a background check. Up to 40 percent of firearm transactions occur through private individuals rather than licensed gun dealers. Allowing 40 percent of those acquiring guns to bypass background checks is like allowing 40 percent of airline passengers to board a plane without going through airport security.

Last October, in Brookfield, Wisconsin, seven women were shot by a prohibited purchaser who was under a domestic violence restraining order. The shooter answered an online ad and was able to buy a gun without a background check. Had the sale required a check, this tragedy could have been prevented.

Background checks work. They stopped nearly 2 million prohibited purchases between 1994 and 2009. We already have a national background check system in place. Therefore, extending background checks to *all* firearm purchasers can easily be implemented – and should be, without delay.

States can't do it alone. Interstate firearms trafficking is a serious problem that must be addressed federally. The problem is rampant: According to the ATF, in 2009, 30 percent of guns recovered at crime scenes had crossed state lines. Submissions to NICS must be improved, especially mental health and drug abuse records. The 2007 massacre at Virginia Tech is a tragic example of a prohibited purchaser slipping between the cracks due to incomplete NICS records.

The ban on assault weapons and high-capacity ammunition magazines must be reinstated. Like assault weapons, high-capacity magazines are not used for hunting, do not belong in our homes and wreak havoc in our communities. Banning these magazines will reduce the number of bullets a shooter can use before having to reload. Reloading can provide a window of time in which to take down a shooter, as we saw in Tucson.

In 1998, four years after the assault weapons and high-capacity ammunition magazine ban was enacted, the percentage of firearms with large-capacity magazines recovered by Virginia police decreased and continued to drop until it hit a low of 9 percent in 2004, the year the ban expired. It hit a high of 20 percent in 2010, according to a Washington Post analysis.

After the 1994 law expired, 37 percent of police agencies saw increases in criminals' use of assault weapons, according to a 2010 PERF survey.

I have been in law enforcement for nearly 35 years, and have seen an explosion in firepower since the assault weapons ban expired. It is common to find many shell casings at crime scenes these days, as victims are being riddled with multiple gunshots.

The common-sense measures we are calling for will not infringe on Second Amendment rights, but will ensure that we keep guns out of dangerous hands and excessive firepower out of our communities.

Generations of Americans, including our youngest ones, are depending on you to ensure they will grow up and fulfill their roles in the great human experience. None of us can fail them. I urge you to follow the will of the American public and stand with law enforcement to enact these common-sense public safety measures.

Thank you.

In: Mass Shootings and Gun Violence in America
Editor: John C. Zandler
ISBN: 978-1-62618-893-8

Chapter 9

TESTIMONY OF GAYLE S. TROTTER, SENIOR FELLOW, INDEPENDENT WOMEN'S FORUM. HEARING ON "WHAT SHOULD AMERICA DO ABOUT GUN VIOLENCE?"*

Chairman Leahy, Ranking Member Grassley, and Members of the Committee, thank you for inviting me to appear before you today. We have seen unspeakable tragedy and now hear calls to action. This Committee has asked what America should do about gun violence.

Asking that question will undoubtedly invite impassioned debate in an area where reasonable and well-intentioned people can disagree on specific approaches. We all want a safer society. We differ on how to make our society safer and on whether some proposals, however appealing they may be, will actually increase public safety. And that is a key element of this debate. We need more than political philosophies to guide our discussion: We should consider the effectiveness of proposed changes. In a similar vein, President Obama said in his first inaugural address, "The question we ask today is not whether our government is too big or too small, but whether it works."

This Committee should ask the same question about proposed gun regulations: What works? We should decline to accept any call to action that will fail to make Americans safer and, in particular, harm women the most.

I would like to begin with the compelling story of Sarah McKinley. Home alone with her baby, she called 911 when two violent intruders began to break down her front door. The men wanted to force their way into her home so they could steal the prescription medication of her deceased husband, who had recently died of cancer. Before the police could arrive, while Ms. McKinley was on the line with the 911 operator, these violent intruders broke down her door. One of the men brandished a foot-long hunting knife. As the intruders forced their way into her home, Ms. McKinley fired her weapon, fatally wounding one of the violent attackers and causing the other to flee the scene. Later, Ms. McKinley reflected on the incident: "It was either going to be him or my son," she said. "And it wasn't going to be my son."

Guns make women safer. Most violent offenders actually do not use firearms, which makes guns the great equalizer. In fact, over 90 percent of violent crimes occur without a

---

* This is an edited, reformatted and augmented version of a testimony presented January 30, 2013 before the Senate Judiciary Committee.

firearm. Over the most recent decade, from 2001 to 2010, "about 6 percent to 9 percent of all violent victimizations were committed with firearms," according to a federal study.[1] Violent criminals rarely use a gun to threaten or attack women. Attackers use their size and physical strength, preying on women who are at a severe disadvantage.

Guns reverse that balance of power in a violent confrontation. Armed with a gun, a woman can even have the advantage over a violent attacker. How do guns give women the advantage? An armed woman does not need superior strength or the proximity of a hand-to-hand struggle. She can protect her children, elderly relatives, herself or others who are vulnerable to an assailant. Using a firearm with a magazine holding more than 10 rounds of ammunition, a woman would have a fighting chance even against multiple attackers. In the Appendix to my testimony, I have summarized news accounts selected from the last twelve months. Each of these accounts involves a woman who, like Sarah McKinley, used a firearm to protect herself or her loved ones against violent men.

Concealed-carry laws reverse that balance of power even before a violent confrontation occurs. In this way, armed women indirectly benefit those who choose not to carry. For a would-be criminal, concealed-carry laws dramatically increase the cost of committing a crime, paying safety dividends to those who do not carry. All women in these jurisdictions reap the benefits of concealed-carry laws because potential assailants face a much higher risk when they attempt to threaten or harm a potential victim. As a result, in jurisdictions with concealed-carry laws, women are less likely to be raped, maimed or murdered than they are in states with stricter gun ownership laws.

Research has shown that states with nondiscretionary concealed handgun laws have 25 percent fewer rapes than states that restrict or forbid women from carrying concealed handguns.[2] The most thorough analysis of concealed-carry laws and crime rates indicates that "there are large drops in overall violent crime, murder, rape, and aggravated assault that begin right after the right-to-carry laws have gone into effect" and that "in all those crime categories, the crime rates consistently stay much lower than they were before the law."[3] Among the ten states that adopted concealed-carry laws over a fifteen-year span, there were 0.89 shooting deaths and injuries per 100,000 people, representing less than half the rate of 2.09 per 100,000 experienced in states without these laws.[4]

Armed security works. Brave men and women stand guard over Capitol Hill, including the building where we are now. Snipers stand guard on the White House roof. Politicians and other high-profile individuals, including prominent gun-control advocates, have admitted to having gun permits either currently or in the past.

Armed guards often serve in the employ of those who themselves advocate for more restrictions on gun rights. Political figures seek to restrict gun rights, and Hollywood celebrities somberly urge Americans to "demand a plan" to reduce gun violence despite their own roles in graphically depicting lethal violence on the screen. In both cases, however, many of these political figures and celebrities already have their own plan: They rely on guns to safeguard their own personal safety. For example, armed guards protected a suburban newspaper in New York after the newspaper published the names and residential addresses of gun permit holders, and the newspaper's own reporter already used a gun for his protection. After publishing the story, the editors disclosed that their reporter owns a Smith & Wesson .357 Magnum and has "a residence permit in New York City."

While armed security works, gun bans do not. Anti-gun legislation keeps guns away from the sane and the law-abiding — but it does not keep guns out of the hands of criminals.

Nearly all mass shootings have occurred in "gun-free" zones. Law-abiding citizens do not bring firearms to gun-free zones, so psychotic killers know they can inflict more harm in these unprotected environments. These laws make easy targets of the sane and the law-abiding. Gun-control advocates cheer the creation of legally mandated gun-free zones, touting increased safety while actually making citizens in those locations more vulnerable to the next horrible monster in search of soft targets. A moment's reflection confirms that statutory provisions and bold signs do not create a gun-free environment. No sober-minded person would advocate that approach when protecting banks, airports, rock concerts and government buildings. Instead, publicly designated gun-free zones have the effect of creating high-visibility soft targets — conspicuous environments where madmen can wreak havoc.

We need sensible enforcement of the gun laws that are already on the books. Currently, we have more than 20,000 under-enforced or selectively enforced gun laws. Gun regulation affects only the guns of the law-abiding. Criminals will not be bound by such gestures, especially as we continually fail to prosecute serious gun violations or provide meaningful and consistent penalties for violent felonies involving firearms.

Recently, a talk show host inadvertently exposed the absurdity of gun regulation in the District of Columbia when he displayed a 30-round magazine on national television, thereby embroiling himself in a police investigation. Ultimately, the Attorney General of the District of Columbia decided not to prosecute the matter. "Despite the clarity of the violation of this important law," he concluded, "a prosecution would not promote public safety."[5] Why is it permissible to possess magazines to persuade people that guns are dangerous, but not for a woman to possess one to defend herself against gang rape? Overbroad anti-gun regulations unduly increase prosecutorial discretion and result in selective enforcement of the law. Equal justice under law should not depend on whether a prosecutor has a political or ideological motivation to seek enforcement. Nor should justice depend on whether a prosecutor has the good sense to decline enforcement of a knowing violation that does nothing more than unwittingly demonstrate the law's absurdity and overbreadth.

In lieu of empty, self-defeating gestures, we should address gun violence by doing what works. By safeguarding our Second Amendment rights, we preserve meaningful protection for women. Our nation made significant progress in that regard when, in recent memory, the United States Supreme Court held that the Second Amendment protects an individual's right to possess a firearm for traditionally lawful purposes, such as self-defense within the home.[6]

For those who believe in safeguarding the civil liberties enshrined in our Bill of Rights, you might consider this an unremarkable conclusion. The constitutional text expressly guarantees the right "to keep and bear Arms," and that right is specifically enumerated — not implied — and guaranteed to "the people." In other words, unlike many of the individual rights that the Supreme Court has recognized — some would say invented — you can actually find the right to bear arms in the literal text of the Second Amendment. Moreover, the Constitution guarantees a "right of the people" only two other times, both of which clearly describe individual rights: The First Amendment protects the "right of the people" to assemble and to petition the government, and the Fourth Amendment protects the "right of the people" against "unreasonable searches and seizures."

Even so, dissenting liberals decried "the Court's announcement of a new constitutional right to own and use firearms for private purposes."[7] Ironically, this claim originated from those who agree with the judicial philosophy that has discovered new fundamental individual rights hiding within "penumbras" that are "formed by emanations" from "specific guarantees in the Bill of Rights." Adherents to this view maintain that the Bill of Rights generates "penumbral emanations" that create assorted individual rights. However, they simultaneously claim that enforcing an individual right expressly written in the black letter of the constitutional text is the "announcement of a new constitutional right." One the one hand, shadowy secretions reveal the hidden meaning of rights secretly embedded in the Constitution and awaiting judicial divination. On the other hand, they view a specifically enumerated guarantee in the Bill of Rights as "a new constitutional right."

Moreover, the dissenting justices claimed that a local law could ban private possession of any form of operable firearm because "the adjacent states do permit the use of handguns for target practice, and those states are only a brief subway ride away."8 They called this a "minimal burden" on the Second Amendment right to bear arms,9 as if a law-abiding citizen who is facing down an attacker might somehow have the ability to coax him onto the subway and take a brief ride to the adjoining jurisdiction's nearest target range. Adherents of this judicial philosophy — which purports to allow the restriction of individual liberties as long as "a brief subway ride" would transport an aggrieved citizen to another jurisdiction where the penumbral emanations flow freely — would assuredly provide more robust protection for rights of their own judicial invention.

These are two dramatically different views of our Bill of Rights. One approach has repeatedly created new rights found nowhere in the Constitution while unflinchingly limiting the Second Amendment's "right of the people to keep and bear Arms" to protect only the right to have a gun in the army, as peculiar as that would be. The other approach, which has twice prevailed in the Supreme Court, takes seriously the people's enumerated rights — the ones actually written in the Constitution — and respects the Second Amendment.

In lieu of empty gestures, we should address gun violence based on what works. Guns make women safer. The Supreme Court has recognized that lawful self-defense is a central component of the Second Amendment's guarantee of the right to keep and bear arms. For women, the ability to arm ourselves for our protection is even more consequential than for men because guns are the great equalizer in a violent confrontation. As a result, we preserve meaningful protection for women by safeguarding our Second Amendment rights. Every woman deserves a fighting chance.

Thank you. It has been a pleasure to be here with you this morning to discuss these issues of such paramount importance to the safety of our citizens. I welcome any questions you may have.

Appendix: Selected News Accounts of Women Using Firearms for Protection Against Violent Men*

Indianapolis, Ind. — A woman used her firearm to stop an intruder who had forced himself into the woman's home and fired a shot. The woman fired several shots at the violent attacker, who fled.[1]

Oklahoma City, Okla. — A woman defended herself from five burglars attempting to break into her home. She shot one of the intruders, causing the others to flee the scene.[2]

Casper, Wyo. — A woman working as a hotel clerk used her gun to thwart a robbery. After two men with covered faces approached her to rob the hotel, the woman brandished a gun from her lunchbox, and the would-be robbers fled.[3]

Loganville, Ga. — A woman hiding in her attic with her children shot a violent intruder and fled to safety. The woman was working at home, saw a man outside her window and took her nineyear-old twins to a crawlspace before the man broke into the home using a crowbar.[4]

Abilene, Tex. — A woman's estranged ex-boyfriend twice attempted to break into her home on Christmas night. After succeeding, he assaulted her while her 16-year-old and newborn child were present. The woman retrieved her firearm and shot the violent intruder.[5]

San Antonio, Tex. — A woman working security in a movie theater shot a gunman who had chased restaurant patrons into the theater's lobby and began shooting, preventing the violent attacker from entering the theater.[6]

Casper, Wyo. — A woman receiving a manicure in a nail salon retrieved a firearm from her purse after a man entered the salon and wielded a pistol. Seeing the woman's weapon, the menacing gunman left.[7]

Atlanta, Ga. — A 77-year-old grandmother used a firearm to defend her home from an intruder trying to gain entry after throwing a brick through her bedroom window. The woman shot twice, and the intruder fled.[8]

Columbia, S.C. — A woman working as a store clerk used her firearm to defend herself from three armed men who attempted to rob the store, demanding money and lottery tickets and shooting into the air. The woman shot one of the violent attackers, and the others fled.[9]

Alcalde, N.M. — A man followed a woman home from a gas station and knocked on her door. While speaking with him at the door, he forced his way into her home, picked up a knife from her kitchen table, put the knife to her chin and ordered her to undress. As he continued to assault her, the woman used a firearm in her home to shoot the violent intruder.[10]

Bryan County, Okla. — A 12-year-old girl was home alone when a man rang the doorbell, went around to the back door and kicked it open. She called her mother, who told her to get the family gun, hide in a closet and call 911. As the mother raced home, the intruder began opening the door to the closet where the girl was hiding. The girl shot the intruder, who immediately fled the house before police caught him.[11]

Blooming Grove, Wis. — A woman heard a robber's footsteps in her home in the middle of the night. As she was dialing 911, the intruder assaulted her with pepper spray. She fired at the man, who fled.[12]

St. Paul, Minn. — A woman walked into her home, where her 34-year-old daughter was asleep at the time, to find a man stealing money from her purse. The burglar struggled with the woman until the daughter entered the room, armed with a handgun. Using the weapon, the women held the man in custody until police arrived.[13]

Athens, Ohio — A 68-year-old woman looked in her driveway at 8 p.m. to see why her dogs were barking. As she rounded her vehicle, a man in a ski mask hit her in the head, knocked her to the ground and kicked her in the stomach. Pulling a handgun from her pocket, the woman fired at the violent attacker, who fled.[14]

Gaffney, S.C. — A woman, home alone with her toddler, hid in her bedroom when she heard an intruder kick in her front door. When the 200-pound man kicked in the woman's bedroom door, she shot at the intruder, who fled.[15]

Detroit, Mich. — As a woman walked out of a store, two carjackers confronted her and shot at her in an attempt to rob her and steal her sport utility vehicle. Although wounded, she used her handgun to return fire, causing the violent attackers to flee.[16]

Fresno County, Calif. — A woman and her two-year old daughter heard a man breaking into her home. The man robbed the woman and tried to kidnap her child. The woman, armed with a shotgun, demanded that the man leave her daughter. The intruder released the child and fled.[17]

Dora, Ala. — A woman called 911 and woke her daughters after hearing the loud crash of an intruder kicking in her front door. Ignoring several warnings, the 25-year-old intruder continued upstairs toward the woman, who shot the man, immobilizing him. "There's so much talk about banning guns and gun control, but they're for protection," she said. "There's no way I could have fought him off."[18]

Blanchard, Okla. — A woman, home alone with her baby, called 911 when two violent intruders attempted to break down her front door. The men wanted to steal medication prescribed to her husband, who had just died of cancer. Before police could arrive, the intruders broke down the door. The woman shot one of the men, brandishing a foot-long hunting knife, and the other fled. "It was either going to be him or my son," she said. "And it wasn't going to be my son."[19]

Gwinnett County, Ga. — A woman getting out of the shower faced a strange man attacking her with a kitchen knife. The attacker, who had stalked her for several days before, forced the woman into her bedroom. Telling him she had money there, she reached her handgun and shot the violent attacker, who ran out of a back door and collapsed in the yard.[20]

Blountville, Tenn. — A woman serving as the resource officer at Sullivan Central High School stopped a violent attacker as he pointed a gun at the principal's head. The woman drew her own gun, pushed the principal to safety and kept the attacker at bay until police arrived, when they shot and killed the violent attacker during a standoff.[21]

End Notes

[1] U.S. Department of Justice Bureau of Justice Statistics, "National Crime Victimization Survey" (Sept. 2011), at 8 (noting that "[d]uring the 10-year period, about 6% to 9% of all violent victimizations were committed with firearms" and that "[t]he percent of violent victimizations involving firearms has remained generally stable from 2004 to 2010").

[2] See John R. Lott, Jr., MORE GUNS, LESS CRIME 46 (3d ed. 2010).

[3] Id.

[4] Id. at 100-01.

[5] Letter from Irvin B. Nathan, Attorney General for the District of Columbia, to Lee Levine (Jan. 11, 2013), at 2.

[6] District of Columbia v. Heller, 554 U.S. 570 (2008) (holding that the Second Amendment guarantees an individual right to possess a firearm unconnected with service in a militia and to use that arm for traditionally lawful purposes, such as self-defense within the home); McDonald v. City of Chicago, 561 U.S. 3025 (2010) (holding that the Second Amendment applies to the states as well as the federal government).

[7] Heller, 554 U.S. at 681 (Stevens, J., dissenting).

[8] Id. at 712 (Breyer, J., dissenting) (citing the online Metrorail System Map of the Washington Metropolitan Area Transit Authority).

[9] Id. (Breyer, J., dissenting).

End Notes for Appendix

[*] This Appendix summarizes selected news accounts, primarily from the last twelve months, involving women who used a firearm to protect themselves and their children against violent attackers or intruders. Many similar stories are aggregated online, such as those available at http://bit.ly/WifldI.

[1] "Resident Fires Back at Intruder" (Jan. 22, 2013), available at http://bit.ly/XAe6DS.

[2] "Burglars Shot in Southeast Oklahoma City" (Jan. 18, 2013), available at http://bit.ly/VGu1mz.

[3] "Casper Hotel Worker Uses Lunchbox Gun to Thwart Robbery" (Jan. 4, 2013), available at http://bit.ly/TPbz9H.

[4] "Woman Hiding With Kids Shoots Intruder" (Jan. 4, 2013), available at http://bit.ly/134dM6d.

[5] "Abilene Woman Shot and Killed Estranged Ex-Boyfriend" (Dec. 26, 2012), available at http://bit.ly/TnvrBO.

[6] "Terror at Southwest Side Movie Theater" (Dec. 17, 2012), available at http://bit.ly/12jVMV9.

[7] "Nail Salon Customer Packs Heat, Gunman Leaves" (Dec. 11, 2012), available at http://bit.ly/W5iZG1.

[8] "Woman, 77, Shoots at Would-Be Burglar" (Dec. 6, 2012), available at http://bit.ly/11ZjJ2W.

[9] "Store Clerk Fears for Her Life, Shoots Robbery Suspect" (Nov. 14, 2012), available at http://bit.ly/Tp4sTt.

[10] "Alcalde Woman In Fatal Shooting Tells Deputies Stranger Barged In, Assaulted Her" (Nov. 7, 2012), available at http://bit.ly/Uv2Efa.

[11] "Twelve-Year-Old Girl Shoots Intruder During Home Invasion" (Oct. 18, 2012), available at http://bit.ly/Xvbrh3.

[12] "Woman Says Shooting at Home Intruder Saved Her Life" (Sept. 22, 2012), available at http://bit.ly/UsmoAJ.

[13] "Mom, Daughter Hold Burglar for Police with Pink Gun" (Sept. 19, 2012), available at http://bit.ly/Ryzf42.

[14] "Rhoric Road Woman Uses Gun to Fend Off Attacker" (Sept. 13, 2012), available at http://bit.ly/RMJNvW.

[15] "Woman Protecting Toddler Fires Shots at Intruder" (Sept. 7, 2012), available at http://bit.ly/UawOmQ.

[16] "Detroit Woman Shoots Back At Would-Be Carjackers" (Aug. 27, 2012), available at http://bit.ly/OqzSdd.

[17] "Fresno County Woman Stops Kidnapping By Pulling Gun on Home Intruder" (Aug. 28, 2012), available at http://bit.ly/SO7gNp.

[18] "Woman Forced to Shoot Intruder to Protect Herself and Children" (Aug. 16, 2012), available at http://bit.ly/Q4ItxX.

[19] "Blanchard Mother Who Shot, Killed Intruder Recalls Home Invasion Terror" (Jan. 1, 2012), available at http://bit.ly/sGcdTr.

[20] "Woman Shot Intruder Nine Times in Self Defense" (May 11, 2011), available at http://bit.ly/HwqfGe.

[21] "Police Officers Kill Gunman at Sullivan Central" (Aug. 30, 2010), available at http://bit.ly/aCuFSl.

In: Mass Shootings and Gun Violence in America
Editor: John C. Zandler
ISBN: 978-1-62618-893-8

Chapter 10

TESTIMONY OF WAYNE LAPIERRE, EXECUTIVE VICE PRESIDENT, NATIONAL RIFLE ASSOCIATION. HEARING ON "WHAT SHOULD AMERICA DO ABOUT GUN VIOLENCE?"*

Mr. Chairman and Members of the Committee:

It's an honor to be here today on behalf of more than 4.5 million moms and dads and sons and daughters, in every state across our nation, who make up the National Rifle Association of America. Those 4.5 million active members are joined by tens of millions of NRA supporters.

And it's on behalf of those millions of decent, hardworking, law-abiding citizens ... to give voice to their concerns ... that I'm here today.

The title of today's hearing is "What should America do about gun violence?"

We believe the answer to that question is to be honest about what works – and what doesn't work.

Teaching safe and responsible gun ownership works – and the NRA has a long and proud history of teaching it.

Our "Eddie Eagle" children's safety program has taught over 25 million young children that if they see a gun, they should do four things: "Stop. Don't touch. Leave the area. Tell an adult." As a result of this and other private sector programs, fatal firearm accidents are at the lowest levels in more than 100 years.1

The NRA has over 80,000 certified instructors who teach our military personnel, law enforcement officers and hundreds of thousands of other American men and women how to safely use firearms. We do more – and spend more – than anyone else on teaching safe and responsible gun ownership.

We joined the nation in sorrow over the tragedy that occurred in Newtown, Connecticut. There is nothing more precious than our children. We have no more sacred duty than to protect our children and keep them safe. That's why we asked former Congressman and Undersecretary of Homeland Security, Asa Hutchison, to bring in every expert available to

* This is an edited, reformatted and augmented version of a testimony presented January 30, 2013 before the Senate Judiciary Committee.

develop a model School Shield Program – one that can be individually tailored to make our schools as safe as possible.

It's time to throw an immediate blanket of security around our children. About a third of our schools have armed security already – because it works.2 And that number is growing. Right now, state officials, local authorities and school districts in all 50 states are considering their own plans to protect children in their schools.

In addition, we need to enforce the thousands of gun laws that are currently on the books. Prosecuting criminals who misuse firearms works. Unfortunately, we've seen a dramatic collapse in federal gun prosecutions in recent years. Overall in 2011, federal weapons prosecutions per capita were down 35 percent from their peak in the previous administration.3 That means violent felons, gang members and the mentally ill who possess firearms are not being prosecuted. And that's unacceptable.

And out of more than 76,000 firearms purchases denied by the federal instant check system, only 62 were referred for prosecution and only 44 were actually prosecuted.4 Proposing more gun control laws – while failing to enforce the thousands we already have – is not a serious solution to reducing crime.

I think we can also agree that our mental health system is broken. We need to look at the full range of mental health issues, from early detection and treatment, to civil commitment laws, to privacy laws that needlessly prevent mental health records from being included in the National Instant Criminal Background Check System.

While we're ready to participate in a meaningful effort to solve these pressing problems, we must respectfully – but honestly and firmly – disagree with some members of this committee, many in the media, and all of the gun control groups on what will keep our kids and our streets safe.

Law-abiding gun owners will not accept blame for the acts of violent or deranged criminals. Nor do we believe the government should dictate what we can lawfully own and use to protect our families.

As I said earlier, we need to be honest about what works and what does not work. Proposals that would only serve to burden the law-abiding have failed in the past and will fail in the future.

Semi-automatic firearms have been around for over 100 years. They are among the most popular guns made for hunting, target shooting and self-defense. Despite this fact, Congress banned the manufacture and sale of hundreds of semi-automatic firearms and magazines from 1994 to 2004. Independent studies, including a study from the Clinton Justice Department, proved that ban had no impact on lowering crime.5

And when it comes to the issue of background checks, let's be honest – background checks will never be "universal" – because criminals will never submit to them.

But there are things that can be done and we ask you to join with us. The NRA is made up of millions of Americans who support what works ... the immediate protection for all – not just some – of our school children; swift, certain prosecution of criminals with guns; and fixing our broken mental health system.

We love our families and our country. We believe in our freedom. We're the millions of Americans from all walks of life who take responsibility for our own safety and protection as a God-given, fundamental right.

Mr. Chairman and members of the Committee, I thank you for your time and consideration.

End Notes

[1] Pre-1981 data from National Safety Council, Accident Facts (annual); 1981 forward from Centers for Disease Control and Prevention, available at http://www.cdc.gov/injury/ wisqars/fatal injury reports.html.

[2] Gary Fields et al., NRA Calls for Arms in School, Wall Street Journal, Dec. 22, 2012, available at http://online.wsj.com/article/SB10001424127887324461604578193364201364432.html.

[3] Calculated from U.S. Department of Justice data available through Transactional Records Access Clearinghouse, http://tracfed.syr.edu.

[4] Ronald J. Frandsen, Enforcement of the Brady Act, 2010: Federal and State Investigations and Prosecutions of Firearm Applicants Denied by a NICS Check in 2010, available at https://www.ncjrs.gov/pdffiles1/bjs/grants/ 239272.pdf.

[5] Jeffrey A. Roth & Christopher S. Koper, "Impact Evaluation of the Public Safety and Recreational Firearms Use Protection Act of 1994, (1997), available at http://www.sas.upenn.edu/jerrylee/research/aw ban.htm.

In: Mass Shootings and Gun Violence in America
Editor: John C. Zandler
ISBN: 978-1-62618-893-8

Chapter 11

STATEMENT OF SENATOR PATRICK LEAHY, CHAIRMAN, SENATE JUDICIARY COMMITTEE. HEARING ON "PROPOSALS TO REDUCE GUN VIOLENCE: PROTECTING OUR COMMUNITIES WHILE RESPECTING THE SECOND AMENDMENT"*

I want to thank Senator Durbin for chairing today's hearing. Two weeks ago, the Committee began the new Congress with a hearing on what our Nation should do to address gun violence in the wake of the tragic shootings in Newtown. We have begun the collective effort to find solutions to help ensure that no family, no school, and no community ever has to endure such a grievous tragedy again. Today's hearing will continue this important discussion and make clear that we are mindful of the constitutional limits of what can be done by Congress.

Today's hearing focuses on ways to reduce gun violence while respecting Americans' Second Amendment rights. As a responsible gun owner and strong supporter of Second Amendment rights, I know we can do both. I have always believed that the Second Amendment affords a fundamental individual right. The Supreme Court has now clearly recognized that right, and it is settled in our law. Following the decisions in Heller and McDonald, there is no question that Americans have a right to self-defense and to keep a firearm to protect their families.

Our conversations take place against a backdrop that recognizes and protects the Second Amendment and the basic rights it secures. But I also agree with Justice Scalia and the other Justices on the Supreme Court that "the right to bear arms is not a right to keep and carry any weapon whatsoever in any manner whatsoever and for whatever purpose." I think we all can agree that the individual right does not include weapons of war like machine guns, or rocket-propelled grenades. And as Justice Scalia has noted, the Second Amendment does not prevent laws restricting "the possession of firearms by felons or the mentally ill."

In the wake of the recent mass killings that have shaken the country, we must consider what more can be done to keep guns out of the hands of criminals and the mentally infirm

* This is an edited, reformatted and augmented version of a statement presented February 12, 2013 before the Senate Judiciary Committee, Subcommittee on the Constitution, Civil Rights and Human Rights.

who threaten our communities. We need to close existing loopholes that allow criminals to avoid the common sense requirement that gun sales should be performed with a background check. Responsible gun store owners in Vermont and around the country carry out these checks every day. Requiring buyers at gun shows to take the same reasonable steps as buyers in stores is a sensible, straightforward solution to help keep firearms out of the wrong hands. In 1999, the NRA fully supported such background checks.

We also need to help our law enforcement officers by providing them with the tools they need to keep our communities safe. We should strengthen law enforcement's ability to prosecute straw purchasers who buy firearms on behalf of criminals who otherwise would not pass a background check. The legislation I introduced with Senator Durbin and other Senators last month to combat this type of illegal trafficking would not affect licensed gun dealers, and in no way alters the rights of those who lawfully trade in guns. It is another commonsense solution that will help make us safer as a Nation.

As we discuss responses to address gun violence, some have proposed changes that would prohibit violence in movies and in video games. As a parent and a grandparent, I share concerns about the pervasiveness of violence in our popular culture. I am also mindful, however, that efforts to regulate content risk undermining our country's strong First Amendment tradition of protecting free speech no matter how objectionable it is. As we reflect on the lessons of recent months, the entertainment industry must renew its efforts to be a responsible leader in this area.

As parents, as lawmakers, as citizens, we must all play a role in addressing the problem of gun violence. We must work together to find reasonable, balanced solutions to improve our laws where they are lacking. I urge us to listen to each other and to work together to find areas of agreement. The American people are looking to us to act.

In: Mass Shootings and Gun Violence in America
Editor: John C. Zandler
ISBN: 978-1-62618-893-8

Chapter 12

STATEMENT OF SENATOR ORRIN G. HATCH. HEARING ON "PROPOSALS TO REDUCE GUN VIOLENCE: PROTECTING OUR COMMUNITIES WHILE RESPECTING THE SECOND AMENDMENT"*

Thank you, Mr. Chairman. Two weeks ago, I participated in the full Judiciary Committee's hearing on what American should do about gun violence. In the statement I submitted for the record at that hearing, I said that legislation in this area must meet three criteria. First, legislation must be consistent with the Constitution in general, and with the Second Amendment in particular. Second, we must draw on the experience of past legislative efforts. Third, we must examine the causes of this problem, not simply its symptoms. Legislation that fails to meet all three criteria will be ineffective and a disservice to victims and their family members.

These criteria bear repeating because this hearing narrows the focus to actual legislative proposals. When I look at the list of proposals offered by the Johns Hopkins Gun Policy Summit, I see item after item that fail one or more of these criteria. And one of the most significant things about this list is what is not there – anything other than guns.

I question whether there actually is a specific, separate, unique category called gun violence. Rather than focusing exclusively on the particular tool used to commit violence, we should be exploring violence in our society more generally.

Like President Obama's list of executive actions, this Johns Hopkins list urges the federal government to approach gun violence as a public health problem. The obvious intent is to encourage the American people to think one day about guns the way they think today about cigarettes. That is a seriously flawed strategy. There is no constitutional right to smoke, there is a constitutional right to keep and bear arms. There is no safe way to smoke, there are many safe ways to use firearms. Cigarettes can take lives, firearms can save lives.

Other items on the list are also troubling. It defines anyone under 21 as a "high risk individual" who should be prohibited from purchasing or even possession a handgun. Tell that to the thousands of young people in the armed forces who are using firearms every day to defend freedom around the world.

---

* This is an edited, reformatted and augmented version of a statement presented February 12, 2013 before the Senate Judiciary Committee, Subcommittee on the Constitution, Civil Rights and Human Rights.

With freedom comes the potential for tragedy. In a free society, we simply cannot ensure that danger will disappear, that violence will never occur, that lives will never be lost. But freedom itself is not the problem. I urge my fellow citizens to help make our country a better and safer place and to preserve the fundamental rights that keep us free.

In: Mass Shootings and Gun Violence in America
Editor: John C. Zandler
ISBN: 978-1-62618-893-8

Chapter 13

STATEMENT OF SENATOR TED CRUZ. HEARING ON "PROPOSALS TO REDUCE GUN VIOLENCE: PROTECTING OUR COMMUNITIES WHILE RESPECTING THE SECOND AMENDMENT"*

Thank you, Mr. Chairman. Let me say it is a particular honor to serve as Ranking Member on this Subcommittee with you. It is also a high honor to serve with two former Ranking Members and Chairmen of this Subcommittee—Senator Cornyn and Senator Hatch—as well as the Ranking Member of the full Committee, Senator Grassley.

All of us were rightly horrified by the tragedy in Newtown, Connecticut. To see young children senselessly murdered takes your breath away. Let me say to each of you who has come here today that are the victims of crimes of violence, my heart goes out to you. Thank you for coming. Thank you for standing for your lost loved ones. I have spent much of my own professional career working in law enforcement to prevent these horrible crimes of violence and ensure that anyone that carries them out is subject to the very strictest punishments.

I am hopeful that the fervor that we see on this Judiciary Committee hearing, for standing up for victims of crimes of violence, will carry over to issues other than gun control. I am hopeful that same fervor will be present when judicial nominees are here who have a record and history of allowing those who have committed violent crimes to walk free. I hope that same fervor on a bipartisan basis will be present when we're talking about how to ensure that laws and resources exist to prevent violent criminals from carrying out their horrific crimes and to ensure that every one of them receives a fair and just punishment.

In my view, the divide on this issue is fairly straightforward. The focus of law enforcement should be on criminals, and we should be unstinting in protecting communities. Sadly, law enforcement has been failing in many of the communities in which each of you has suffered losses. We should be working to fix that problem.

At the same time, we should continue to respect and protect the constitutional rights of law-abiding citizens. It is often lost in the debate over guns that the Second Amendment is a vital part of our Constitution. It is part of the Bill of Rights. It is indeed, as Justice Joseph

* This is an edited, reformatted and augmented version of a statement presented February 12, 2013 before the Senate Judiciary Committee, Subcommittee on the Constitution, Civil Rights and Human Rights.

Story put it, the "palladium of the liberties of a republic." Stripping the constitutional rights of law-abiding citizens does nothing to prevent criminals from carrying out violent crime.

The overwhelming weight of the empirical evidence demonstrates that violent crime increases when the rights of law-abiding citizens to protect themselves, to protect their homes, and to protect their families are taken away. Defenseless citizens are more vulnerable to violent criminals.

For that reason, the two cities with the strictest gun control policies in the country, Washington, D.C., and Chicago, have suffered from some of the highest crime and murder rates, notwithstanding those laws. Both cities had, for years, effectively total bans on firearms ownership and both still have among the highest murder rates in the nation.

Likewise, when Australia banned guns, violent crime went up. And after Great Britain banned guns, its violent crime rate was more than four-times higher than the rate in the United States. If you look in contrast to jurisdictions that have protected the constitutional right to bear arms, you have consistently seen lower crime and murder rates, as individual citizens are able to protect their families.

Aggressive gun control would restrict the constitutional rights of every American. We cannot outlaw evil, but we can remain vigilant in working to deter and punish violent criminals. And we should vigorously defend the constitutional right of law-abiding citizens to protect themselves and others from deadly attacks.

The Supreme Court's decisions in Heller and McDonald were landmark decisions. They concerned the question whether each of us is protected by the Bill of Rights. The cities took the position, in those cases, that individuals have no right whatsoever under the Second Amendment and that the Second Amendment does not apply to the States. The position of the litigants in those cases, I would suggest, was quite extreme.

Heller made crystal clear that individuals have a Second Amendment right to keep and bear arms. Like virtually all constitutional rights, however, everyone acknowledges that there are some limits on this right. For example, the government may prohibit felons and the mentally ill from possessing firearms, as Heller explained.

The key question, which I hope we will explore in this hearing, is the scope of an individual's Second Amendment right to keep and bear arms. But we are not discussing this in a vacuum, as Heller and McDonald should guide our inquiry. McDonald explicitly stated that an individual's Second Amendment right "is fundamental to our scheme of ordered liberty" and is "deeply rooted in this Nation's history and tradition."

And Heller establishes that the Second Amendment protects in particular those firearms that are in "common use." So the Second Amendment does not give citizens the right to have "dangerous and unusual" weapons, like fully automatic machine guns—which are already functionally illegal under current law. But it does give individuals the right to keep and bear firearms that are widely used. I therefore have serious doubts about the constitutionality of the proposed Assault Weapons Ban and a ban on magazines with more than 10 rounds—because both of these bans would cover millions of firearms that are "commonly used" by Americans.

In any event, we should not pass legislation that the evidence has proven is utterly ineffective. In particular, the Department of Justice has already concluded that the so-called "assault weapons ban," when it was in effect from 1994 to 2004, had no impact on reducing crime. This is unsurprising, because real assault weapons—machine guns—have been functionally illegal since 1934. All an "assault weapons ban" would do is restrict cosmetic features of firearms, in effect, banning "scary-looking guns." Instead of passing ineffective show legislation—sound and fury, signifying nothing—we should be acting to deter and punish violent criminals and to prevent those with dangerous mental illness from illegally acquiring firearms.

There is wide agreement that guns should not be in the hands of the mentally ill. Current law seeks to identify those individuals, but it relies on states submitting relevant medical records. Not all states are doing this. A July 2012 GAO report explained that the federal government is not enforcing or implementing a 2007 law that was supposed to reward states for submitting mental health records and to punish states that do not. We should make sure current law is enforced and work with states to help them get past the challenges that prevent them from providing more robust data. This is an area of bipartisan agreement and a direct way to address the real problem of the mentally ill getting guns.

In doing so, we can respect the Second Amendment rights of all Americans. So today, as we discuss the limits on the Second Amendment right to bear arms, we should keep in mind that the Supreme Court made absolutely clear that the Second Amendment is a constitutional right of every American. And I would point out that constitutional rights are designed to be protected not just when they are popular but especially when passions are seeking to restrict and limit those rights. I look forward to this hearing underscoring the vital protections of the Second Amendment to every American.

In: Mass Shootings and Gun Violence in America
Editor: John C. Zandler
ISBN: 978-1-62618-893-8

Chapter 14

STATEMENT OF SENATOR TIMOTHY J. HEAPHY, U.S. ATTORNEY, DEPARTMENT OF JUSTICE. HEARING ON "PROPOSALS TO REDUCE GUN VIOLENCE: PROTECTING OUR COMMUNITIES WHILE RESPECTING THE SECOND AMENDMENT"*

Good morning, Chairman Durbin, and Members of the Subcommittee, it is a privilege to appear before you today on behalf of the Department of Justice. As the United States Attorney for the Western District of Virginia, I am pleased to speak with you about the continuing work of the United States Attorney community and the Department of Justice to address gun-related violence. In particular, I want to talk to you today about our efforts to bring to justice those individuals and criminal organizations who have endangered our communities and undermined public safety through the illegal possession and use of firearms.

Recent tragedies at Sandy Hook Elementary School in Newtown, Connecticut; at a nursing school in Oakland, California; at a movie theater in Aurora, Colorado; and at a Sikh Temple in Oak Creek, Wisconsin have reminded us of the overwhelming tragedy caused by gun-related violence. In my district, we experienced the same kind of tragedy several years ago, on the campus of Virginia Tech. We also confront the awful reality of gun violence in the diverse communities in which we serve, from Chicago, Illinois to Roanoke, Virginia. All of these incidents reinforce our continuing obligation to enforce the federal firearms laws we currently have, and of the need to find additional tools to help prevent violent crime in all its forms.

As the chief federal law enforcement officer in my district, I have taken an oath to uphold the Constitution and the laws of the United States. Like my fellow United States Attorneys, I am duty-bound to do everything within my authority to ensure the safety of the citizens of our communities. As a former line prosecutor who has handled numerous violent crime cases, including one trial involving 17 defendants charged with a total of 31 murders, I have seen firsthand the crucial role that federal law enforcement plays in this effort. My colleagues and I consider it a solemn obligation and a privilege to bear the responsibility of keeping our people

* This is an edited, reformatted and augmented version of testimony given on February 12, 2013 before the Senate Judiciary Committee, Subcommittee on the Constitution, Civil Rights and Human Rights.

safe, and today I want to discuss with you what we have done to address the particular challenges of gun-related violence – through both prevention and enforcement efforts.

I. Combatting Violent Crime Is a Key Department of Justice Priority

Attorney General Holder has consistently emphasized that combatting violent crime and fostering safe communities is a top priority of the Department of Justice. To that end, he has tasked the United States Attorneys with the responsibility to develop localized strategies to apprehend and prosecute individuals, street gangs, and other criminal organizations that engage in gun-related violence. In a meeting of federal prosecutors in New Orleans dedicated to the protection of our communities in July of 2010, Attorney General Holder urged United States Attorneys to be more than mere "case processors" and to embrace the additional role of "problem solvers" when it comes to the gun violence plaguing our communities. He instructed us "to bring innovative, evidence-based solutions to the work of addressing our most overwhelming and intractable challenges – namely, the prevalence and consequences of gun-, gang-, and drug-related violence, as well as the devastating impact of childhood exposure to violence." We continue to follow these instructions in our ongoing efforts to protect our children and communities while holding violent offenders accountable for their criminal actions.

Each United States Attorney, working with federal, state, local and tribal prosecutors, law enforcement, and community leaders, has implemented a district-specific, anti-violence strategy, consistent with the Attorney General's direction. These local strategies provide specific plans that combine targeted enforcement with support for crime prevention and viable offender reentry. We work closely with our state and local partners to apply this comprehensive approach to violence prevention in communities both large and small, urban and rural.

Our work reflects the priority we put on preventing gun violence in every district in the country. We must continually strive to make the most of the finite number of federal prosecutors, agents, and state and local officers we have deployed in this fight. This requires us to work smarter by gathering intelligence and targeting our enforcement efforts at the most dangerous and complicated criminal justice threats in our communities. By doing so, we are bringing impactful cases that help change neighborhoods. This data-driven approach makes us more effective. We work cooperatively with state and local law enforcement to identify and support their efforts where it makes the most sense for them to be in the lead. We continue to do all we can to vigorously prosecute gun crime, relying on close coordination with ATF and our other federal, state, and local partners in a targeted approach.

II. Prevention

As the Attorney General has said repeatedly, any effective response to a criminal justice challenge must combine enforcement with prevention – violent crime is no exception. In this regard, preventing prohibited persons from even obtaining a firearm is a crucial component in the overall strategy to reduce gun-related violence. Federal law precludes certain categories of "prohibited persons" from receiving or possessing firearms, including those who have been convicted of, or are currently under indictment for, a felony; are an unlawful user of a controlled substance; have been involuntarily committed to a mental institution; are illegally or unlawfully present in the United States; have been dishonorably discharged from the Armed Forces; have renounced their citizenship; are subject to a domestic violence order of protection; or have been convicted of a misdemeanor crime of domestic violence.

Federal law also requires licensed gun dealers to ensure that they are not selling firearms to prohibited persons. Specifically, before a federal firearms licensee (FFL) can transfer a firearm to an unlicensed individual, the dealer must request a background check through the FBI's National Instant Criminal Background Check System (NICS) to determine whether the prospective transfer would violate federal or state law. During the NICS check, personal information provided by the prospective firearms purchaser is used to search national databases containing criminal history and other relevant records to determine if the person is disqualified by law from receiving or possessing a firearm. The information in NICS is largely furnished by state and local governments, and we're doing all we can to create incentives and provide assistance to state actors to ensure that NICS information is complete and thorough.

Since it was created in 1998, the NICS background check system has kept more than 1.5 million guns out of the wrong hands. That's why expansion of this system is so vital to public safety. Many individuals who are prohibited by law from purchasing a firearm have been stopped from making a firearms purchase. Approximately 83,000 of these sales were prevented in FY 2012 in states that rely on the FBI to process the background checks.

Of course, these denials only represent instances where the prohibited person attempted to purchase a firearm from a FFL. Under current law, in most states, when a prohibited person attempts that same purchase from an unlicensed seller at a gun show, from an unlicensed private individual, or from any source other than a licensed FFL, no background check is required. As a result, prohibited persons are able to evade background checks. A recent case in the Western District of Oklahoma provides a good example of the problem. Local law enforcement officers in Oklahoma City observed a previously convicted felon and gang member of the Southside Locos – a violent street gang known for its long history of violent crime – visit multiple vendors at a local gun show. Law enforcement officers watched as the felon deliberately avoided purchasing firearms from any of the FFLs in attendance. Instead, he purchased, without any paper trail, a machine pistol with a high-capacity magazine and another gun from non-licensed vendors who were not required to perform background checks. It was only because this individual was already known to law enforcement and law enforcement happened to be on-site at the time he visited the gun show that this gang member was prosecuted by the United States Attorney's Office for being a felon in possession of a firearm, and was sentenced to 46 months in federal prison. Without this unique confluence of events, this prohibited person would have had all too-easy access to firearms.

Cases like these provide strong support for universal background checks. Without a comprehensive background check system, it is too easy for violent criminals to seek out sellers – whether at gun shows, on the Internet, or in the Yellow Pages – who are not licensed dealers, who the criminals know do not require paperwork. And unlicensed sellers of these guns, whether at a gun show or for any private sale, would have no systematized way of being informed of the defendant's felony record unless they conduct the transaction through an FFL. The most effective way to ensure that the only people able to buy guns are those who are legally able to own them is to require background checks for all private sales. This rule should admit some important, limited exceptions – such as certain transfers between family members and temporary transfers for hunting and sporting purposes. Except for these private, non-commercial transfers, however, any sale of a firearm should trigger the background check requirement. Quite simply, requiring universal background checks is our best opportunity to keep firearms out of dangerous hands and to help keep our children and communities safe.

III. Criminal Enforcement

Enforcement of the federal firearms laws is one of the Department's core missions and the primary focus of our approach to combatting violent crime. We use the firearms laws to apprehend violent offenders, those who possess firearms illegally, and those who facilitate gun distribution and gun trafficking.

United States Attorneys recognize that "one-size-does-not-fit-all" and that the prosecution strategies for firearms offenses will vary depending on the nature of the problem in a given judicial district or community. Our enforcement strategies must necessarily take into account differences in state laws and state prosecution priorities. With many firearms cases, the question is not whether any given defendant will be prosecuted – they will be. The question is whether it is most effective for the case to be prosecuted at the federal or state level. Working in conjunction with our state and local partners, United States Attorneys make strategic judgments about the most effective approach for their district. Our overall goal is the pursuit of impactful cases that help change neighborhoods, not simply locking up everyone with a gun. We have to develop good intelligence about where the need is greatest and be smart about how we deploy our investigative and prosecutorial resources. Notwithstanding variations from district-todistrict, the mission remains the same across the country: apprehending those who threaten the safety of our children, our families, and our communities. Yet, despite our commitment to enforcing the laws, more must be done to enhance the laws available to law enforcement to keep our communities safe.

A. Prosecutions of Prohibited Persons in Possession of Firearms and Those Who Sell to Them

One component of our enforcement strategy across the country is keeping prohibited persons, such as the convicted felon in the Western District of Oklahoma described above, from obtaining and possessing firearms. Our statistics are reflective of our work in this area. The statistical report released by the Executive Office of United States Attorneys (EOUSA) reveals that the number of defendants charged nationwide with violations of 18 U.S.C. § 922 or 18 U.S.C. § 924 – which, generally speaking, prohibit the sale, receipt, or possession of firearms to prohibited persons and the use of firearms to commit other crimes – remained fairly consistent from FY 2007 to FY 2011, ranging from 11,421 in FY 2010 to 12,087 in FY

2007. These numbers are significantly higher than they were back in FY 2000 (when the total was 8,054), FY 2001 (when the total was 8,845), and FY 2002 (when the total was 10,634). In FY 2005, when federal gun prosecutions peaked at 13,062, there were 17,128 murders nationwide according to the FBI's uniform crime report data. Since FY 2005, murders nationwide have declined by 13.7 percent. The number of defendants prosecuted federally for gun crimes has declined by 9.6 percent.

On the supply side, we prosecute individuals who are engaged in the business of dealing with firearms without a license and who ignore or disregard the law preventing gun sales to prohibited persons. A recent case in my district is a good example. Don Simonpietri ran a pawn shop in Front Royal, Virginia. After losing his federal firearms license in 2005, he continued to sell multiple firearms from the pawn shop and at gun shows in Virginia. Undercover agents working with a task force of agents from the ATF, the Virginia State Police, and the Shenandoah County Sheriff's Office made several controlled purchases of firearms from Mr. Simonpietri, each time indicating to him that the purchaser was a convicted felon. Mr. Simonpietri sold guns – including an AR-15 Bushmaster assault rifle – to these undercover officers acting as felons. On one occasion, Mr. Simonpietri directed the sale to the undercover officer through a "straw purchaser" who he did not believe was a felon, in direct violation of law. ATF agents later seized 1,350 guns from Mr. Simonpietri at his pawn shop and his residence. In 2010, my office charged Mr. Simonpietri and three others with unlawful firearms transfers, resulting in forfeiture of all 1,350 guns and jail sentences for all four defendants.

B. Prosecutions of Firearms Trafficking and Straw Purchasing Cases

In addition to prosecuting prohibited persons illegally in possession of firearms and illegal gun dealers who sell to them, the Department emphasizes building and prosecuting firearms trafficking and straw purchasing cases. A recent prosecution from the Southern District of Mississippi is an excellent example. After an investigation of gun trafficking among the Simon City Royals street gang and its affiliates, the United States Attorney's Office secured a 30-count indictment charging 15 defendants with firearms-conspiracy charges. The defendants were part of a group that procured and sold weapons to the gang. In November of 2012, 12 of these defendants – only one of whom was a previously convicted felon – were sentenced. One defendant received a sentence of only 33 months in prison and another defendant received a sentence of only 41 months. Similarly, ATF and ICE investigators in the Middle District of Florida developed information about a firearms ring that was moving more than 200 guns from Florida to Puerto Rico. Last year, the trafficker pled guilty and was sentenced to 38 months of imprisonment.

We pursue these trafficking cases despite the fact that they present an enormous challenge for federal agents and prosecutors. United States Attorneys have only a limited range of statutory "tools" in our collective tool-box, and the penalties for many of these offenses remain relatively low. These cases are also made more difficult by the fact that no single federal statute is specifically devoted to punishing firearms trafficking or straw purchasing. This requires prosecutors to try to find other gun-related criminal statutes that can be applied to the facts of a particular trafficking scheme. While we can and do use every tool we have to bring unlawful gun traffickers to justice, without more meaningful penalties for those who traffic in firearms, we will continue to find it difficult to dismantle the criminal networks that exploit these statutory gaps.

C. Prosecutions of "Lie and Try" Cases

There has been much public discussion lately about the Department's prosecution philosophy with regard to individuals who improperly attempt to purchase a firearm by lying to an FFL. We do prosecute these cases. For example, the United States Attorney's Office in Maine recently prosecuted a defendant who falsely completed an application form in the attempted acquisition of a Colt, Model 1911A1, .45 Caliber pistol. The defendant did not reveal that he was subject to a domestic violence protection order obtained by his abused, live-in girlfriend. He was denied the firearm and subsequently prosecuted for violating 18 U.S.C. §922(a)(6), which prohibits making false representations in connection with the acquisition of a firearm. He was convicted at trial and sentenced to six months' imprisonment. The victim's family expressed deep appreciation for the officers and prosecutors who helped avert a potentially lethal domestic incident. Despite the nominal sentence, this case provides an example of the type of "lie and try" case that it makes sense for the Department to prosecute, given the defendant's history of violence, the existence of a domestic violence protection order, and the fact that the woman he had abused continued to reside in the home they had previously shared together.

For the most part, however, the Department prioritizes prosecuting prohibited persons who actually *obtain* guns – people who have gotten around the background check system and acquired weapons illegally – rather than those who attempted to purchase a firearm through the background check system but were unsuccessful. In cases where a prohibited person attempted to purchase a firearm and was denied as a result of the background check, the system worked at the front end. That prohibited person was prevented from obtaining the gun he was attempting to purchase. In some cases, the prohibited person may not have known that they were prohibited and, therefore, may not have committed the crime of making an intentional misrepresentation when filling out the form. As I said before, United States Attorneys around the country work with our state and local counterparts to make thoughtful decisions about how to use our finite prosecution resources to best protect public safety in our communities.

D. Use of Statutory and Sentencing Guidelines Enhancements in Violent Crime Cases

Lastly, federal prosecutors rely on gun charges and sentencing enhancements in broader violent crime cases. Section 924(c) of Title 18 provides a mandatory, consecutive sentence when a gun is used to commit a federal crime. While that provision is not perfect, I can say that we use that overall statute in connection with a variety of underlying crimes – everything from drug sales to robberies to homicides. Similarly, the Sentencing Guidelines provide for an enhancement in the defendant's recommended sentencing range if he or she uses a firearm during the course of any criminal offense. We use these provisions to hold violent offenders accountable. The serious penalties they carry allow us to obtain actionable intelligence about drug organizations, violent street gangs, and other criminal enterprises. These provisions help us build the kind of large, impactful cases that we have prioritized.

CONCLUSION

In sum, we need to implement both front and back end solutions to the problem of gun violence in America. As the Attorney General articulated in his anti-violence strategy, the combination of prevention and enforcement works. As we try to prevent kids from joining gangs, we must prevent unlawful firearms transfers and ensure that we do all we can to keep guns out of the hands of dangerous persons. We must also react swiftly and with certainty when people break the law. We have to make impactful cases that remove dangerous criminals and their guns out of our communities. Our efforts to stop gun violence must be targeted and coordinated. Nothing less will be successful.

Those of us who work within the Department of Justice are doing what we can to rid communities across the country from the scourge of gun violence. We are implementing a comprehensive strategy, working in tandem with our state partners, and letting reliable intelligence guide our work. We will continue to do all we can to rise to this challenge and promote public safety. The legislative proposals put forth by the President would provide much needed additional tools for us to deploy in this important effort.

Thank you for the opportunity to appear before you today and to reiterate my commitment and the commitment of my colleagues in the Department of Justice to ensure the safety of our families and the peace of our communities.

In: Mass Shootings and Gun Violence in America
Editor: John C. Zandler
ISBN: 978-1-62618-893-8

Chapter 15

TESTIMONY OF LAURENCE H. TRIBE, CARL M. LOEB UNIVERSITY PROFESSOR, HARVARD LAW SCHOOL. HEARING ON "PROPOSALS TO REDUCE GUN VIOLENCE: PROTECTING OUR COMMUNITIES WHILE RESPECTING THE SECOND AMENDMENT"*

Mr. Chairman and members of the Committee:

I am honored and grateful for the invitation to testify before you today. I know I am not alone in wanting us to do all we can, consistent with the Constitution, to reduce the awful specter of rampant gun violence and the far too frequent massacres of our children, our friends, and our fellow citizens.

Like all decent Americans, I felt a pang of unspeakable horror on December 14, when I learned that twenty first-grade children had been brutally slaughtered in their first-grade classroom in Newtown, Connecticut. Those children, and the brave grown-ups who died at Adam Lanza‘s hands as they tried to save the young lives entrusted to their care, deserve every effort to translate our shared grief into shared national action. That action must not be deterred by the defeatist argument that, because we will never solve this problem in its entirety, we might as well give up. Nor should it be deterred by distorted interpretations of the United States Constitution. As others have often reminded us about that great and enduring document, it is many things to many people, but one thing it is *not* is a suicide pact.

While we debate the pending proposals to reduce gun violence through measures focused on gun safety as part of a holistic national response, it‘s crucial that we not permit any part of our Constitution to become a collateral casualty of our conversation. Proposals to disarm the American people, to leave firearms solely in the hands of the military and the police, have been decisively taken off the table – if they were ever truly *on* the table – by the Supreme Court‘s Second Amendment decisions in 2008 and 2010. —Slippery slope|| arguments predicated on the unsettled state of the law prior to 2008 have been rendered irrelevant. The

* This is an edited, reformatted and augmented version of testimony given on February 12, 2013 before the Senate Judiciary Committee, Subcommittee on the Constitution, Civil Rights and Human Rights.

only proposals under serious consideration in this body are reasonable measures that would fully respect the basic rights of responsible citizens to use ordinary firearms for self-defense and other lawful purposes. They cannot lead to unacceptably extreme measures as long as the Supreme Court sits.

Having examined those proposals, having looked at the steps announced by the President under his power faithfully to execute the laws of the United States, and having studied the decisions of the Supreme Court and lower courts around the country, I am convinced that nothing under discussion in the Senate Judiciary Committee represents a threat to the Constitution or even comes close to violating the Second Amendment or the Constitution‘s structural limits either on congressional power or on executive authority.

Undoubtedly we should have a national debate about how best to reconcile the Second Amendment rights of every individual with the full range of proposals to reduce gun violence in America. As someone who has studied and taught constitutional law for four decades and argued dozens of cases in the Supreme Court and dozens more in the lower courts, I am obviously interested in engaging those questions. In today‘s testimony, however, I will focus not on competing theories of how the Second Amendment ought to have been interpreted but on the law as it stands. I am here not as an academic theorist but as a constitutional lawyer. As a lawyer, I‘ve won some and I‘ve lost some, and I know a losing argument when I see it. And the argument that any of the proposals to reduce gun violence currently being considered here might be struck down as unconstitutional is decidedly a losing argument.

There is plenty of room for policy debate over the best steps to take to reduce gun violence, but we mustn‘t confuse those policy differences or the ideological and cultural divisions that underlie them with genuine constitutional doubts about whether any of those steps crosses the constitutional line. Everyone in this room knows that anything Congress or the President does in this field will confront opposition. And in a nation as litigious as ours, some of that opposition will no doubt find its way into the courts. But there is no basis to suppose that the courts will or should rebuff any of the steps being debated here today. They should not, and they will not.

What I hope to do this morning, setting all hyperbole aside and approaching the law on the books with a fair-minded eye, is explain why reforms such as those this committee is considering clearly pass constitutional muster.

I. Introduction: Taking the Second Amendment Seriously, But Applying It Cautiously

I begin by reaffirming my agreement with the Supreme Court that the Second Amendment guarantees Americans the right as individuals to possess guns for reasonable self-defense. Some of my friends and colleagues devoted to the cause of responsible firearms regulation evidently wish to relitigate this point. They continue to insist that the best reading of the Second Amendment would secure gun rights only in connection with service in the state militia and not for individual possession and use. For nearly a decade and a half, I have disagreed with them and have defended the individual rights view ultimately taken by the Supreme Court in 2008. In October of 1999, for example, I joined a fellow constitutional law scholar in publishing an op-ed in *The New York Times* arguing that —bearing arms [is] a ‗privilege‘ of each citizen.[1] I continue to defend this position today.

That matters only insofar as it bears on my credibility as a witness in today‘s hearing. If I were among those who had *opposed* the individual rights interpretation adopted by the Supreme Court in *Heller*, some might wonder whether my conclusions about the regulations *Heller* permits Congress to adopt reflect wishful thinking rather than a realistic and sympathetic appraisal of what the Court that decided *Heller* would in fact permit. But there is no wishful thinking here. I am being a hard-headed realist in reading the *Heller* decision and extrapolating conclusions from the majority opinion.

Although many in the community advocating gun rights had long assumed that the individual rights interpretation governed the scope of the Second Amendment, it was not until the Supreme Court‘s 2008 ruling in *District of Columbia v. Heller*[2] that a majority of the Court‘s Justices agreed. In so doing, the Court recognized that the core individual liberty protected by the amendment affords Americans the right to purchase and store operable firearms for self-defense in the home. Two years later, in *McDonald v. City of Chicago*,[3] the Court extended the *Heller* ruling to cover restrictions imposed by state and local governments, making it unmistakably clear that the right at issue was not and is not simply a right of the state-organized militia against being overrun by federal authority.

Despite this fundamental affirmation, the *Heller* decision is exceedingly narrow in many important respects. As Judge Brett Kavanaugh of the D.C. Circuit Court of Appeals recently put it, "It bears emphasis that *Heller,* while enormously significant jurisprudentially, was not revolutionary in terms of its immediate real-world effects on American gun regulation." "Indeed," he continued, "*Heller* largely preserved the status quo of gun regulation in the United States."[4] To understand what he meant, it helps to look first to the Washington, DC ordinance implicated in the *Heller* case. The District had in place one of the most restrictive firearms regulations in the nation; it essentially outlawed the possession of handguns in the home, where the need for self-defense is, as Justice Scalia wrote, "most acute."[5] For the majority on the Court, a policy like the one the District had adopted, a policy on the outer edge of gun control‘s reach in the United States, was irreconcilable with the Second Amendment.

The *Heller* decision took great pains to emphasize its relative modesty. It repeated the mantra that the Second Amendment right "is not unlimited"[6] and devoted an entire section to listing types of regulation – for example, limits on gun ownership "by felons and the mentally ill" and, most relevant to today‘s hearing, regulation of "dangerous and unusual weapons" – the constitutionality of which the Court had no intention of casting into doubt.[7] The decision paused to note that, by specifically giving a constitutional green light to some regulatory efforts, the Court did not mean to signal that others were constitutionally dubious.[8] Justice Scalia closed his opinion for the Court with an expression of solicitude for the regulatory goals that Washington, DC sought to advance and, more importantly, an invitation to pursue those goals with the "variety of tools" still available to the District and to other states and localities across the country even in *Heller*‘s wake.[9]

Since that decision and its extension to state and local laws in 2010, the vast majority of federal and state courts to adjudicate Second Amendment claims have responsibly hewed to the cautious approach espoused by the Supreme Court in *Heller* and *McDonald*. For example, in a ruling highly relevant to the topic of this hearing, the D.C. Circuit recently upheld the constitutionality of Washington D.C.‘s assault weapons ban, which included a restriction on high-capacity magazines, as well as gun registration requirements.[10] The majority in the case, following the broad consensus that has emerged among federal and state judges,[11] evaluated the regulations against a standard of heightened judicial scrutiny while preserving both the option to adopt a more skeptical mode of review for restrictions on core self-defense firearm possession and the option to exempt other laws from Second Amendment review entirely when they do not enter the amendment‘s zone of protected conduct.[12] In another notable decision staking out a similar approach, a panel of the Seventh Circuit Court of Appeals struck down Chicago‘s firing-range ban given the close nexus between regular firing practice and training and safe, responsible self-defense in the home.[13] And state appellate courts from North Carolina to Wisconsin to California have joined with their federal brethren in upholding state restrictions on firearms ownership under this middle-of-the-road approach that molds the degree of judicial scrutiny to the extent of a law‘s burden on the core self-defense right secured by the Second Amendment.[14]

The central message of *Heller* and its lower-court progeny is thus to take the application of the Second Amendment seriously but also cautiously. When necessary to vindicate the core right to self-defense respected by *Heller*, neither courts nor lawmakers should be shy about invoking the Second Amendment. But because few public responsibilities are as important to good governance as legislating to secure public safety, lawmakers and jurists should not casually give the amendment an expansive scope nor unduly scrutinize reasonable firearm regulations. In the wake of the Newtown massacre and the push to propose sensible new rules about firearms, the Obama administration and many leaders in Congress have conducted themselves precisely along these lines.

II. The Second Amendment Propriety of Recent Policy Proposals

Limits on Large-Capacity Magazines

A core feature of the Assault Weapons Ban of 2013, introduced by Senator Dianne Feinstein, as well as the primary component of a freestanding bill championed by Senator Frank Lautenberg, is a ban on magazines capable of firing more than ten rounds of ammunition without reloading.[15] Before moving into the weeds of the constitutional analysis, it would be useful to contrast such a high-capacity magazine restriction to the law *Heller* struck down. *Heller* axed a local ordinance that adopted about as blunt an approach to restraining gun violence as possible: By its very design, the DC law espoused disagreement with the whole idea of law-abiding gun ownership for self-defense in the home. A limit on large-capacity magazines, by contrast, is a regulation of an entirely different caliber. It does not challenge the fundamental recognition that gun possession for self-defense is a right of every citizen; it merely seeks to reset the parameters of responsible ownership to advance the cause of public safety. It operates with a scalpel rather than an ax. Even Robert Levy, the man who largely funded the challenge to DC‘s sweeping handgun ban in *Heller* and served as an attorney on the case, concedes that bans on both high-capacity magazines and assault weapons almost certainly do not infringe the Second Amendment rights he successfully fought to vindicate in court.[16]

By any reasonable reckoning, this crucial measure might not even trigger heightened Second Amendment review at the threshold stage that the *Heller* ruling requires courts to undertake. But even if the high-capacity magazine prohibition does require further analysis, it safely falls within a zone of regulations that do not unconstitutionally abridge Second Amendment rights.

Most constitutional challenges require lawyers and scholars to carry out two stages of analysis. First, we must assess whether a given government policy even *implicates* a given right in the first place. For example, in 1915, the Supreme Court entertained a First Amendment challenge to a filmmaker‘s punishment under an Ohio censorship law but, in a clear misjudgment the Court would later correct, decided that movies were not even a form of "speech" entitled to First Amendment protection.[17] More recently, in a ruling that may perhaps give pause to members of this committee (despite the distinct protections of the Constitution‘s Speech and Debate Clause), the Court concluded that votes by legislators are not a form of "speech" over which any public official can claim a personal First Amendment right.[18] Assuming that a law *does* implicate the right in question, the government must then proceed to justify the challenged law so that the court hearing the challenge may evaluate, roughly speaking, whether the justification is strong enough to permit the law to stand or, alternatively, whether the measure goes too far and thus violates the Constitution.

I begin with this return to fundamentals because it never ceases to surprise me how often those engaged in legal debate talk past one another by conflating these distinct steps. In the Second Amendment context particularly, there is no excuse for making that mistake. For *Heller* itself makes it absolutely plain that not every gun regulation even triggers Second Amendment review. In other words, sometimes governments may enact regulations addressing the manufacture, transfer, possession or use of firearms that categorically fall outside the Second Amendment‘s scope, freeing governments of any burden even to make detailed defenses of the provisions in question. For example, the *Heller* opinion specifically named "longstanding prohibitions on the possession of firearms by felons and the mentally ill, or laws forbidding the carrying of firearms in sensitive places such as schools and government buildings" as illustrative examples of regulations that should not even receive further constitutional review.[19] The importance of this point should not be underemphasized. If too many entirely reasonable firearm regulations, like assault weapon bans and background checks, or rules about trafficking and straw purchases, are subjected to heightened Second Amendment review, it will become difficult if not impossible to separate those regulations categorically from the restrictions that *Heller* specifically approved without subjecting them to any "scrutiny" at all.

Beyond the examples appearing in the decision, *Heller* also identifies the three primary factors to consider in judging whether other types of regulation trip the Second Amendment‘s alarm. First, the Court carefully frames the scope of the Second Amendment to cover *only* firearms "in common use at the time."[20]

Second, *Heller* recognized that "dangerous or unusual" weapons may be and have historically been heavily regulated or banned.[21] It is not inconceivable – indeed, it seems quite likely – that the Court‘s pause to distinguish unusually dangerous weapons from widely possessed handguns had precisely the 1994 Assault Weapons Ban, which included a prohibition on high-capacity magazines, in mind. At the very least, the *Heller* majority recognized that the government could keep machine guns —"M-16 rifles and the like"—out of the hands of civilians.[22] The Supreme Court thus emphatically rejected the extravagant, or as Justice Scalia characterized it, "startling" notion, still promoted by some, that the Second Amendment could fulfill its original purposes only if citizens were guaranteed a right to arm themselves to the teeth, matching in their private armories essentially the full array of weapons possessed by the United States Military.[23]

Third and finally, the Court emphasized the importance of a nexus to core self-defense needs.[24] The majority in *Heller* had no trouble recognizing that handguns represented the "quintessential self-defense weapon," particularly in the home.[25] Moreover, handguns were not categorically more dangerous than other types of firearms. So Washington D.C.'s handgun ban clearly fell within the scope of the Second Amendment.

The clarity of *Heller*'s guidance on how to apply these threshold factors begins to dissipate, however, when they no longer align so strikingly in one direction. To begin with, the Court left "dangerousness" undefined, and what the Court meant by that term is not entirely self-evident. In an obvious sense, *all* firearms are dangerous; that is what makes them effective instruments of self-defense. The *Heller* ruling, therefore, asks us to balance any *exceptional* dangerousness of particular firearm design features against the potential self-defense value of those features. For example, even if home possession of machine guns for self-defense might, on rare occasion, deter criminal trespassers more than home possession of handguns, that benefit is simply not sufficient to overcome the substantial hazards to innocent bystanders and intentional targets, in particular the police. *Heller* obviously does not contemplate asking the government to provide an intricately reasoned justification for banning machine guns; instead, it recognizes – and it surely authorizes Congress, and indeed all of us, to recognize – excessive dangerousness in the inherent design of the weapon[26] so as to cut off Second Amendment review at the threshold.

All things considered, I conclude that reasonably restricting magazine size and availability does not implicate the core Second Amendment right as *Heller* conceived of it. The reason is not the first factor, that of —common use," because, of course, large-capacity ammunition magazines and the firearms outfitted for them are, by any reasonable measure, in quite common use in the United States. I note here just a few examples. The standard Glock pistol, the firearm that one reporter called —America's handgun" in a recent book on the subject, comes equipped with a seventeen-round magazine.[27] And America's most popular rifle, the AR-15 model,[28] typically comes with a thirty-round magazine and can accommodate magazines with even larger capacities.[29]

But to contend that the sizeable market presence of a particular firearm feature is sufficient in itself to trigger full Second Amendment scrutiny is to misrepresent the lesson of *Heller*. The relative dangerousness and self-defense-serving capacity of a firearm or design feature are also crucial considerations. This approach makes complete sense. The common use and possession of a given firearm feature is, at best, just one helpful indicator of whether restricting that feature will stymie or frustrate the exercise of the core Second Amendment protection of lawful self-defense to a constitutionally cognizable degree. For instance, in the case of high-capacity magazines, significant market presence does not necessarily translate into heavy reliance by American gun owners on those magazines for self-defense. Analysis of the modern development of the U.S. gun market demonstrates that the firearms industry, driven by an obvious profit motive, ushered in a revolution in the state of the market during the 1980s. Manufacturers began to roll out increasing numbers of pistols with ever-larger-capacity magazines rather than revolvers, which take just six rounds of ammunition and had traditionally been the most popular firearm for personal self-defense.[30] The frequent purchase of such large-capacity magazines, then, may not be attributable purely or even primarily to actual gun-owner preferences, much less to gun-owner needs. Rather, guns equipped with or ready for large-capacity magazines may simply be the weapons most readily made available on the market. And even if this market presence begins to influence more Americans to purchase firearms with high-capacity magazines because they fear attacks from criminals possessing guns outfitted with the same high-capacity magazines, nothing in *Heller* suggests that it is improper for the government to halt the escalation of this arms race in its tracks. The one-way ratchet of ever more powerful firearms is not a constitutional inevitability. For unlike the doctrine of mutually assured destruction that some say maintained an uneasy peace during the nuclear arms buildup of the Cold War, the propagation of increasingly dangerous guns on American streets has already taken an all-too- violent toll. In other words, tempering the trend toward more dangerous weapons actually *vindicates* the core Second Amendment right of self-defense and personal safety that *Heller* recognizes. In this context, as in many others, less is more.

But even looking beyond the market saturation of large-capacity magazines, this feature runs headlong into the other threshold obstacles that *Heller* requires Second Amendment claims to clear. As experts in effective firearms regulation have preached for years and particularly fervently in recent weeks, higher-capacity magazines pose greater dangers to public safety. By permitting shooters using semi-automatic weapons to continue firing more bullets without interruption, these magazines increase the potential lethality of armed killers.[31] Though well-trained gun users can change magazines quickly, this interruption may, as we saw last year in the Arizona shooting of Rep. Gabby Giffords, afford time for heroic men or women to intervene and disarm the shooter.[32] Moreover, this interruption gives our police a chance to return fire.[33] And it may even provide time for reflection and rethinking before murder becomes massacre.

Against the evident dangerousness of high-capacity magazines as a design feature, we must evaluate the strength and plausibility of asserted self-defense interests. Critics of recent proposals to reestablish a limit on high-capacity magazines have argued that firing more than ten rounds without changing a magazine is necessary for effective self-defense. While I have no doubt that subscription to this perspective among some law-abiding gun owners is sincere, I doubt that it is well-founded. It‘s rhetorically effective to ask, ―How many bullets do *you* want in your magazine when an intruder breaks into your home?‖ But the answer tells us little that is of relevance to the Second Amendment as *Heller* conceives that provision. I might want a magazine with twice as many bullets as any possible home intruder; I might want a machine gun too. But in the end that can‘t be the measure of what the Second Amendment says I have a *right* to own and deploy.

Despite the emotional resonance of this kind of appeal, incidents like burglaries and home invasions – even when they lead to the exchange of fire – are unlikely to *require* firing many shots. The NRA publishes a regular column featuring newspaper clippings of gun owners protecting themselves against intruder attacks, and an analysis of these reports over a five-year period demonstrated that in 50% of all cases, two or fewer shots were fired, and the average number of shots fired across the entire data sample was also about two.[34] Of course, this data comes from the episodes the NRA chooses to report, so selection bias is possible, meaning the average number of shots fired per incident could be even lower.[35] Even police officers traditionally found revolvers with six-bullet magazines sufficient for their own safety until more dangerous guns flooded the market.[36] And we should not lose track of the bigger picture: studies show that self-defense in the home with firearms is rare.[37] Additionally, firearms accidents are all too common: between 1965 and 2000, unintentional shootings accounted for the deaths of over 60,000 Americans.[38] Firing more bullets quickly may compound their damage.

Another version of the critics‘ response is that in scary situations, like home invasions, gun owners may go through bullets too quickly in a fit of nervousness or panic.[39] That may be true, but it also aggravates the downside hazard in cases of error,[40] so it is not at all clear that increased access to large-capacity magazines for shooters subject to fragile nerves represents a net gain for home security or public safety. Finally, some critics of magazine-capacity limits have pointed out that, realistically, many gun owners have not received proper training and for that reason, may fire bullets indiscriminately; a larger magazine – so the thinking presumably goes – will increase the chances that at least one of their wayward shots will hit its mark.[41] As the Supreme Court recognized in *Heller*, however, the Second Amendment protects only the right of ―*responsible* citizens to use arms in defense of hearth and home.‖ [42] In other words, a dangerous firearms feature otherwise outside the Second Amendment‘s scope cannot become subject to heightened constitutional scrutiny because of the shortcomings of *irresponsible* gun owners.

To be sure, *some* gun owners may struggle to change magazines quickly not for lack of adequate training but rather by reason of disability or old age.[43] Perhaps a ban on high-capacity magazines without any exception for the disabled or elderly might, for this reason, trigger heightened scrutiny of such a ban as applied specifically to those individuals. But the possibility that a prohibition could raise constitutional questions in some subset of its applications does not mean that the prohibition is constitutionally vulnerable on its face.[44] And it remains the case that large-capacity magazines are highly unlikely to be necessary to self-defense in the vast majority of home invasions or burglaries, even those that resort to the exchange of fire. The facial validity of a high-capacity magazine ban is therefore clear.

Despite the considerable market presence of high-capacity magazines, the danger they pose to public safety and the weakness of the self-defense justification for their possession means that two of the three threshold *Heller* factors point strongly against extending Second Amendment protection to high-capacity magazines. The D.C. Circuit Court of Appeals, in a case challenging Washington D.C.‘s restriction on magazines with more than ten rounds, recently struggled with this first stage of analysis and determined that the court did not have before it sufficient evidence to decide whether the Second Amendment even *reached* large-capacity magazines.[45] However, the court went on to conclude that, even if it was proper to extend coverage of the amendment to large-capacity magazines, the government‘s interest in banning them was strong enough to do so without violating Second Amendment rights.[46]

Having now reviewed the best evidence and argumentation advanced by defenders of high-capacity magazine possession, I doubt that the Supreme Court would find it necessary to reach that second stage of review in dealing with a ban on high-capacity magazines and am quite confident that, in any event, the Court would agree with the ultimate conclusion that, even if the amendment applies, a ban on high-capacity magazines withstands Second Amendment scrutiny.

In explaining that conclusion, I emphasize that commonly advanced rejections of a legitimate government interest in banning high-capacity magazines are deeply misleading. Many opponents of reasonable firearms regulation insist that we tried banning large-capacity magazines in 1994: the results are in, they say, and we failed. One favorite trope is to cite to a

1997 Department of Justice study, which, according to the recent testimony of Wayne LaPierre, —proved that [the] ban had no impact on lowering crime."[47] But no one is even *arguing* that a ban on high-capacity magazines (or on assault weapons, for that matter) will necessarily decrease crime rates; highly lethal firearms will still be widely available on the market, and some criminals will use them, just as they do now.

What defenders of a ban on high-capacity magazines *do* argue is that such a ban will help prevent these criminals from killing or maiming as many people when they commit violent crimes. And that argument is solidly grounded. One study, for example, found that between 1984 and 1993, criminals using guns with high-capacity magazines or assault weapons as defined by the 1994 Assault Weapons Ban killed or injured an average of 29 victims, compared to the average 13 victims shot by criminals unequipped with large-capacity magazines.[48] Another study suggests that, since the lapse of the ban in 2004, high-capacity magazines have once again become common in episodes of violent crime after the beginnings of a decline, which probably took place because the black market for these magazines had begun to dry up.[49]

Even more misleading is the suggestion that in 1997 we could (or even today that we can) draw meaningful conclusions from the absence of unmistakable evidence of a decrease in violence following the 1994 ban. That legislation grandfathered or exempted many thousands of weapons already owned, and those could still be sold or transferrei[50] In other words, the 1994 ban was crafted with long-term effects in mind; to measure its effects notwithstanding its untimely end is to misunderstand fundamentally how the legislation was designed to work. It is therefore all the more telling that supporters of reasonable regulation can cite studies based upon identifiable trends emerging during the latter years of the ban, as well as evidence from both before and after the ban, showing that the legal availability of large-capacity magazines is indeed correlated with increased deaths and injuries caused by gun violence. Considered alongside the dangerousness inherent in a large-capacity magazine as a design feature, this evidence provides the government with a sufficient basis to satisfy the Second Amendment under any plausible understanding of the Supreme Court's jurisprudence surrounding that amendment.

Assault Weapons Ban

By many accounts, the most important component of the newly proposed assault weapons ban is its prohibition on high-capacity magazines.[51] But that does not mean that the remaining features of the proposal stand on weaker constitutional ground. Far from it. Application of *Heller*'s three threshold factors – dangerousness, commonness of use, and connection to core self-defense interests – demonstrates that the Second Amendment does not provide legal shelter to the features that trigger a firearm's prohibition under the ban.

Opponents of the legislation as well as some proponents of new firearms regulation have observed that some of the "military characteristics" that can lead to prohibition under the legislation[52] (and, by some accounts, under assault weapons bans in general[53]) are mostly cosmetic traits designed to make a gun *appear* dangerous and are not, in fact, intrinsically hazardous. But Congress would surely be acting within its constitutional authority if it were to reject this characterization as self-serving or otherwise unreliable. For example, the Brady Campaign to Prevent Gun Violence insists that "[p]istol grips . . . help stabilize the weapon during rapid fire and allow the shooter to spray-fire from the hip position [and that] [b]arrel shrouds on assault pistols protect the shooter's hands from the heat generated by firing many rounds in rapid succession.[54] Moreover, even if the characterization of these features as cosmetic were accurate, it would make little difference as a constitutional matter. In a recent televised interview, Justice Scalia explained the basis in history for exempting certain types of regulations from Second Amendment review. Certain limitations on gun ownership are constitutionally permissible, he contended, "because there were some [regulations] that were acknowledged at the time [of the Founding]. For example, there was a tort called affrighting . . . if you carried around a really horrible weapon just to scare people, like a head ax or something. . . . 55 What the Justice evidently meant was that regulating weapons because they are chosen specifically for their intimidating appearance is constitutionally unproblematic because the very use of intimidation is unnecessarily disruptive to organized society.[56]

Even more important to the constitutionality of the assault weapons ban is the absence of any connection to the core Second Amendment right to defend oneself with a firearm. At this committee‘s hearing on January 30, several witnesses criticized the assault weapons ban on policy grounds, but in my role as a constitutional lawyer listening intently for arguments relevant to the proposal‘s Second Amendment propriety, I was struck by the failure of anyone‘s testimony to support these features as essential to self-defense. In fact, I have searched in vain for any reasoned arguments that pistol grips, forward grips, telescoping stocks, grenade or rocket launchers, and barrel shrouds are indispensable or even contribute to self-defense.

Finally, it is relevant to ask how many assault weapons Americans currently own. Data is hard to come by in large part because firearms manufacturers refuse to release data tracking their sales.[57] What we do know is that the number of weapons that would qualify under either the proposed ban‘s so-called —characteristics test|| or its explicit list of banned models is smaller than the number of guns with standard-issue high-capacity magazines.[58] One reporter‘s painstaking analysis estimated that there are 3.75 million AR-15-style rifles owned in the U.S. today, and AR-15s are the most popular although not the exclusive type of qualifying assault weapon.[59] The NRA‘s lobbying arm estimates that, depending upon the definition of assault weapon, assault weapons represent 15% of all semi-automatic guns owned in the U.S., which in turn represent about 15% of all firearms owned in the U.S.[60] Given that the Congressional Research Service recently found that, as of 2009, Americans own about 310 million guns,[61] the NRA‘s estimate would translate into approximately 7 million assault weapons owned today. Although 7 million is hardly a negligible figure, it still corresponds to quite a small portion of the overall gun market – hardly enough to justify calling such weapons —common within the meaning of *Heller*.

But for the purposes of constitutional analysis, debating how to characterize the significance of assault weapons‘ market presence would be a waste of time. To make a difference to *Heller*‘s threshold inquiry, which must take notice of the complete lack of any connection of assault-weapon features to self-defense as well as these features‘ dangerousness in both fact and appearance, the market presence of assault weapons would have to be overwhelmingly large (and even then, I doubt seriously the bottom line would change as a constitutional matter). And overwhelmingly large it assuredly is not.

Universal Registration and Background Checks

All responsible participants in the gun safety debate agree that some groups of people simply should not be allowed to own, keep, or carry guns. Those groups include children, dangerous felons, and those with serious mental illnesses that preclude safe gun ownership. When some observers casually compare the Second Amendment to the First, they forget this essential difference: Although freedom of speech sometimes comes at a price, and although speech can at times pose dangers, our constitutional system addresses those dangers by permitting government to impose carefully crafted limits on speech, not by limiting or licensing eligible speakers. The Constitution‘s strategy with respect to guns is entirely different. It addresses the dangers of guns in the wrong hands by permitting government to keep them out of those hands in the first place, and, of course, by permitting government to regulate where and under what conditions people can bear those weapons in possible confrontation with others.

Accordingly, this Congress might be called upon to consider measures designed to minimize the risk that guns fall into the hands of such prohibited purchasers and owners. Measures dealing with straw purchases and trafficking are obviously important in that effort and are clearly constitutional. Rather than spending the committee‘s time on those measures, I will focus here on provisions that mandate universal registration requirements or a universal background check, closing the many notorious loopholes that characterize current laws on the subject. There is no serious doubt that requiring universal registration or a universal background check would comply with the Second Amendment.

It is important to recognize, at the outset, that prohibiting particular groups of people from owning or possessing guns is fully compatible with the Second Amendment. In the first place, such prohibitions are consistent with the original and traditional understanding of the Second Amendment. It was widely accepted at the time of the framing that not every person had a right to keep and bear arms; instead, the right was closely tied to the notion of responsible citizenship, and it has long been denied to criminals and others whose possession of guns would pose a severe danger to the public.[62] On this point, precedent aligns closely with history. The Supreme Court said in *District of Columbia v. Heller*: ―[N]othing in our opinion should be taken to cast doubt on longstanding prohibitions on the possession of firearms by felons and the mentally ill ..."[63] The Court fortified this conclusion in *McDonald v. City of Chicago*, when it added: "We made it clear in *Heller* that our holding did not cast doubt on such longstanding regulatory measures as ‗prohibitions on the possession of firearms by felons and the mentally ill‘ ... We repeat those assurances here."[64]

Once the constitutionality of prohibiting gun possession by some people is accepted, the constitutionality of a reasonable system of registration or background checks follows automatically. The most powerful argument for this inference is not a technical legal point; it is, instead, common sense. And, although it shouldn‘t be necessary to cite authority for the point, it‘s worth noting that as eminent an authority as Alexander Hamilton wrote in *The Federalist* that "[t]he rules of legal interpretation are rules of *common sense*," and that the "true test" of a "just application" of these rules is whether the resulting interpretation is "consistent with reason and common sense."[65]

Consider, then, whether the Constitution would be "consistent with reason and common sense" if it allowed prohibitions on firearms purchases by felons but disallowed background checks to determine whether a felon was the would-be purchaser of a firearm. As a matter of common sense, we all know that guns do not of their own accord stay out of the hands of prohibited purchasers. Nor are prohibited purchasers likely to confess their legal inability to buy guns when talking to gun dealers. The prohibitions, in short, do not enforce themselves. In order to be effective, in order to be meaningful, in order to be anything more than rules on paper, they must be comprehensive and must be carried into operation by the government. It contradicts common sense—it ignores the fact that "the framers of the Constitution were not mere visionaries, toying with speculations or theories, but practical men"[66]—to say on the one hand that prohibiting felons from owning guns is constitutional, but to insist on the other hand that the background checks that seek to make those prohibitions effective are unconstitutional.

The Supreme Court's decisions in *District of Columbia v. Heller* and *McDonald v. City of Chicago* confirm the constitutionality of reasonable background check requirements. *Heller* expressly affirms that the Court was not calling into doubt "laws imposing conditions and qualifications on the commercial sale of arms."[67] The *McDonald* Court "repeat[ed] those assurances," observing that its holding "does not imperil every law regulating firearms."[68] The universal registration requirement or background check is simply a "condition[]" on the transfer of arms; it is therefore expressly within the zone of permissible regulation identified by *Heller* and *McDonald*.

Analogous Supreme Court doctrine points in the same direction. The right to vote, like the right to keep and bear arms, is a fundamental right of Americans.[69] But no serious legal scholar doubts that before letting a citizen cast his ballot, the government may require the citizen to register and may take steps to check whether he or she really is an eligible voter. And the Supreme Court agrees; in *Crawford v. Marion County Election Board*, for example, it concluded that Indiana's voter ID law was a permissible means of ensuring that only eligible voters participate in an election.[70] Checking whether a voter is eligible before giving that voter a ballot is comparable to checking whether a purchaser is eligible before letting her acquire a gun. Just as the former is constitutional, so is the latter. And the argument is of course even stronger in the instance of firearms. For, unlike a ballot in the hands of an ineligible voter, which might in the end prove to make no difference to who wins or loses the election at issue, a gun in the hands of even one ineligible owner poses a deadly danger all by itself.

History reinforces common sense and case law in this regard. The Supreme Court in *Heller* and *McDonald* stressed the role of history in interpreting the scope of the Second Amendment; —longstanding|| prohibitions upon gun ownership, the Court indicated, are presumptively exempt from Second Amendment scrutiny.[71] Lower courts have likewise noted that history plays an important, though not exclusive, role in determining the scope of permissible regulation under the Second Amendment.[72] Measures to keep guns out of the hands of prohibited owners – owners who could not safely be entrusted with control of a lethal weapon – have a strong historical pedigree. For example, many states have longstanding laws— sometimes, laws dating back a century or more—requiring sellers to keep registers of all firearm purchasers; the registers had to be open to peace officers.[73] The government could use thus use these registers to determine whether any of the purchasers had obtained weapons in violation of the law.

To be sure, modern computerized background checks differ from the more cumbersome historical enforcement measures known to hisory. But —a constitution [is] intended to endure for ages to come.[74] Just as the Second Amendment covers modern weapons, like handguns, that did not exist when the Bill of Rights was ratified in 1791, so too does it cover modern enforcement measures, like mandatory computerized background checks, that could not have been anticipated in 1791. Reasonable background checks fit into the long historical tradition to which registration requirements belong, and that is enough to sustain them without further ado under the tests established by the Supreme Court in *Heller* and *McDonald*.

In short, all relevant legal considerations—logic and common sense, directly applicable precedent, analogies to surrounding legal doctrines, and history and tradition—point to the same conclusion. The Second Amendment does not prohibit Congress from passing laws to carry into effect concededly constitutional prohibitions on firearm purchases. The universal background check, in particular, easily passes constitutional muster as a permissible regulation of the transfer of firearms.

This is not to say that all conceivable background check systems would comport with the Constitution. Suppose, for example, that Congress were to pass a law requiring handgun purchasers to undergo an extensive check on the purchasers themselves and all their family members and housemates, a check that took years to complete. Such a scheme would plainly impose a very severe burden on the right to keep and bear arms for self-defense. The burden would be entirely disproportionate to the objective the government is seeking to pursue. Where a background check is taken to such lengths that it effectively destroys the right to keep and bear arms, rather than ensuring that the right is enjoyed only by those constitutionally entitled to it, the government has overstepped the lawful boundaries of its power.

Such concerns are entirely out of place here, however. Whether a particular background check scheme that Congress adopts would go too far obviously depends on the specific details of that scheme. But none of the proposals seriously under consideration at the present come remotely close to overstepping constitutional boundaries. The proposed background check frameworks, especially those that rely on checks conducted instantaneously through the National Instant Background Check System, impose a constitutionally insignificant burden upon law-abiding citizens. Indeed, an instant background check is much *less* onerous than the Voter ID law that the Supreme Court upheld in *Crawford v. Marion County Election Board*; it is also much less cumbersome than longstanding registration requirements and other conditions on sale[75] that are concededly constitutional. Ultimately, therefore, I see no merit to the constitutional objections to the background check proposals presently being seriously considered by Congress.

III. The Consistency of the President's Measures with the Separation of Powers

This January, President Obama announced twenty-three steps that his Administration would take to prevent gun violence.[76] The President has begun to implement these steps by using the executive powers vested in him by the Constitution and laws of the United States. Because the President adopted these measures by executive action, without specific congressional involvement, some have concluded that the President violated the separation of powers established by the Constitution. This claim is legally untenable; the President is acting well within his powers as head of the executive branch.

Some of the President's measures involve nothing beyond communicating with members of the public. Measure 23, for example, is to "[l]aunch a national dialogue ... on mental health." There is plainly no constitutional problem with executive steps of this sort. The President obviously does not need congressional permission every time he decides to give a speech or publish a press release.

Another category of measures—and this covers the great majority of the actions that the President has committed to take—includes steps that will improve the enforcement of federal laws already on the books. Thus, the President has agreed to "[m]aximize enforcement efforts to prevent gun violence and prosecute gun crime."[77] He has likewise decided "to require federal law enforcement to trace guns recovered in criminal investigations."[78] These improvements to federal law enforcement efforts plainly fall within the President's constitutional power—and constitutional responsibility—to —take Care that the Laws be faithfully executed."[79]

A third group of measures involves the making of rules and regulations under preexisting congressionally granted authority. For instance, step 21——[f]inalize regulations clarifying essential health benefits and parity requirements within ACA exchanges"—simply carries into effect authority granted by the Patient Protection and Affordable Care Act.[80]

Step 11, —[n]ominate an ATF director," is equally clearly within the President's constitutional powers; the Constitution expressly states that the President —shall nominate, and by and with the Advice and Consent of the Senate, shall appoint ... Officers of the United States."[81]

Likewise, the Constitution plainly authorizes the President's requests for information from executive branch officials, such as step 15, —direct[ing] the Attorney General to issue a report on the availability and most effective use of new gun safety technologies and challenge the private sector to develop innovative technologies"; Article II provides that the President —may require the Opinion, in writing, of the principal Officer in each of the executive Departments, upon any Subject relating to the Duties of their respective Offices."[82]

Finally, and perhaps most controversially, some of the President's measures entail the issuance of interpretations of existing laws. To this class belongs, for instance, step 16, —[c]larify[ing] that the Affordable Care Act does not prohibit doctors asking their patients about guns in their homes." To be sure, the Article III judiciary must ultimately interpret laws when applying those laws in the context of concrete cases or controversies. But it is well established that the President also has the authority to interpret the law—and especially the power to announce legal interpretations concerning issues that have not yet been settled by the courts.

In fact, the tradition of presidential clarifications of the law goes back to President George Washington's Neutrality Proclamation. The tradition also has a solid grounding in the text of the Constitution; it is based on the Constitution's vesting in the President of —the executive Power," and in its imposition on the President of the power and duty to —take Care that the Laws be faithfully executed."[83]

In sum, although some opponents of gun regulation might disagree with some of the President's executive actions as a matter of policy, those disagreements cannot plausibly be translated into constitutional objections. From a separation-of-powers perspective, the President has acted well within the bounds of his constitutionally assigned authority.

***

In closing, I note that I share the beliefs of many that the prevalence of guns in our country is by no means the only significant contributor to the tragedy at Newtown and to the many other gun-related massacres we have seen in recent months and recent years, or to the deaths of an average of over 30 Americans, nearly 5 of them children, *each and every day* as a result of gunfire homicides in less visible, and often virtually unnoticed, tragic incidents. 84

Violence has many causes. Violent video games, for example, some of them simulating mass shootings, may well play a significant role in the inculcation of violent attitudes among children.[85] And mental illness plainly played a significant part in bringing about the massacre at Newtown. If our country is to reduce the incidence of similar unspeakable violence in the future, the widespread availability of high-powered guns to people who should not possess them and who have no constitutional right to do so is by no means the only phenomenon that our government, our society, and our families need to address.

But it is simply not true that the presence of other causes of gun violence means that we neither can nor should do anything significant about the prevalence, too often in the wrong hands, of high-powered guns and high-capacity magazines that turn those guns from means of self-defense into weapons of mass destruction. It is not true constitutionally, it is not true politically, and it is not true morally. We must do our best to address in a serious way *every* source of avoidable death by firearms that we can, and if we always point to other problems still waiting to be solved we will never get started.

The time to get started on sensible gun regulation is not now—it was weeks, months, years, even decades ago. The Second Amendment is not a barrier. We have already delayed too long, and our society has paid a terrible price. We should delay no longer.

End Notes

[1] Laurence H. Tribe & Akhil Reed Amar, *Well Regulated Militias and More*, N.Y. TIMES, Oct. 28, 1999, at A25; 1 Laurence H. Tribe, *American Constitutional Law* 900–902 (3d ed. 2000).

[2] 554 U.S. 570 (2008).

[3] 130 S.Ct. 3020 (2010).

[4] Heller v. Dist. of Columbia, 670 F.3d 1244, 1270 (D.C. Cir. 2011) (Kavanaugh, J., dissenting).

[5] *Heller*, 544 U.S. at 628.

[6] *Id.* at 595, 626.

[7] *Id.* at 626 – 28.

[8] *Id.* at 627 n. 26. There is no doubt, for instance, that regulatory provisions targeting firearms and ammunitions *manufacturers* in addition to those who transfer, possess, carry, or use the resulting weapons are at least as easy to defend from Second Amendment challenge as are measures that do not take effect until the point of sale.

[9] *Id.* at 636.

[10] Heller v. Dist. of Columbia, 670 F.3d 1244 (D.C. Cir. 2011).

[11] *See, e.g.*, Kachalsky v. County of Westchester, 701 F.3d 81, 93 – 94 (2d Cir. 2012); United States v. Booker, 644 F.3d 12, 25 (1st Cir. 2011) cert. denied, 132 S. Ct. 1538 (U.S. 2012); United States v. Masciandaro, 638 F.3d 458, 469-70 (4th Cir. 2011) cert. denied, 132 S. Ct. 756 (U.S. 2011); United States v. Marzzarella, 614 F.3d 85, 97 (3d Cir. 2010);

[12] *Heller*, 670 F.3d at 1256 – 58.

[13] The court applied what it called —not quite strict scrutiny|| because the law's burden struck so close to the core Second Amendment right to self-defense in the home. Ezell v. City of Chicago, 651 F.3d 684, 708 (7th Cir. 2011).

[14] *See, e.g.*, Johnston v. State, 735 S.E.2d 859 (N.C. Ct. App. 2012); State v. Brown, 815 N.W.2d 407 (Ct. App. Wisc. 2012); People v. Ellison, 196 Cal. App. 4th 1342, 1347 (2011).

[15] The Assault Weapons Ban of 2013 also prohibits firearms with fixed magazines capable of holding more than ten rounds of ammunition.

[16] Interview with Robert A. Levy by the Washington Post (Jan. 10, 2013), *transcript available at* http://articles.washingtonpost.com/2013-01-10/lifestyle/36272630 1 assault-weapons-highcapacity-magazines-military-style-guns.

[17] Mut. Film Corp. v. Indus. Comm'n of Ohio, 236 U.S. 230, 243 (1915).

[18] Nevada Comm'n on Ethics v. Carrigan, 131 S. Ct. 2343, 2350 (2011).

[19] Dist. of Columbia v. Heller, 554 U.S. 570, 626 - 27 (2008).

[20] *Id.* at 627.

[21] *Id.*

[22] *Id.*

[23] *Id.* at 624.

[24] *Id.* at 599 ("Justice Breyer‘s assertion that individual self-defense is merely a _subsidiary interest‘ of the right to keep and bear arms . . . is profoundly mistaken. He bases that assertion solely upon the prologue—but that can only show that self-defense had little to do with the right's *codification;* it was the *central component* of the right itself." (emphasis in original)).

[25] *Heller*, 544 U.S. at 629.

[26] Throughout this debate, opponents of restrictions on large-capacity magazines have repeatedly demanded empirical evidence showing a link between magazine capacity and gun violence. Studies in that mold certainly exist, and I discuss them later. *See, e.g.,* text accompanying notes 48 – 50. But at this threshold stage of the Second Amendment inquiry, the *Heller* decision‘s meaning of dangerousness cannot be equivalent to an empirically demonstrated effect on public safety. Rather, the standard is one that asks us to examine design features to assess whether the weapon poses an aggravated threat to safety as a common-sense matter. First, if the former were the meaning of dangerousness, the threshold inquiry, which may lead courts to conclude that the Second Amendment does not even apply, would become indistinguishable from the more advanced stage of review, in which courts scrutinize a government‘s public safety rationale. Second, making empirical evidence of salutary public-safety impacts a prerequisite to gun regulation would defeat efforts to respond to new technologies and lethal features that pose a substantial threat to public safety. The Second Amendment does not require that Americans afford the gun industry a —wait and see" grace period on the (in)famous theory that even a vicious dog deserves one free bite.

[27] Erin McCarthy, *Why the Glock Became America's Handgun,* POPULAR MECHANICS (Jan. 12, 2012, 6:30 AM), http://www.popularmechanics.com/technology/military/weapons/why-theglock-became-americas-handgun

[28] Erica Goode, *Rifle Used in Killings, America's Most Popular, Highlights Regulation Debate*, N.Y. TIMES (Dec. 16, 2012), http://www.nytimes.com/2012/12/17/us/lanza-used-a-popular-ar15-style-rifle-in-newtown.html?pagewanted=all.

[29] Steven Almasy, *Newton Shooter's Guns: What We Know*, CNN (Dec. 19, 2012, 10:11 AM), http://www.cnn.com/2012/12/18/us/connecticut-lanza-guns/index.html.

[30] *See* DC Reedy & CS Koper, *Impact of handgun types on gun assault outcomes: a comparison of gun assaults involving semiautomatic pistols and revolvers*, 9 INJURY PREVENTION 151, 151 (2002), *available at* http://injuryprevention.bmj.com/content/9/2/151.full#aff-1. VIOLENCE POLICY CENTER, BACKGROUNDER ON GLOCK 19 PISTOL AND AMMUNITION MAGAZINES USED IN ATTACK ON REPRESENTATIVE GABRIELLE GIFFORDS AND OTHERS 1 (2011), *available at* www.vpc.org/fact sht/AZbackgrounder.pdf.

[31] BRADY CAMPAIGN TO PREVENT GUN VIOLENCE, ASSAULT-STYLE WEAPONS: HIGH-CAPACITY MAGAZINES, http://www.bradycampaign.org/legislation/msassaultweapons/highcapacity (last visited Feb. 2, 2013).

[32] Ken Dolak & Justin Wealer, *Woman Wrestled Fresh Ammo Clip From Tucson Shooter as He Tried to Reload*, ABC NEWS (Jan. 9, 2011), http://abcnews.go.com/Politics/patricia-maischdescribes-stopping-gunman-reloading/story?id=12577933.

[33] I believe I can speak for many Americans when I thank Baltimore County Police Chief Jim Johnson for the illuminating insights he has publicly offered on the threats of high-capacity weapons not just to public safety in general but also law enforcement officer safety more specifically. *See, e.g.*, John Quinones, *Baltimore*

Police Chief Wants to Ban High-Capacity Firepower, ABC NEWS (Dec. 20, 2012), http://abcnews.go.com /US/baltimore-police-chief-banhigh-capacity-firepower/story?id=18030163

[34] Claude Verner performed the analysis of reporting over the period 1997 to 2001. The findings further show that when many shots were fired, a (presumably frightened) gun owner finished an entire magazine rather than firing the number of shots that necessarily had to be fired in light of the scenario. The analysis can be found reprinted with the author‘s permission at *Analysis of Five Years of Armed Encounters (With Data Tables)*, GunsSaveLives.net (March 12, 2012), http://gunssavelives.net/self-defense/analysis-of-five-years-of-armed-encounters-with-datatables/.

[35] It seems likely, for example, that merely brandishing a weapon may often lead intruders to flee. A non-exhaustive review of the NRA column reveals several examples of exactly this scenario, giving me the impression that the NRA‘s reporting is not demonstrably biased toward extreme scenarios or even those in which some shots are fired. *See, e.g.*, Armed Citizen, NRA (March 2012), http://www.nrapublications.org/index.php/12492/armed-citizen-23/ ("[The resident] met the intruder at her bedroom door, pointed the gun at him and demanded he leave. The trespasser fled without hesitation.").

[36] *See* Eugene Volokh, *Implementing the Right to Keep and Bear Arms for Self-Defense: An Analytical Framework and A Research Agenda*, 56 UCLA L. REV. 1443, 1489 (2009).

[37] A study of Atlanta police records, for example, found that victims of burglaries used guns in self-defense just 3% of the time. For a description of the study and a rich discussion of self-defense uses for firearms, see DAVID HEMENWAY, PRIVATE GUNS, PUBLIC HEALTH 67 (2004). The study is A.L. Kellermann et al., *Weapon involvement in home invasion crises*, 273 J. OF THE AM. MED. ASSOC. 1759 (1995).

[38] HEMENWAY, *supra* note 38, at 27 – 35.

[39] *See, e.g.*, Heller v. Dist. of Columbia, 670 F.3d 1244, 1261 (D.C. Cir. 2011); Emily Miller, *The High Capacity Magazine Myth*, WASHINGTON TIMES (Jan. 27, 2013), http://www.washingtontimes.com/news /2013 /jan/27/the-high-capacity-magazine-myth/; Jacob Sullum, *The Threat Posed by Gun Magazine Limits*, REASON (Jan. 16, 2013), http://reason.com/archives/2013/01/16/the-threat-posed-by-gun-magazine-limits.

[40] *Heller*, 670 F.3d at 1263 - 64 ("[T]he tendency is for defenders to keep firing until all bullets have been expended, which poses grave risks to others in the household, passersby, and bystanders." (internal quotations omitted)).

[41] *See, e.g.*, Stephen Hunder, *Why 33 rounds makes sense in a defensive weapon*, WASHINGTON POST (Feb. 6, 2011), http://www.washingtonpost.com/wp-dyn/content/article/2011/02/04/AR2011020407083.html

[42] Dist. of Columbia v. Heller, 554 U.S. 570, 635 (2008) (emphasis added).

[43] Yih Chau-Chang, *High-Capacity Magazines And Their Critical Role In Lawful Self-Defense*, THE EXAMINER (March 10, 2011), http://www.examiner.com/article/high-capacity-magazinesand-their-critical-role-lawful-self-defense

[44] The Supreme Court has exhibited an extreme reluctance to strike down laws on their face – meaning in all applications – when only some applications would fall afoul of a constitutional provision (with the exception of the First Amendment, as facially overbroad laws may chill protected free speech). *See* RICHARD H. FALLON, DANIEL J. MELTZER & DAVID L. SHAPIRO, HART AND WECHSLER'S THE FEDERAL COURTS AND THE FEDERAL SYSTEM 162, 168 (6th ed. 2009).

[45] *Heller*, 670 F.3d at 1261.

[46] *Id.* at 1263 – 64.

[47] *See, e.g.*, *What Should America Do About Gun Violence?: Hearing Before the S. Judiciary Comm.*, 113th Cong. (2013) (prepared testimony of Wayne LaPierre, Executive Vice President and Chief Executive Officer of the National Rifle Association).

[48] This study considered all —mass shooting" incidents: those in which six or more were killed or twelve or more were wounded. For an explanation of this study, see Christopher S. Koper, *America's Experience with the Federal Assault Weapons Ban*, *in* REDUCING GUN VIOLENCE IN AMERICA 167 (Daniel W. Webster & Jon S. Vernick, eds., 2013). The study is Christopher S. Koper & Jeffrey A. Roth, *The Impact of the 1994 Federal Assault Weapon Ban on Gun Violence Outcomes: An Assessment of Multiple Outcome Measures and Some Lessons for Policy Evaluation*, 17 J. OF QUANTITATIVE CRIMINOLOGY 33 (2001).

[49] *See* David S. Fallis and James V. Grimaldi, *Va. data show drop in criminal firepower during assault gun ban*, WASH. POST (Jan. 23, 2011), http://www.washingtonpost.com/wpdyn/content/article/2011/01/22/AR2011012203452.html (finding that in Richmond, Virginia, the percentage of guns with high-capacity magazines seized from criminals by police fell to a low of 10% by 2004, when the federal assault weapons ban expired, but has since rebounded to 22%).

[50] Koper, REDUCING GUN VIOLENCE IN AMERICA, *supra* note 49, at 165 – 66.

[51] Tom Diaz, a researcher for the Violence Policy Center, has repeatedly called on lawmakers to focus their attention on a high-capacity magazine ban. *E.g.*, Tom Diaz, *Ten Ways to Spot a Sell-Out on Gun Control*, FAIRLY CIVIL (Jan. 14, 2013, 2:26 PM), http://tomdiazgunsandgangs.com/2013/01/14/ten-ways-to-spot-a-sell-out-on-gun-control/ ("An effective law will focus on one prime feature—the ability to accept a high-capacity magazine.").

[52] *See, e.g.*, *What Should America Do About Gun Violence?: Hearing Before the S. Judiciary Comm.*, 113th Cong. (2013) (statement by Sen. Ted Cruz) ("Now, what the assault weapons ban instead targets are cosmetic features.").

[53] See, e.g., Nicholas J. Johnson, *Supply Restrictions at the Margins of Heller and the Abortion Analogue: Stenberg Principles, Assault Weapons, and the Attitudinalist Critique*, 60 HASTINGS L.J. 1285, 1295 (2009).

[54] Brady Campaign to Prevent Gun Violence, The Top 10 NRA Myths About Assault Weapons, http:// www.bradycampaign.org/issues/assaultweapons/nramyths/.

[55] Interview with Justice Antonin Scalia by Chris Wallace, FOX NEWS SUNDAY (July 29, 2012), *transcript available at* http://www.foxnews.com/on-air/fox-news-sunday/2012/07/29/justiceantonin-scalia-issues-facing-scotus-and-country#p//v/1760654457001.

[56] Justice Scalia's point about the tort of affrighting surfaces in the *Heller* decision itself: the majority opinion cited three illustrative examples of state courts entertaining such actions in the nineteenth century. *See* Dist. of Columbia v. Heller, 554 U.S. 570, 627 (2008) (citing, e.g., State v. Lanier, 71 N.C. 288, 289 (1874) ("The elementary writers say that the offence of going armed with dangerous or unusual weapons is a crime against the public peace by terrifying the good people of the land, and this Court has declared the same. . . .‖)).

[57] Justin Peters, *How Many Assault Weapons Are There in America? How Much Would It Cost the Government To Buy Them Back?,* SLATE (Dec. 20, 2012), http://www.slate.com/blogs/crime/2012/12/20/assault rifle stats how many assault rifles are there in america.html.

[58] *See* Koper, REDUCING GUN VIOLENCE IN AMERICA, *supra* note 49, at 161 (explaining that the universe of large-capacity magazine equipped firearms is broader than the universe of weapons satisfying the criteria for categorization as an assault weapon).

[59] Peters, *supra* note 58.

[60] *Top Ten Frequently Asked Questions*, NRA-ILA, http://www.gunbanfacts.com/FAQ.aspx (last visited February 2, 2013).

[61] WILLIAM J. KROUSE, CONG. RES. SERV., RL32842, GUN CONTROL LEGISLATION 8 (2012).

[62] *See United States v. Rene E.*, 583 F.3d 8, 15–16 (1st Cir. 2009).

[63] 554 U.S. 570, 626 (2008).

[64] 130 S. Ct. 3020, 3047 (2010) (plurality opinion).

[65] *The Federalist* No. 83, at 495 (Alexander Hamilton) (Clinton Rossiter ed., 1961).

[66] *NFIB v. Sebelius*, 132 S. Ct. 2566, 2589 (2012) (opinion of Roberts, C.J.) (quoting *South Carolina v. United States*, 199 U.S. 437, 449 (1905)).

[67] 554 U.S. at 626–27.

[68] 130 S. Ct. at 3047 (plurality opinion).

[69] *Compare Harper v. Virginia State Board of Elections*, 383 U.S. 663 (1966) (holding that the right to vote is fundamental), *with McDonald v. City of Chicago*, 130 S. Ct. 2020 (2010) (holding that the right to keep and bear arms is fundamental).

[70] 553 U.S. 181 (2008) (plurality opinion).

[71] *See* 554 U.S. at 626–27; 130 S. Ct. at 3047 (plurality opinion).

[72] *See, e.g.*, *Heller v. District of Columbia*, 670 F.3d 1244, 1253 (D.C. Cir. 2011); *Ezell v. City of Chicago*, 651 F.3d 684, 701–04 (7th Cir. 2011); *United States v. Marzzarella*, 614 F.3d 85, 89 (3d Cir. 2010); *United States v. Chester*, 628 F.3d 673, 680 (4th Cir. 2010); *United States v. Reese*, 627 F.3d 792, 800–01 (10th Cir. 2010).

[73] *See Heller*, 670 F.3d at 1253–54.

[74] *McCulloch v. Maryland*, 17 U.S. 316, 415 (1819).

[75] *See Heller*, 670 F.3d at 1253.

[76] *See, e.g.*, Colleen Curtis, *President Obama Announces New Measures to Prevent Gun Violence*, Jan. 16, 2013, available at http://www.whitehouse.gov/blog/2013/01/16/presidentobama-announces-new-measures-prevent-gun-violence.

[77] Measure 13.

[78] Measure 9.

[79] U.S. Const. art. II, § 3.

[80] Patient Protection and Affordable Care Act of 2010, Pub. L. 111-148, § 1321(a).

[81] U.S. Const. art. II, § 2, cl. 2.
[82] U.S. Const. art. II, § 2, cl. 1.
[83] U.S. Const. art. II, §§ 1, 3.
[84] The Center for Disease Control reports that in 2010, 11,078 individuals in the U.S. died from firearm-related homicides. 1,773 of them were between the ages of 0 and 19. *See* CENTER FOR DISEASE CONTROL, NATIONAL CENTER FOR INJURY PREVENTION & CONTROL, *WISQARS Fatal Injury Reports, National and Regional, 1999 – 2010*, http://webappa.cdc.gov/sasweb/ncipc/mortrate10us.html (last visited Feb. 4, 2013). 85 *See Brown v. Entertainment Merchants Ass'n*, 131 S. Ct. 2729, 2767–71 (2011) (Breyer, J., dissenting).

In: Mass Shootings and Gun Violence in America
Editor: John C. Zandler

ISBN: 978-1-62618-893-8

Chapter 16

TESTIMONY OF DANIEL W. WEBSTER, PROFESSOR AND DIRECTOR, JOHNS HOPKINS CENTER FOR GUN POLICY AND RESEARCH. HEARING ON "PROPOSALS TO REDUCE GUN VIOLENCE: PROTECTING OUR COMMUNITIES WHILE RESPECTING THE SECOND AMENDMENT"*

Mr. Chairman, members of the Committee, I appreciate the opportunity to testify before you today. I am the director of the Johns Hopkins Center for Gun Policy Research.

The Center engages in original scholarly research, policy analysis, and agenda-setting public discourse with the goal of bringing public health expertise and perspectives to the complex policy issues related to gun violence prevention.

An important part of the Center's mission is to provide objective information and analysis to policymakers.

THE BURDEN OF GUN VIOLENCE IN THE UNITED STATES

The burden of gun violence on American society is substantial, whether measured in years of productive life lost, disability, fear, or economic costs. More than 31,000 people a year in the United States die from gunshot wounds.[1] Because victims are disproportionately young, gun violence is one of the leading causes of premature mortality in the U.S.[2] In addition to these deaths, in 2010 there were an estimated 337,960 non-fatal violence crimes committed with guns, and 73,505 persons treated in hospital emergency departments for non-fatal gunshot wounds.[3]

There are enormous economic costs associated with gun violence in the U.S. Firearm-related deaths and injuries resulted in medical and lost productivity expenses of about $37 billion in 2005.[4] But the overall cost of gun violence goes well beyond these figures. When lost quality of life, psychological and emotional trauma, decline in property values, and other

* This is an edited, reformatted and augmented version of testimony given on February 12, 2013 before the Senate Judiciary Committee, Subcommittee on the Constitution, Civil Rights and Human Rights.

legal and societal consequences are included, the cost of gun violence in the U.S. in 2010 was estimated to be $174 billion with government absorbing $12 billion of those costs.[5]

Addressing Weaknesses in Current Gun Laws Would Reduce the Burden of Gun Violence

On January 14-15, 2013, I along with more than twenty other top researchers and gun policy experts gathered to participate in a Summit on Reducing Gun Violence in America at Johns Hopkins. After the experts shared their research and analyses at the summit, the experts evaluated various proposals to reduce gun violence, and I would refer to the Committee the full presented findings and analyses that were just published in a book that I co-edited with Jon Vernick entitled *Reducing Gun Violence in America: Informing Policy with Evidence and Analysis*.[6] Collectively, the summit participants recommended a set of reforms to current gun laws that we believe would reduce the burden of gun violence in the United States, including the establishment of a universal background check system, strengthening laws to reduce firearms trafficking, banning the future sale and possession of assault weapons and large capacity ammunition magazines, expanding incentives for states to provide information about disqualifying mental health conditions to the National Instant Check System for gun buyers, and encouraging research to better understand the causes and solutions of gun violence. A full list of the summit's recommendations is included as an appendix to this testimony. Information presented at the summit demonstrated that these policies would enhance public safety and have broad public support. Further, as constitutional experts from across the ideological spectrum have explained, policies such as these would not violate constitutional rights.[7]

Opponents of the types of reforms recommended by the experts who participated in the summit make several common arguments. At the summit and in the book, compelling evidence was put forward to rebut those arguments. In my testimony today I would like to discuss several of those arguments and summarize the evidence that refutes them.

Opponents' Claim #1: Our Nation's High Rate of Homicide Has Nothing to Do with Firearm Availability

Evidence in Response: Dr. Matthew Miller and his colleagues at Harvard[8] presented data demonstrating that the homicide in the United States is nearly seven times higher than the average homicide rate among other high-income countries due to the fact that our rate of homicides with firearms is 20 times higher than the average rate of firearm homicide in those countries.[9] Arguments that this gross disparity in homicide rates is due to the United States being more violent and crime-ridden than other high-income countries are inconsistent with available data. Rates of robbery, sexual assault, aggravated assault, burglary, car theft, and adolescent fighting in the United States are not significantly different from that of other high-income countries.[10,11]

Opponents' Claim #2: Gun Control Laws Don't Work Because Criminals Won't Obey Them and Will Always Find a Way to Get a Gun through Theft or the Illegal Market

Evidence in Response: First, the logic of this argument is flawed. Using this logic, laws against drunk driving are pointless because drunks will always disobey those laws. Just as drunk driving laws provide law enforcement with the tools to arrest individuals who break those laws and deter others from driving drunk, laws such as background check requirements for all gun sales will help law enforcement combat illegal gun trafficking and keep guns from prohibited individuals.

Opponents of gun control point to the frequency with which criminals obtain firearms through unregulated private transactions as proof that regulations are pointless. However, I and many of the experts convened for our conference believe that the weaknesses in current federal firearms laws are the reason that many gun traffickers, criminals, underage youth, and other prohibited individuals are able to obtain firearms in the underground market.[12,13,14, 15,16]

Second, the argument is based on invalid claims about how criminals acquire their guns. I analyzed 2004 survey data from a nationally-representative sample of state prison inmates to identify those who were incarcerated for crime committed with handguns. Only 9.9 percent of these offenders reported that they acquired their handgun by stealing it. Nearly eighty percent had acquired their handguns via a transaction with unlicensed private sellers, a category of transactions that current federal law illogically exempts from mandatory background checks or record-keeping by sellers.[14†]

Third, this argument implies that criminals have no difficulty in obtaining firearms which is also inconsistent with the facts. Most criminologists as well as the general public would consider people who commit robberies to fit the definition of "criminals." Although a firearm would seem an excellent tool to use if you are a robber for increasing compliance of victims to hand over their goods, only 29 percent of robberies reported in the National Crime Victimization Survey involved the robber's use of a firearm.[17] Furthermore, in an in-depth, multi-method study of the underground gun market in Chicago only twenty percent of male arrestees who participated in an anonymous survey reported that they had owned a handgun and sixty percent of those who did own one reported that it had taken them more than a week to search for and obtain a handgun. Criminals reported wariness of purchasing firearms from sellers they did not know or trust, a dearth of trusted suppliers of guns, and considerable mark-ups in price from the legal market.[18]

Fourth, gun sales regulations do impact the illegal gun market. My research has shown that when states enact laws to increase gun seller and purchaser accountability including universal background checks, strong regulation and oversight of licensed gun dealers, and mandatory reporting of theft of loss of firearms, far fewer guns are diverted from the legal to the illegal market.[14,19] Unfortunately, the success of these state gun laws in reducing the diversion of guns to criminals is undermined by gaps in federal laws which facilitate interstate trafficking of firearms from states with the weakest gun control laws to those with comprehensive policies to keep firearms from dangerous people.[14,16,20]

† Sources of handguns used in crime included family and friends (39.5%), "street or black market" (37.5%), gun shows/flea markets (1.7%), licensed gun dealers (11.4%), and theft (9.9%).

Missouri's repeal of its permit-to-purchase licensing law for handgun sales in late August 2007 provides an example of the value of policies designed to reduce the diversion of guns to criminals. The law had required handgun purchasers, whether they were purchasing a handgun from a licensed gun dealer or a non-licensed private seller, to obtain a permit from the local sheriff following a background check. My colleagues and I used annual state-level data on crime guns recovered by police in Missouri and traced by the ATF during the period 2002 – 2011 to examine changes in a commonly-used indicator of illegal gun diversion – the number and proportion of guns with short sale-to-crime intervals – before and after the state repealed the law.

Immediately following the repeal of the law, the share of guns recovered by Missouri police agencies that had an unusually short time interval from retail sale to crime indicative of trafficking more than doubled. Importantly, the sharp increase in short time-to-crime guns coincided with the length of time between the repeal of the law and a crime gun's recovery by police. Crime guns with a sale-to-crime interval of less than three months increased from a pre-repeal stable mean of 2.9 percent to 4.5 percent in 2007 when the repeal was in effect for only four months, and then increased further to a mean of 8.4 percent for 2008 through 2011. Crime guns with sale-to-crime intervals of 3-12 months increased sharply beginning in 2008 from a pre-repeal mean of 5.9 percent to 13.9 percent for 2008-2011. Following this same pattern, the percentage of crime guns recovered one to two years after retail sale increase beginning in 2009 from a mean of 6.4 percent to 12.8 percent during 2009-2011. The sharp increase in very short sale-to-crime intervals for guns in Missouri cannot be explained away as being part of a national trend toward shorter time-to-crime guns because the average sale-to-crime interval for the U.S. increased from 10.2 years in 2006 to 11.2 years in 2011.[14]

States with stricter gun sales laws tend to attract guns originating in states with weaker gun laws, resulting in proportionately fewer crime guns being sold by in-state gun dealers.[21] This is likely to be due to a relative scarcity of guns to criminals in states with more comprehensive gun sales regulations which drives up the price and attracts suppliers from states with weaker gun laws. Following the repeal of Missouri's purchase permit law requiring handgun purchasers to obtain licenses from local sheriffs who would photograph and fingerprint applicants, the percentage of crime guns that had been sold by in-state gun dealers increased from 55.6 percent when the law was in place to 70.8 percent by 2011. This is a significant change for an indicator that tends to change very little over time in most states.[14]

I am just beginning a study of the effects of Missouri's repeal of its permit-to-purchase licensing system on violent crime. Preliminary evidence suggests that the increase in the diversion of guns to criminals linked to the law's repeal may have translated into increases in homicides committed with firearms. From 1999 through 2007, Missouri's age-adjusted homicide rate was relatively stable, fluctuating around a mean of 4.66 per 100,000 population per year. In 2008, the first full year after the permit-to-purchase licensing law was repealed, the age-adjusted firearm homicide rate in Missouri increased sharply to 6.23 per 100,000 population, a 34 percent increase. For the post-repeal period of 2008-2010, the mean annual age-adjusted firearm homicide rate was 5.82, 25 percent above the pre-repeal mean. This increase was out of synch with changes during that period in age-adjusted homicide rates nationally which decreased ten percent and with changes in other states in the Midwest which declined by 5%.[‡]

In our new book, researchers reported several examples in which state laws prohibiting high-risk groups – perpetrators of domestic violence, violent misdemeanants and the severely mentally ill – from possessing firearms reduced violence,[22,23] especially if necessary records are available for law enforcement to deny prohibited individuals.[24] Such laws would be even more effective if gaps and weaknesses in federal laws were addressed.

A case study from Brazil provides useful lessons relevant to the debate over the ability of gun control laws to curtail criminal use of firearms.[25] Brazil has historically had one of the highest homicide rates in the world amid enormous challenges including well-armed organized crime syndicates, income inequality, and high rates of substance abuse, as well as corruption within the military, law enforcement, and criminal justice system. Seventy percent of Brazil's homicides were committed with firearms.

Efforts to strengthen Brazil's gun control laws were met with skepticism and the same arguments used to dismiss calls to reform U.S. guns laws, principally that the illicit gun market is awash with guns that criminals will have little difficulty accessing. Yet in December 2003, the Brazilian government responded to an outcry for change from its people and enacted an array of gun control measures. Prior to the new gun laws, Brazil's deaths from firearms had been steadily increasing, but this trend was reversed following the new gun control laws.

Researchers estimated that the laws reduced firearm-related deaths by 15.8 percent nationally.[26] Brazil has had approximately 5,000 fewer firearm-related deaths per year following the enactment of the gun law reforms.[25]

Opponents' Claim #3: We Don't Need to Pass New Gun Laws, We Just Need to Enforce Current Ones

Evidence in Response: This is a common response to calls for strengthening current gun laws. But federal gun laws are currently written in ways that make it very difficult to hold firearm sellers, whether licensed dealers or private sellers, accountable if they sell firearms to criminals or traffickers.[27,28]

Non-licensed sellers of firearms have no obligation to ensure that the prospective purchasers have passed a background check and can legally possess firearms. There is no statute defining and outlawing straw purchases or gun trafficking. To prosecute gun traffickers, federal prosecutors must use laws against being in the business of selling firearms without a license or intentionally providing false information on the form used to process background checks for firearm sales by licensed dealers. Standards of evidence are high while penalties are weak relative to the seriousness of the crime of supplying criminals with firearms. Legislation has been proposed in the Senate that addresses these weaknesses.

---

‡ Annual age-adjusted firearm homicide rates in the U.S. averaged 4.03 during 1999-2007 and 3.81 for 2008-2010. Firearm homicide rates in states in the Midwest other than Missouri averaged 3.52 during 1999-2007 and 3.33 for 2008-2010. Data taken from National Center for Injury Prevention and Control, Fatal Injury Reports. Web-based Injury Statistics Query and Reporting System (WISQARS), Centers for Disease Control and Prevention, Accessed February 1, 2013.

Congress would do well to rewrite several prior laws that shield scofflaw gun dealers from scrutiny, civil penalties, and criminal prosecution.

The 1986 Firearm Owners Protection Act weakened penalties for gun sales violations, increased standards of proof for prosecutions and actions against licensed gun dealers, and limited ATF law compliance inspections. The Protection of Lawful Commerce in Arms Act provided special immunity from lawsuits for negligent practices which enable criminals and other prohibited individuals to obtain guns. The Tiahrt Amendments provided further protections to licensed gun dealers who sell many guns that subsequently are recovered from criminals by restricting the use of crime gun trace data.[15]

Laws that increase gun seller accountability and increase the risk to those involved in illegal gun transactions significantly reduce the number of guns diverted for criminal use.[14] Whereas the Tiahrt Amendments, which reduce firearm seller accountability, have been shown to increase the diversion of guns to criminals from suspect gun dealers,[29] strong regulation and oversight of gun dealers reduces guns diverted to criminals as does being vulnerable to lawsuits for making illegal sales.[30,31]

Opponents' Claim #4: Requiring Background Checks for All Firearms Sales Is too Great of a Burden to Gun Purchasers to Justify

Evidence in Response: My colleagues and I just completed a large survey of a nationally-representative sample of adults and found that 84 percent of gun owners and 74 percent of NRA members reported that they supported laws requiring a background check for all gun sales.[32] In the 14 states that currently require background checks for all handgun sales, 89 percent of gun owners supported universal background checks for gun sales. More broadly, large majorities of gun owners supported an array of policies intended to keep guns from criminals and the severely mentally ill.

Thus the overwhelming majority of gun owners apparently consider any inconvenience associated with pre-gun-sale background checks to be acceptable given the importance of keeping firearms out of the hands of dangerous people.

Opponents' Claim #5: Proposed Universal Background Checks Would Allow the Federal Government to Create a Registry of Gun Owners

Evidence in Response: Under current federal law, the FBI must destroy records from background checks within 24 hours of the background check being completed. Current federal law explicitly forbids the federal government from creating anything remotely related to a registry of gun owners - even preventing the ATF from automating records from out of business firearms dealers in order to facilitate crime gun trace requests. There is no evidence that proposals to fix the gap in current law that exempts individuals purchasing firearms from private sellers from having to pass a background check would alter current prohibitions against creating a registry of gun owners or their guns.

Opponents' Claim #6: Limits on Assault Weapons and Large Capacity Magazines Would Not Enhance Public Safety

Evidence in Response: Assault weapons and large capacity magazines (LCMs) or ammunition feeding devices are common characteristics of guns discussed in policy debates because they are disproportionately used in mass shootings.

Mass shootings involving assault weapons typically involve more victims per incident than mass shootings with other weapons.[33] Recent examples of firearms with LCMs being used in mass shootings include the Glock 9mm semi-automatic pistol, with a magazine holding 33 rounds of ammunition, used to murder six and wound 13 others, including Congresswoman Gabrielle Giffords. The suspect assault rifle with a 100-round magazine used in the mass shooting at a movie theater in Aurora, Colorado that left 12 dead and 58 injured.

A Bushmaster XM15 assault rifle was used in the Newtown, Connecticut mass-murder of 20 children and six adults. Weapons with LCMs were also used in the mass shootings at Virginia Tech University and Fort Hood, Texas. It is impossible to determine if these and other perpetrators of mass shootings would have been able to acquire assault weapons or LCMs had the weapons and magazines been banned. But if the perpetrators had used firearms that were not equipped with LCMs, it is very likely that fewer people would have been injured and killed. Indeed, it has been shown that there is a positive correlation between the ammunition capacity of firearms used in mass shootings and the number of victims murdered or wounded.[34]

Christopher Koper conducted an evaluation of the federal ban of assault weapons and LCMs and found that the ban led to a significant reduction in the use of assault weapons, but no statistically change in the use of guns with LCMs in the cities where data were available.[35] An analysis of data collected on firearms recovered in crimes in Virginia found, however, that use of firearms with LCMs declined significantly after the federal ban and abruptly increased when the ban expired.[36] Although Koper's study assessed the effects of the federal ban of assault weapons and LCMs on overall homicides and shootings, relatively few shooting incidents involve more than 10 rounds fired from a single firearm – about three percent of shooting incidents and five percent of victims shot in one city.[37]

Thus, his analysis is unlikely to be able to detect the small and gradual effects that might be expected population-wide.

Koper indicated that the lack of statistically significant findings does not mean that the law did not prevent a small percentage of the over 10,000 firearm-involved homicides and nonfatal woundings of nearly 50,000 people annually. Even if the ban eventually prevented only 1 of every 5 of the five percent of incidents in which LCMs are relevant, that would translate into about 100 fewer homicides and 500 fewer people wounded by gunshots per year. Such effects would not be definitively detectable with national data, but would be nonetheless meaningful, given the magnitude of the problem. Further, focusing solely on the "body count" glosses over the considerable psychological trauma and other social costs resulting from mass shootings. We have decided to regulate the design of numerous consumer products, such as cribs and small, high-powered magnets, in order to prevent far fewer deaths than could be prevented with a ban of LCMs. Opponents of such bans do not have a compelling reason why law-abiding citizens need to have firearms with unlimited ammunition capacity.

Opponents' Claim #7: "The Only Thing That Can Stop a Bad Guy with a Gun, Is a Good Guy with a Gun"

Evidence in Response: First of all, I am not aware of any current Congressional proposal to reform federal gun laws that would disarm any law-abiding citizen who is not prohibited from possessing firearms under current law. Second, this call to arms suggests that the way to reducing violence in the United States is to allow or even encourage anyone who can legally possess a firearm to arm themselves not only in their homes, but in public places. The best evidence on the effects of so-called right to carry laws shows that they do not reduce violent crime[38] and may lead to small increases in aggravated assaults.[39,40]

Arguments to expand concealed carrying of firearms suggests that everyone who is a legal firearm possessor is a "good guy (or gal)," yet my own research on the backgrounds of persons who were incarcerated for crimes committed with guns in states where conditions for legal firearm possession mirror those stated in federal law indicate that sixty percent of these offenders were legally qualified to possess firearms in their home prior to committing the crime with a gun that led to their incarceration. Many had prior arrests and convictions for misdemeanors involving violence, guns, drugs, or alcohol abuse or had committed more serious crimes processed in juvenile courts.[41]

Conclusion

In summary, Congress could significantly reduce the availability of guns to dangerous individuals by enacting the recommendations made by our summit participants such as requiring background checks for all firearms sales, strengthening laws against illegal straw purchasing and gun trafficking, and doing away with laws that offer special protections that law-abiding gun dealers don't need and scofflaw dealers don't deserve. Evidence demonstrates that these reforms would translate into fewer lives lost, safer streets and homes, increased quality of life, and reduce government expenditures on health care, disability payments, criminal justice, and corrections. Furthermore, the reforms would not involve unreasonable burdens on law-abiding gun owners and are supported by the vast majority of Americans including large majorities of gun owners.

End Notes

[1] National Center for Injury Prevention and Control. Fatal Injury Reports. Web-based Injury Statistics Query and Reporting System (WISQARS). Centers for Disease Control and Prevention, Atlanta, GA, accessed February 9, 2013.

[2] National Center for Injury Prevention and Control. Leading Causes of Death. Web-based Injury Statistics Query and Reporting System (WISQARS). Centers for Disease Control and Prevention, Atlanta, GA, accessed February 9, 2013.

[3] National Center for Injury Prevention and Control. Nonfatal Injury Data 2002-2011. Web-based Injury Statistics Query and Reporting System (WISQARS). Centers for Disease Control and Prevention, Atlanta, GA, accessed February 9, 2013.

[4] National Center for Injury Prevention and Control. Cost of Injury Reports, 2005. Web-based Injury Statistics Query and Reporting System (WISQARS). Centers for Disease Control and Prevention, Atlanta, GA, accessed February 9, 2013.

[5] Miller TR. *The Cost of Firearm Violence.* Children's Safety Network Economics and Data Analysis Resource Center, at Pacific Institute for Research and Evaluation, December 2012.

[6] Webster, Daniel W. and Jon S. Vernick. *Reducing Gun Violence in America: Informing Policy with Evidence and Analysis.* Baltimore, MD: Johns Hopkins University Press, 2013.

[7] Statement of Professors of Constitutional Law: The Second Amendment and the Constitutionality of the Proposed Gun Violence Prevention Legislation, Jan. 30, 2013, available at http://www.huffingtonpost.com/geoffrey-r-stone/the-second-amendment_b_ 2581625.html,.

[8] Miller M, Azrael D, Hemenway D. "Firearms and Violent Death in the United States," pages 3-20 in *Reducing Gun Violence in America: Informing Policy with Evidence and Analysis,* Daniel W. Webster and Jon S. Vernick, Eds. Baltimore, MD: Johns Hopkins University Press, 2013.

[9] Richardson EG, Hemenway D. Homicide, suicide, and unintentional firearm fatality: comparing the United States with other high-income countries, 2003. *Journal of Trauma Injury, Infection and Critical Care* 2011;70:238-243.

[10] van Kesteren J, Mayhew P, Nieuwbeerta P. Criminal victimization in seventeen industrialized countries: key findings from the 2000 international crime victimization survey. In *Netherlands Ministry of Justice: Research and Documentation Centre Netherlands*, 2001.

[11] Picket W, Elgar FJ, Brooks F, de Looze M, Rathman K. Trends and socioeconomic correlates of adolescent fighting in 30 countries. *Pediatrics* 2013;131:18-26.

[12] Cook PJ, Ludwig J. "The Limited Impact of the Brady Act: Evaluation and Implications," pages 21-32 in *Reducing Gun Violence in America: Informing Policy with Evidence and Analysis.* Daniel W. Webster and Jon S. Vernick, Eds. Baltimore, MD: Johns Hopkins University Press, 2013.

[13] Wintemute GJ. "Comprehensive Background Checks for Firearms Sales: Evidence from Gun Shows," pages 95-108 in *Reducing Gun Violence in America: Informing Policy with Evidence and Analysis.* Daniel W. Webster and Jon S. Vernick, Eds. Baltimore, MD: Johns Hopkins University Press, 2013.

[14] Webster DW, Vernick JS, McGinty EE, Alcorn T. "Preventing the diversion of guns to criminals through effective firearm sales laws." Pages 109-122 in *Reducing Gun Violence in America: Informing Policy with Evidence and Analysis.* Daniel W. Webster and Jon S. Vernick, Eds. Baltimore, MD: Johns Hopkins University Press, 2013.

[15] Vernick JS, Webster DW. "Curtailing dangerous sales practices by licensed firearms dealers: legal opportunities and obstacles," pages 133-142 in *Reducing Gun Violence in America: Informing Policy with Evidence and Analysis,* Daniel W. Webster and Jon S. Vernick, Eds., Baltimore, MD: Johns Hopkins University Press, 2013.

[16] Braga AA, PL Gagliardi. "Enforcing federal firearms laws against firearms traffickers: Raising operational effectiveness by lowering enforcement obstacles." Pages 143-156 in *Reducing Gun Violence in America: Informing Policy with Evidence and Analysis,* Daniel W. Webster and Jon S. Vernick, Eds., Baltimore, MD: Johns Hopkins University Press, 2013.

[17] Truman JL. Criminal Victimization, 2010. National Crime Victimization Survey. NCJ 235508. Washington, DC: United States Department of Justice, Bureau of Justice Statistics; September 2011.

[18] Cook PJ, Ludwig J, Venketesh S, Braga AA. Underground gun markets. *The Economic Journal* 2007;117;F588-F618.

[19] Webster DW, Vernick JS, Bulzacchelli MT. Effects of state-level firearm seller accountability policies on firearms trafficking. *Journal of Urban Health* 2009;86:525-537.

[20] Braga AA, Cook PJ, Kennedy DM, Moore MH. "The Illegal Supply of Firearms." In *Crime and Justice: A Review of Research* Volume 29, Chicago: University of Chicago Press, 2002.

[21] Webster DW, Vernick JS, Hepburn LM. The relationship between licensing, registration and other state gun sales laws and the source state of crime guns. *Injury Prevention* 2001;7: 184-189.

[22] Wintemute GJ. "Broadening denial criteria for the purchase and possession of firearms: Need, feasibility, and effectiveness." Pages 77-94 in *Reducing Gun Violence in America: Informing Policy with Evidence and Analysis,* Daniel W. Webster and Jon S. Vernick, Eds., Baltimore, MD: Johns Hopkins University Press, 2013.

[23] Zeoli AM, Frattaroli S. "Evidence for optimism: policies to limit batters' access to firearms. Pages 53-64 in *Reducing Gun Violence in America: Informing Policy with Evidence and Analysis,* Daniel W. Webster and Jon S. Vernick, Eds., Baltimore, MD: Johns Hopkins University Press, 2013.

[24] Swanson JW, Robertson AG, Frisman LK, Norko MA, Lin HJ, Swartz MS, Cook PJ. "Preventing gun violence involving people with severe mental illness. Pages 33-52 in *Reducing Gun Violence in America: Informing Policy with Evidence and Analysis,* Daniel W. Webster and Jon S. Vernick, Eds., Baltimore, MD: Johns Hopkins University Press, 2013.

[25] Bandeira AR. "Brazil – Gun control and homicide reduction," pages 213-222 in *Reducing Gun Violence in America: Informing Policy with Evidence and Analysis,* Daniel W. Webster and Jon S. Vernick, Eds., Baltimore, MD: Johns Hopkins University Press, 2013.

[26] de Souza MDM, Macinko J, Alencar AP, Malta DC, Neto OLD. Reductions in firearm-related mortality and hospitalizations in Brazil after gun control. *Health Affairs* 2007;26:575-584. With updated statistics from the Brazilian Ministry of Health, Secretariat for Epidemiological Surveillance.

[27] Braga AA, PL Gagliardi. "Enforcing federal firearms laws against firearms traffickers: Raising operational effectiveness by lowering enforcement obstacles." Pages 143-156 in *Reducing Gun Violence in America: Informing Policy with Evidence and Analysis,* Daniel W. Webster and Jon S. Vernick, Eds., Baltimore, MD: Johns Hopkins University Press, 2013.

[28] Vernick JS, Webster DW. "Curtailing dangerous sales practices by licensed firearms dealers: legal opportunities and obstacles". Pages 133-142 in *Reducing Gun Violence in America: Informing Policy with Evidence and Analysis,* Daniel W. Webster and Jon S. Vernick, Eds., Baltimore, MD: Johns Hopkins University Press, 2013.

[29] Webster DW, Vernick JS, Bulzacchelli MT, Vittes KA. Recent federal gun laws, gun dealer accountability and the diversion of guns to criminals in Milwaukee. *J Urban Health* 2012;89:87-97.

[30] Webster DW, Zeoli AM, Bulzacchelli MT, Vernick JS. Effects of police stings of gun dealers on the supply of new guns to criminals. *Injury Prevention* 2006;12:225-230.

[31] Webster DW, Vernick JS. "Spurring responsible firearms sales practices through litigation: the impact of New York City's lawsuits against gun dealers on interstate gun trafficking." Pages 123-132 in *Reducing Gun Violence in America: Informing Policy with Evidence and Analysis.* Daniel W. Webster and Jon S. Vernick, Eds. Baltimore, MD: Johns Hopkins University Press, 2013.

[32] Barry CL, McGinty EE, Vernick JS, Webster DW. After Newtown – public opinion on gun policy and mental illness. *New England Journal of Medicine* Jan. 28, 2013; DOI: 10.1056/NEJMp1300512

[33] Roth JA, Koper CS. Appendix A in *Impact Evaluation of the Public Safety and Recreational Firearm Use Protection Act of 1994*. Urban Institute: Washington, DC, 1997.

[34] Koper CS, Roth JA. The impact of the 1994 federal assault weapons ban on on gun violence outcomes: an assessment of multiple outcome measures and some lessons for policy evaluation. *Journal of Quantitative Criminology* 2001;17:33-74.

[35] Koper CS. "America's Experience with the Federal Assault Weapons Ban, 1994-2004: Key Findings and Implications," pages 157-171 in *Reducing Gun Violence in America: Informing Policy with Evidence and Analysis.* Daniel W. Webster and Jon S. Vernick, Eds. Baltimore, MD: Johns Hopkins University Press, 2013.

[36] Fallis DS, Grimaldi JV. Va. Data Show Drop in Criminal Firepower During Assault Gun Ban, *The Washington Post*, January 23, 2011.

[37] Reedy DC, Koper CS. Impact of handgun types on gun assault outcomes: a comparison of gun assaults involving semi-automatic pistols and revolvers. *Injury Prevention* 2003;9;151-155.

[38] National Research Council. *Firearms and Violence: A Critical Review.* Committee to Improve Research Information and Data on Fireaerms. Charles F. Wellford, John V. Pepper, and Carol V. Pietre, Eds. Washington, DC: National Academies Press. 2005.

[39] Aneja A, Donohue JJ, Zhang A. The Impact of Right-to-Carry Laws and the NRC Report: Lessons for the Empirical Evaluation of Law and Policy. American Law and Economics Review. 2011;13(2):565-632.

[40] Ayers I, Donohue JJ. Shooting down the more guns, less crime hypothesis. Stanford Law Review. 2003;55:1993-312.

[41] Vittes KA, Vernick JS, Webster DW. Legal status and source of offenders' firearms in states with the least stringent criteria for gun ownership. *Injury Prevention* 2013;19:26-31.

APPENDIX TO TESTIMONY

Summit on Reducing Gun Violence in America Policy Recommendations

JANUARY 15, 2013

A Summit of more than 20 of the world's leading gun policy experts has identified several research-based policies to reduce gun violence in the United States. The policy recommendations were the result of a two-day Summit on gun violence convened by The Johns Hopkins University on January 14 and 15, The Summit on Reducing Gun Violence in America: Informing Policy with Evidence and Analysis.

During the Summit, experts presented and analyzed research-based approaches to reducing gun violence. Collectively, the Summit participants recommend[#] the following:

Background Checks

Fix the background check system by:

- Establishing a universal background check system, which would require a background check for all persons purchasing a firearm (inheritance exception).
- All sales would be facilitated through a federally licensed gun dealer. This would have the effect of mandating the same record keeping for all firearm transfers.
- Increase the maximum amount of time for the FBI to complete a background check from 3 to 10 business days.
- Require all firearm owners to report the theft or loss of their firearm within 72 hours of becoming aware of its loss.
- Persons who have a license to carry a firearm, permit to purchase, or other firearm permit must still be subject to a background check when purchasing a firearm.

Prohibiting High-Risk Individuals from Purchasing Guns: Expand the Conditions for Firearm Purchase to Include

- Persons convicted of a violent misdemeanor would be prohibited from firearm purchase for a period of 15 years.
- Persons who committed a violent crime as a juvenile would be prohibited from firearm purchase until age 30.
- Persons convicted of 2 or more crimes involving drugs or alcohol within a three-year period would be prohibited from firearm purchase for a period of 10 years.
- Persons convicted of a single drug-trafficking offense would be prohibited from firearm purchase.
- Persons determined by a judge to be a gang member would be prohibited from firearm purchase.
- Establish a minimum age of 21 years for handgun purchase or possession.
- Persons who have violated a restraining order issued due to the threat of violence (including permanent, temporary and emergency) are prohibited from purchasing firearms.
- Persons with temporary restraining orders filed against them for violence or threats of violence are prohibited from purchasing firearms.

[#] These recommendations represent the consensus of the experts presenting at the Johns Hopkins Gun Policy Summit. However, it may not be the case that every expert endorsed every specific recommendation.

- Persons who have been convicted of misdemeanor stalking are prohibited from purchasing firearms.

Mental Health

- Federal restrictions of gun purchase for persons with serious mental illness should be focused on the dangerousness of the individual.
- Fully fund federal incentives for states to provide information about disqualifying mental health conditions to the National Instant Check System for gun buyers.

Trafficking and Dealer Licensing

- A permanent director for the ATF should be appointed and confirmed.
- ATF should be required to provide adequate resources to inspect and otherwise engage in oversight of federally licensed gun dealers.
- Restrictions imposed under the Firearm Owners Protections Act limiting ATF to one routine inspection of gun dealers per year should be repealed.
- Provisions of the Firearm Owners Protection Act raising the evidentiary standard for prosecuting dealers who make unlawful sales should be repealed.
- ATF should be granted authority to develop a range of sanctions for gun dealers who violate gun sales or other laws.
- The Protection of Lawful Commerce In Arms Act, providing gun dealers and manufacturers protection from tort liability, should be repealed.
- Federal restrictions on access to firearms trace data, other than for ongoing criminal investigations, should be repealed.
- Federal law mandating reporting of multiple sales of handguns should be expanded to include long guns.
- Adequate penalties are needed for violations of the above provisions.

Personalized Guns

- Congress should provide financial incentives to states to mandate childproof or personalized guns.
- The Federal Consumer Product Safety Commission should be granted authority to regulate the safety of firearms and ammunition as consumer products.

Assault Weapons

- Ban the future sale of assault weapons, incorporating a more carefully crafted definition to reduce the risk—compared with the 1994 ban—that the law can be easily evaded.

High Capacity Magazines

- Ban the future sale and possession of large capacity (greater than 10 rounds) ammunition magazines.

Research Funding

- The federal government should provide funds to CDC, NIH and NIJ adequate to understand the causes and solutions of gun violence, commensurate with its impact on the public's health and safety.
- The Surgeon General should produce a regular report on the state of the problem of gun violence in America and progress towards solutions.

"The purpose of putting forth these recommendations is to provide a research-based framework for reducing the staggering toll of gun violence in America," said Summit organizer Daniel Webster, ScD, MPH, director of the Center for Gun Policy and Research at the Johns Hopkins Bloomberg School of Public Health. "Importantly, most recommended policies have broad public support and would not violate constitutional rights."

New national public opinion polling data presented during the Summit from Johns Hopkins researchers showed the majority of Americans—including gun owners—support a universal background check system, more oversight on gun dealers, restricting access to guns among high-risk individuals such as those with previous criminal convictions, and banning the sale of large-capacity ammunition clips or magazines that allow some guns to shoot more than 20 bullets.

Presentations included research findings from experts at Johns Hopkins, Harvard, Yale, Duke, Rutgers, Michigan State, George Mason and Howard universities, the universities of Chicago, Connecticut and California-Davis, and insights from former federal law enforcement officials. Experts from Great Britain, Australia and Brazil presented evaluations of gun policy reforms in their nations.

"This has been an important two days," said Ronald J. Daniels, president of The Johns Hopkins University. "We knew that a critical outcome of this Summit would be a set of research-based recommendations designed to inform the current debate. These will help lawmakers and opinion leaders identify the policy changes that are most likely to reduce gun violence in the United States."

Last month's shootings in Newtown, Conn., opened the door to new federal action to reduce gun violence in the United States. Johns Hopkins University's Center for Gun Policy and Research believes that any action should be based on the best available research.

"The research-informed measures address not only mass shootings but also the less publicized U.S. gun violence that takes an average of 30 lives every day," said Summit organizer Jon Vernick, JD, MPH, co-director of the Center for Gun Policy and Research at the Johns Hopkins Bloomberg School of Public Health. "We can reduce this number through implementation of such measures as expanding conditions which would prohibit high-risk individuals from possessing guns, strengthening the background check system by covering all firearm sales, and ensuring that necessary records for prohibited individuals are available."

The Summit convened by the University, its Bloomberg School of Public Health and the Center for Gun Policy and Research is believed to be the most extensive summit meeting ever of gun policy researchers to discuss the evidence and make specific action recommendations.

"Gun violence is an urgent public health problem facing our country. I'm proud of our faculty for their contributions to the prevention of gun violence and for their leadership in this important summit," said Michael J. Klag, dean of the Johns Hopkins Bloomberg School of Public Health. "Efforts like this Summit showcase what we do best, providing the science and evidence to solve the major challenges to our health."

According to the Centers for Disease Control and Prevention, guns kill more than 31,000 people each year in the U.S., including more than 11,000 homicides. The U.S. homicide rate is seven times the average of other high-income countries.

Within weeks of the Summit, the Johns Hopkins University Press will publish the book, *Reducing Gun Violence in America: Informing Policy with Evidence and Analysis*. Collected for the first time in one volume, this reliable, empirical research and legal analysis will inform the policy debate by helping lawmakers and opinion leaders identify the policy changes that are most likely to reduce gun violence in the U.S. The book will be available in late January. Copies of the book will be delivered to policymakers from across the country, including members of Congress and the Administration.

In: Mass Shootings and Gun Violence in America
Editor: John C. Zandler
ISBN: 978-1-62618-893-8

Chapter 17

TESTIMONY OF SANDRA J. WORTHAM. HEARING ON "PROPOSALS TO REDUCE GUN VIOLENCE: PROTECTING OUR COMMUNITIES WHILE RESPECTING THE SECOND AMENDMENT"*

Good morning Chairman Durbin, Ranking Member Cruz, and members of the committee. My name is Sandra Wortham, and I want to thank you for the opportunity to testify today. It is an honor.

On May 19, 2010 I was having a good day. During the early evening I went to line dancing class with my mother, as we did every Wednesday. We had fun. When I got home a friend asked me to go out with her to scout locations for her birthday party. I of course said yes. So, we went out. Again, we had fun. Then, we got in the car to head home.

The fun ended then.

When we were about 5 minutes away from my house my mother called me. It wasn't unusual for her to call because we talk a thousand times a day. But this call was different. She was crying. She said, “Sandy, come home.” She continued to speak through her tears, “They tried to rob him.” The “him” my mother spoke of was my older brother, Thomas E. Wortham IV.

Thomas and I grew up in a strong family. Our parents taught us that we could be anything we wanted to be. But they also taught us that we had a responsibility to help others along the way. That is how Thomas lived his life. Like many other siblings we often fought like cats and dogs, but he always watched out for me.

Thomas dedicated his professional life to serving others. He joined the National Guard, serving two tours in Iraq. He was also a Chicago Police Officer, and he worked to protect our community on the South Side of Chicago. Earlier that week he'd traveled here, to Washington, D.C., to participate in activities for National Police Week honoring our Nation's fallen law enforcement officers. He then traveled to New York City to run in a race in honor of Chicago Police Officer Alex Valadez, who was shot and killed in the line of duty the year before. So, on the night of May 19th Thomas stopped by to show our parents his pictures

* This is an edited, reformatted and augmented version of testimony given on February 12, 2013 before the Senate Judiciary Committee, Subcommittee on the Constitution, Civil Rights and Human Rights.

from Police Week. When they finished, he walked to the front door to leave. My father followed him to the door to watch him out.

I wasn't there, but this is what reports say happened. As Thomas walked over to his motorcycle two men walked towards him, pulled out a gun, and tried to take his motorcycle. Two more men were in a car nearby. Thomas was armed, and he identified himself as a police officer. My father, a retired Chicago Police Sergeant, also had a gun and when he saw what was happening he ran back into the house to get it. There was an exchange of gunfire between Thomas, my father, and the robbers.

When I got the call from my mother I had no idea how bad it was. My friend tried to drive me to the house but shortly after I got the call the traffic stopped. When I looked ahead I saw that the police had blocked off all of the streets on our route. Again, it didn't even occur to me that this had anything to do with Thomas. But I knew I needed to get home. So I got out of the car and started to run. As I ran an ambulance passed me. I know now that the ambulance was carrying my brother. He had been shot.

We went to the hospital and we waited. I prayed, and we waited. But Thomas died.

Just a few days before my brother was killed he was interviewed by the Chicago Tribune about recent shootings in our neighborhood. He said, "When people think of the South Side of Chicago, they think violence." He went on to say, "We're going to fix it, so it doesn't happen again." I am here today because I want to fix it too.

This hearing has been called to show that we can protect our communities while respecting the Second Amendment. I have to be honest and say I'm not sure where there can be serious disagreement on this. My family and I are not anti-gun people. My brother and my father were police officers- they were trained with guns and carried them most of the time. I value and respect the rights provided by our Constitution. However, I find it hard to believe that our founders intended those rights to go unreasonably unchecked.

This isn't about taking away the right to lawfully own guns. This is about trying our best to keep guns out of the hands of people like the ones who killed my brother. They didn't walk into a gun store and buy a handgun, because if the news reports are right they wouldn't have been eligible to buy one. So they got the gun the same way many ill-intentioned individuals obtain weapons-- -they bought it on the street.

It is also reality that the gun used to kill my brother didn't get to Chicago on its own. It was trafficked from a pawn shop in Mississippi. According to news reports, a gun trafficker went to Mississippi, used straw purchasers to buy multiple handguns from that shop and other shops, and then brought those guns to Chicago to sell to gang members.

I cannot accept the notion that we can't fix this. If we know, as we do, that in many places criminals have fairly easy street access to guns, don't we have a responsibility to address that issue to the best of our ability? I would say yes. Common sense gun laws to keep guns out of the wrong hands do not hurt decent people. The only people who should be disturbed by them are those people that shouldn't have guns in the first place and those who participate in funneling guns to those criminals.

When we speak about rights and the Constitution I think we would all be well served to remember the words of another important document in our Country's history---"life, liberty and the pursuit of happiness." Those rights were taken away from my brother at age 30.

My brother carried a gun. My father carried a gun. But the fact that my brother and father were armed that night did not prevent my brother from being killed. We need to do more to keep guns out of the wrong hands in the first place. I don't think that makes us anti-gun, I think it makes us pro-decent, law abiding people.

I am not here to say that any one law would necessarily have stopped what happened to my brother. But I am saying that we can do better.

This isn't about me, Thomas or our family alone. This is about our country. We are just one of too many families who have experienced horror and death as a result of gun violence. Some of our loved ones were killed with assault weapons. Some with guns that were straw purchased or sold without background checks. All of us want to prevent any more families from going through what we have endured. Gun violence is a problem in our country that needs to be fixed, and we have an opportunity, through this process, to help save lives. I hope we can do it.

Thank you for your time.

In: Mass Shootings and Gun Violence in America
Editor: John C. Zandler
ISBN: 978-1-62618-893-8

Chapter 18

STATEMENT OF CHARLES J. COOPER, PARTNER, COOPER & KIRK, PLLC. HEARING ON "PROPOSALS TO REDUCE GUN VIOLENCE: PROTECTING OUR COMMUNITIES WHILE RESPECTING THE SECOND AMENDMENT"*

Good morning Mr. Chairman, and Members of the Subcommittee. Thank you for inviting me to participate in today's hearing entitled "Proposals to Reduce Gun Violence: Protecting Our Communities While Respecting the Second Amendment." I am honored to be included among the very distinguished members of this panel and to share with you my thoughts on the constitutional issues raised by this important subject.[1]

It is critical, of course, that any legislation enacted to reduce gun violence respect the Second Amendment, which provides: "A well regulated Militia, being necessary to the security of a free State, the right of the people to keep and bear Arms, shall not be infringed." The Supreme Court's recent decisions in *District of Columbia v. Heller*, 554 U.S. 570 (2008), and *McDonald v. City of Chicago*, 130 S. Ct. 3020 (2010), provide authoritative guidance for interpreting and applying the Second Amendment. I believe that the principles established by these decisions cannot be reconciled with certain gun control measures pending before the Congress, including the proposed ban on certain semiautomatic rifles, pistols, and shotguns tendentiously dubbed "semiautomatic assault weapons" and the proposed 10-round limitation on the capacity of ammunition magazines.

I. PRINCIPLES ESTABLISHED BY *HELLER* AND *MCDONALD*

In analyzing the constitutional implications of the proposed gun control measures, one must first identify the pertinent principles established by the *Heller* and *McDonald* decisions.

First, the Second Amendment protects an "*individual right*" that "*belongs to all Americans*." *Heller*, 554 U.S. at 581, 595 (emphasis added). The Court thus rejected the

* This is an edited, reformatted and augmented version of testimony given on February 12, 2013 before the Senate Judiciary Committee, Subcommittee on the Constitution, Civil Rights and Human Rights.

notions that the Second Amendment protects only a "collective" right and that it protects a right only to bear arms in connection with militia service. While the right to arms was "*codified* . . . to prevent elimination of the militia . . ., most [Americans] undoubtedly thought it even more important for self-defense and hunting." *Id.* at 599 (emphasis added). Indeed, the Court repeatedly emphasized in both *Heller* and *McDonald* that the "inherent" and "pre-existing" right of self-defense is the "core" and "the *central component* of the right itself."[2]

Second, the right to keep and bear arms is a *fundamental* right, implicit in our constitutional scheme of ordered liberties and "deeply rooted in this Nation's history and tradition." *McDonald*, 130 S. Ct. at 3042. It "was considered . . . fundamental by those who drafted and ratified the Bill of Rights" and by the "Framers and ratifiers of the Fourteenth Amendment," *id.* at 3037, 3042, and it is still considered fundamental by countless millions of Americans today. The fundamental Second Amendment right to arms, accordingly, is entitled to no less respect than the other fundamental rights protected by our Constitution. As the Court emphasized in *McDonald*, it is not to be "treat[ed] . . . as a second-class right" or "singled out for special – and specially unfavorable – treatment." *Id.* at 3043, 3044.

Third, the line between permissible and impermissible arms regulations is established by looking to the Second Amendment's *text* and *history* and to the history of arms regulations in this country. The Second Amendment is "enshrined with the scope [it was] understood to have *when the people adopted [it]*, whether or not future legislatures or (yes) even future judges think that scope too broad." *Heller*, 554 U.S. at 634-35 (emphasis added). This passage from *Heller* is an express admonition that all government officials, including Members of this body, are oath-bound to respect and obey the command of the Second Amendment as it was understood in 1791, no matter how much they may disagree with the breadth of that constitutional command. To be sure, this does not mean that the Second Amendment right has no limits. Rather, it means that the Second Amendment's scope is determined through "historical analysis" and that any limits on the right must be supported by "historical justifications." *Id.* at 627, 635. Indeed, even as the Court in *Heller* recognized the presumptive validity of certain "longstanding prohibitions on the possession of firearms," it expressly reserved for future cases the ultimate question whether "the historical justifications for [those] exceptions" would suffice to uphold their validity. *Id.* at 626, 635.

Fourth, and relatedly, the line between permissible and impermissible arms regulations *is not* to be established by balancing the individual right protected by the Second Amendment against purportedly competing government interests. This balance has already been struck, for the Second Amendment "is the very *product* of an interest-balancing by the people," and "[t]he very enumeration of the right takes out of the hands of government . . . the power to decide on a case-by-case basis whether the right is *really worth* insisting upon." *Id.* at 634-35 (original emphasis).

Thus, while *Heller* made clear that the District of Columbia's handgun ban would fail "any of the standards of scrutiny that [the Court has] applied to enumerated constitutional rights," *id.* at 628, the Court pointedly did not apply any of those standards but rather flatly and categorically struck down the ban after finding it irreconcilable with the Second Amendment's text and history. Likewise, the Court categorically invalidated the so-called "trigger-lock requirement" – the separate, independent provision of D.C. law requiring "that firearms in the home be rendered and kept inoperable at all times" – without subjecting it to any form of heightened scrutiny. *Id.* at 630. Indeed, the Court squarely rejected the "interest-balancing" approach proposed by Justice Breyer in dissent, *see id.* at 634-35, an approach that was in substance if not in name a form of intermediate scrutiny, *see, e.g., Heller*, 554 U.S. at 704-05 (Breyer, J., dissenting) (finding "no cause here to depart from the standard set forth in *Turner* [*Broadcasting System, Inc. v. FCC*, 520 U.S. 180 (1997)]," a "First Amendment case[] applying intermediate scrutiny"). *McDonald* reiterated that *Heller* "expressly rejected the argument that the scope of the Second Amendment right should be determined by judicial interest balancing." 130 S. Ct. at 3047. Indeed, *McDonald* emphasized that resolving Second Amendment cases *would not* "require judges to assess the costs and benefits of firearms restrictions and thus to make difficult empirical judgments in an area in which they lack expertise." *Id.* at 3050.[3]

In sum, *Heller* and *McDonald* establish that the Second Amendment guarantees a fundamental, individual right to keep and bear arms, the scope of which is established by the Second Amendment's text and history and which cannot be circumscribed by appeal to countervailing government interests.

II. The Second Amendment's Protection of Certain "Arms" Is Absolute

As noted earlier, the text of the Second Amendment provides that "the right of the people to keep and bear *Arms*, shall not be infringed." U.S. CONST. amend. II (emphasis added). The amendment is thus one of the few enumerated constitutional rights that specifically protects the possession and use of a particular kind of personal property – "arms." It follows that there are certain "instruments that constitute bearable arms," *Heller*, 554 U.S. at 582, that law-abiding, responsible adult citizens have an absolute, inviolable right to acquire, possess, and use. Indeed, the Court in *Heller* made clear that the Second Amendment's "core protection" – the right to armed self-defense, including, most acutely, in the home – is no less absolute than the First Amendment's protection of the expression of unpopular opinions: "The First Amendment contains the freedom-of-speech guarantee that the people ratified, which included exceptions for obscenity, libel, and disclosure of state secrets, but not for the expression of extremely unpopular and wrong headed views. The Second Amendment is no different. . . . And whatever else it leaves to future evaluation, it surely *elevates above all other interests* the right of law-abiding, responsible citizens to use arms in defense of hearth and home." *Id.* at 634-35 (emphasis added).

The key question, then, is what arms are protected by the Second Amendment. For again, under the Supreme Court's categorical approach, the Second Amendment guarantees a fundamental, inviolable right to own and possess the arms that fall within its scope.

While *Heller* and *McDonald* instruct that we look to history to determine the types of arms that fall within the Second Amendment's scope, those cases have already done the analysis and answered the question: The arms protected by the Second Amendment are those weapons that are "of the kind in common use . . . for lawful purposes like self-defense." *Heller*, 554 U.S. at 624. Conversely, "the Second Amendment *does not* protect those weapons not typically possessed by law-abiding citizens for lawful purposes, such as short-barreled shotguns." *Id.* at 625 (emphasis added).

This distinction – between firearms in common use by ordinary Americans and unusual, sophisticated weapons historically confined to military use – is hardly novel.[4] Indeed, the distinction was central to the Supreme Court's 1939 decision in *United States v. Miller*, 307 U.S. 174 (1939), which rejected a Second Amendment challenge to convictions for unlawfully transporting in interstate commerce a short-barreled shotgun. As *Heller* emphasized, the *Miller* Court's "basis for saying that the Second Amendment did not apply . . . was that the type of weapon at issue was not eligible for Second Amendment protection." *Heller*, 554 U.S. at 622 (emphasis omitted). "*Miller* said . . . that the sorts of weapons protected [by the Second Amendment] were those 'in common use at the time.' " *Id.* at 627. According to *Heller*, then, possession and use of short-barreled shotguns, like modern-day "M-16 rifles" and other "sophisticated arms that are highly unusual in society at large," can be banned or otherwise regulated without constitutional concern. *Id.* But possession and use of firearms of the kind in common use for self defense and other lawful purposes are constitutionally protected.

Applying this "common use" test, *Heller* flatly and categorically struck down the District of Columbia's handgun ban. "The handgun ban," the Court reasoned, "amounts to a prohibition of an entire class of 'arms' that is overwhelmingly chosen by American society for [the] lawful purpose [of self-defense]." *Id.* at 628; *see also id.* at 628-29 (Handguns are "the most preferred firearm in the nation to 'keep' and use for protection of one's home and family.") (quotation marks omitted); *id.* at 629 ("[T]he American people have considered the handgun to be the quintessential self-defense weapon."); *id.* ("[H]andguns are the most popular weapon chosen by Americans for self-defense in the home . . . ."). The Court thus held "that the District's ban on handgun possession in the home violates the Second Amendment," and ordered that, "[a]ssuming that Heller is not disqualified from the exercise of Second Amendment rights, the District must permit him to register his handgun and must issue him a license to carry it in the home." *Id.* at 635. Because "[t]he vast majority of handguns today are semi-automatic," *Heller II*, 670 F.3d at 1286 (Kavanaugh, J., dissenting), *Heller* necessarily holds that semiautomatic handguns are constitutionally protected and cannot be banned. *See id.* at 1289 ("semi-automatic handguns are constitutionally protected under the Supreme Court's decision in *Heller*").

The constitutionality of the pending proposals to ban certain "arms" thus turns on whether the banned rifles, shotguns, and pistols are in common use for lawful purposes in this Nation. The answer to that question is plainly yes.

Indeed, the answer to that question should be apparent from the very term that one of the pending bills, S.150, uses for the weapons it seeks to ban: "*semiautomatic* assault weapons." As explained below, "assault weapon" is a term of opprobrium invented for political and public relations purposes. But "semiautomatic" *is* a term that has a distinct meaning, and it is a weapon type that has been in existence for over a hundred years. *See* David B. Kopel, *Rational Basis Analysis of "Assault Weapon" Prohibition*, 20 J. CONTEMP. L. 381, 413 (1994) ("semiautomatics are more than a century old"). And unlike "machineguns, sawed-off shotguns, and artillery pieces," semiautomatic firearms "traditionally have been widely accepted as lawful possessions." *Staples v. United States*, 511 U.S. 600, 611-12 (1994). "Automatic" refers to the fact that the user need not manipulate the firearm (via mechanisms such as a bolt or lever) to place another round in the chamber after each round is fired. *See id.* at 602 n.1. A fully automatic firearm on one pull of its trigger will fire continuously until the trigger is released or until the ammunition in the firearm's magazine is expended. *See id.* But a semiautomatic firearm requires the user to pull the trigger each time he or she wants to discharge a bullet – hence the qualifier "semi."

A large percentage of firearms in common civilian use in the United States are semiautomatic, including many handgun, rifle, and shotgun models that fall outside S.150's definition of "assault weapons." *See Heller II*, 670 F.3d at 1269 (Kavanaugh, J., dissenting) ("the vast majority of [handguns] today are semi-automatic"); Declaration of Mark Overstreet 13 ("Overstreet Decl."), *Heller v. District of Columbia*, No. 08-1289 (D.D.C. July 23, 2009), ECF No. 23-8 ("Annual firearm manufacturing and export statistics published by ATF indicate that semiautomatic pistols rose as a percentage of total handguns made in the United States and not exported, from 52 percent of 1.3 million handguns in 1986, to 77 percent of 1.5 million handguns in 2007."); Nicholas J. Johnson, *Supply Restrictions at the Margins of* Heller *and the Abortion Analogue*, 60 HASTINGS L.J. 1285, 1293-95 (2009) (noting that in a 1994 survey "sixty percent of gun owners reported owning some type of semiautomatic firearm" and that "it is just not credible to say that semiautomatic technology is unusual or uncommon"). Again, all semiautomatic firearms – including so-called "semiautomatic assault weapons" banned under S.150 – discharge only a single shot per trigger pull. They are thus functionally distinguishable from fully automatic, military weapons. But the semiautomatic "assault weapons" that would be banned by S.150 are *not* functionally distinguishable from the semiautomatic firearms that would be permitted under the measure.

Indeed, Americans own millions of the very semiautomatic firearms S.150 seeks to ban. Take, for example, the AR-15 rifle, which S.150 would prohibit along with any "copies, duplicates, variants, or altered facsimiles with the capability . . . thereof." § 2(a)(1). The AR-15 "is the most popular semi-automatic rifle; since 1986, about two million semi-automatic AR-15 rifles have been manufactured. In 2007, the AR-15 *alone* accounted for 5.5 percent of firearms and 14.4 percent of rifles produced in the United States for the domestic market." *Heller II*, 670 F.3d at 1287 (Kavanaugh, J., dissenting) (citation omitted, original emphasis); *see also id.* at 1261 (majority opinion); Johnson, 60 HASTINGS L.J. at 1296 ("the AR-15" is "now the bestselling rifle type in the United States"). Indeed, the AR-15 is the very firearm that the Supreme Court in *Staples* deemed among those weapons that "traditionally have been widely accepted as lawful possessions." 511 U.S. at 611-12.

The AR-15, of course, is just one of scores of specific firearm types singled out by S.150. In addition to these specifically identified firearms, S.150 would also outlaw an untold number of other weapons through its ban on semiautomatic rifles, handguns, and shotguns with certain features. Semiautomatic rifles with the capacity to accept detachable magazines, for example, are banned if they have one additional enumerated feature such as a pistol grip, a folding stock, or a threaded barrel. A detachable magazine does nothing to distinguish a semiautomatic weapon from the mine-run of familiar, commonly-possessed firearms. Indeed, most semiautomatic firearms in America have a detachable magazine. *See* Johnson, 60 HASTINGS L.J. at 1298 n.100 (citing David B. Kopel, *Assault Weapons*, in GUNS: WHO SHOULD HAVE THEM? 159, 165 (David B. Kopel, ed., 1995)).

To be sure, under S.150 a detachable magazine, standing alone, is not enough to transform an otherwise lawful pistol or rifle into a "semiautomatic assault weapon" (a detachable magazine standing alone would make a semiautomatic shotgun unlawful). But to the extent the additional attributes that, when combined with a detachable magazine, push a firearm over the line from acceptable to contraband make a difference in the functionality of the firearm at all, they tend to *improve* the firearm's utility and safety for self-defense and other lawful purposes. A pistol grip, for example, makes it easier to hold and stabilize a rifle or shotgun when fired from the shoulder, and therefore promotes accuracy. *See* Kopel, 20 J. CONTEMP. L. at 396 ("The defensive application is obvious, as is the public safety advantage in preventing stray shots."). A grip that can be held by the non-trigger hand – such as a forward grip on a long gun or a second pistol grip on a handgun – also promotes better control by the user. A threaded barrel facilitates the attachment of a muzzle brake, which "reduces the gun's recoil and makes it easier to control," resulting in a weapon that is "significantly more accurate . . . and more comfortable to shoot." *Id.* at 396-97. A telescoping or folding stock not only makes it easier to transport a firearm in a vehicle or to store it in the home, *id.* at 398-99, but, more importantly, also promotes accuracy by allowing the stock to be adjusted to fit the individual user's physique, thickness of clothing, and shooting position.

What, then, can possibly explain why S.150 singles out the firearms that it does? A little history goes a long way towards providing an explanation. The term "assault weapon" is a neologism – a recent invention that does not denote any pre-existing category of weapon recognized in the history of firearms. "Prior to 1989, the term 'assault weapon' did not exist in the lexicon of firearms. It is a political term, developed by anti-gun publicists to expand the category of 'assault rifles' so as to allow an attack on as many additional firearms as possible on the basis of undefined 'evil' appearance." *Stenberg v. Carhart*, 530 U.S. 914, 1001 n.16 (2000) (Thomas, J., dissenting) (quotation marks omitted)). The leaders of this movement were not coy about the political agenda behind their invention of this term:

> Assault weapons . . . are a new topic. The weapons' menacing looks, coupled with the public's confusion over fully automatic machine guns versus semiautomatic assault weapons – anything that looks like a machine gun is assumed to be a machine gun – can only increase the chance of public support for restrictions on these weapons.

Josh Sugarmann, *Assault Weapons and Accessories in America* (Violence Policy Center 1988), *available at* http://www.vpc.org/studies/awaconc.htm (emphasis omitted). *See also* Johnson, 60 HASTINGS L.J. at 1289-90 ("Some people still believe the assault weapons debate is about machine guns. This is not surprising given that proponents of the 1994 ban were counting on precisely that confusion. The calculation was political.").

In accord with this pedigree, S.150's definition of "assault weapons" turns not on a firearm's value or appropriateness for self-defense or other lawful civilian purposes, nor on features that render a firearm "unusually dangerous" to the public or the police. *Heller*, 554 U.S. at 627. Rather, firearms are classified (and banned) based primarily on whether they have features used on military firearms – which, like their civilian defensive counterparts, are designed to be accurately fired under life-threatening circumstances – or are believed simply to have particularly "menacing looks." Sugarmann, *Assault Weapons and Accessories in America*. This is perhaps best exemplified by S.150's ban on semiautomatic pistols that both (a) have the capacity accept a detachable magazine and (b) are "[a] semiautomatic version of an automatic firearm." § 2(a)(1). The *only* thing that distinguishes these pistols from other, permissible semiautomatic pistols that accept a detachable magazine is that they *look like* (but in fact are not) automatic weapons.

III. THE PUBLIC INTEREST

Because S.150 outlaws firearms that are "of the kind in common use . . . for lawful purposes," *Heller*, 554 U.S. 624, it is unconstitutional – period. But even if some sort of "interest balancing" test were allowed, S.150's ban on such firearms would not pass constitutional muster.

As an initial matter, the only balancing test that possibly could be appropriate is strict scrutiny, which requires that a restriction on a fundamental constitutional right be narrowly tailored to serve a compelling governmental interest. As explained above, the Supreme Court held in *McDonald* that the Second Amendment right to keep and bear arms is *fundamental*. And when a law interferes with "fundamental constitutional rights," it generally is subject to "strict judicial scrutiny." *San Antonio Indep. Sch. Dist. v. Rodriguez*, 411 U.S. 1, 16 (1973). *See also, e.g.*, *Clark v. Jeter*, 486 U.S. 456, 461 (1988) ("classifications affecting fundamental rights . . . are given the most exacting scrutiny"); *Perry Educ. Ass'n v. Perry Local Educators' Ass'n*, 460 U.S. 37, 54 (1983) ("strict scrutiny [is] applied when government action impinges upon a fundamental right protected by the Constitution"). Because S.150 strikes directly at the fundamental, enumerated right to keep and bear arms, nothing less than strict scrutiny would be appropriate.

At any rate, S.150's ban on "semiautomatic assault weapons" could not pass even intermediate scrutiny, for it is not even "substantially related to the achievement" of the government's objective of advancing public safety. *United States v. Virginia*, 518 U.S. 515, 533 (1996). As an initial matter, it is wholly implausible that criminals bent on committing murder or other acts of deadly violence would give serious thought to whether their weapon of choice would be legal for them to possess. And even if this were not the case, a criminal could simply substitute for a banned "semiautomatic assault weapon" another equally powerful – or even more powerful – semiautomatic weapon. *See* GARY KLECK, TARGETING GUNS: FIREARMS AND THEIR CONTROL 128 (1997) (Assault rifles "are generally less lethal than ordinary hunting rifles, while ['assault weapon'] pistols are no more lethal than [non-'assault weapon'] handguns."). Again, the term "semiautomatic assault weapon" does not denote any mechanically distinct category of semiautomatic firearms, but rather bans certain semiautomatic firearms because of certain user-friendly features or simply because of the way they look, while leaving other functionally indistinguishable and equally (or more) lethal firearms untouched. *See id.* at 121 (noting that "[t]he few dozen models of semiautomatic guns that ha[d] been banned as ['assault weapons' by the 1994 federal ban and similar State laws] are, as a group, mechanically identical to the hundreds of models not banned" in relevant respects, and "[t]herefore, there is no basis for expecting that the outcomes of *any* shootings would be different . . . if unbanned semiautomatic guns capable of accepting detachable magazines were used instead of mechanically identical, though cosmetically different, banned ['assault weapons']") (original emphasis). Indeed, as explained above, several of the forbidden features singled out by S.150 actually serve to *enhance* a firearm's utility and safety for self-defense. Thus, far from *substantially serving* its goal of advancing public safety, S.150's ban on certain types of semiautomatic firearms is actually at war with it. Indeed, such a ban on "semiautomatic assault weapons," as Professor Randy Barnett has recently noted, "is simply irrational and therefore unconstitutional" under any standard of review. Randy Barnett, *Gun Control Fails Rationality Test*, WASH. EXAMINER, Jan. 29, 2013, http://washingtonexaminer.com/gun-control-fails-rationality-test/article/2519971.

Not surprisingly, empirical evidence from the now-expired 1994 federal ban on semiautomatic "assault weapons" supports the commonsense proposition that S.150 will not materially advance public safety. To begin, this evidence indicates that criminals use "assault weapons" so infrequently that it cannot reasonably be expected that banning them will have a significant impact on crime or homicide rates. Assault weapons "were used in only a small fraction of gun crimes prior to the [1994] ban: about 2% according to most studies and no more than 8%." Christopher S. Koper et al., Report to the National Institute of Justice, United States Department of Justice, *An Updated Assessment of the Federal Assault Weapons Ban: Impacts on Gun Markets and Gun Violence, 1994-2003* 2 (2004); *see also* KLECK, TARGETING GUNS at 41- 42, 112. These results are consistent with studies conducted in prisons indicating that "criminals not only did not 'prefer' military-style guns, they were strongly *dis*inclined to carry them during commission of their crimes, even when they owned one." KLECK, TARGETING GUNS at 116-17 (original emphasis). Police officers also report that criminals prefer not to use "the sophisticated and expensive assault weapons as commonly thought." Thomas E. Romano, *Firing Back: Legislative Attempts to Combat Assault Weapons*, 19 SETON HALL LEGIS. J. 857, 890 & n.171 (1995) (citing George R. Wilson, chief of the firearms division for the Washington, D.C. police department).

Of course, one could "artificially increase the share of crime guns that are ['assault weapons'] simply by expanding the definition of an ['assault weapon']," KLECK, TARGETING GUNS at 112-13, and S.150's definition of prohibited weapons is broader than that contained in the 1994 ban. But a definition of assault weapons that sweeps in a broader range of guns used by criminals simply means that more criminals will either ignore the law or use a different semiautomatic gun that is equally effective for their criminal purposes. In other words, at most "violent criminals will simply resort to more easily attainable, equally lethal weapons." Romano, 19 SETON HALL LEGIS. J. at 892; Eugene Volokh, *Implementing the Right to Keep and Bear Arms for Self-Defense: An Analytical Framework and A Research Agenda*, 56 UCLA L. REV. 1443, 1468 (2009) ("[A]nyone who is denied an 'assault weapon' will almost certainly substitute another gun that is equally lethal. It's therefore hard to see how assault weapons bans will do much to reduce danger of crime or injury."); KLECK, TARGETING GUNS at 106 ("restrictions on one subtype of firearms encourage criminals to substitute other gun types, and in some cases the most likely substitutes are even more dangerous than the targeted"). This is not mere conjecture, it has already occurred. *See* Koper, Report to the National Institute of Justice at 2 (noting that following the 1994 federal ban any "decline in ['assault weapon'] use was offset throughout at least the late 1990s by steady or rising use of other guns equipped with" magazines holding more than 10 rounds).

Therefore, it is not surprising that the 10-year national "assault weapons" ban had "very modest effects on homicide" which were "statistically insignificant." Peter Reuter & Jenny Mouzos, *Australia: A Massive Buyback of Low-Risk Guns*, *in* EVALUATING GUN POLICY 121, 141 (Jens Ludwig & Philip J. Cook eds., 2003); National Research Council, *Firearms and Violence: A Critical Review* 97 (Charles F. Wellford et al. eds., 2005) ("[G]iven the nature of the [1994 assault weapons ban], the maximum potential effect of the ban on gun violence outcomes would be very small and, if there were any observable effects, very difficult to disentangle from chance yearly variation and other state and local gun violence initiatives that took place simultaneously."). Indeed, before the 1994 ban expired in 2004, a study sponsored by the National Institute of Justice reported that, if the ban were continued, "effects on gun violence [were] likely to be small at best and perhaps too small for reliable measurement." Koper, Report to the National Institute of Justice at 3. *See also* Johnson, 60 HASTINGS L.J. at 1290, 1302; Kopel, 20 J. CONTEMP. L. at 404-13.

In sum, given S.150's arbitrary classification of firearms on the basis of largely cosmetic differences and the ready ability of criminals to substitute functionally indistinguishable lawful weapons for the weapons it would ban, enacting the Bill's ban on certain semiautomatic firearms plainly will not improve public safety. This dooms S.150 under intermediate scrutiny, for a legislative restriction on a constitutional right is presumed invalid unless it can be shown to serve an important government interest in a direct and substantial way. *See, e.g.*, *Nguyen v. I.N.S.*, 533 U.S. 53, 73 (2001) (upholding sex classification because it was based on "basic biological differences" between men and woman, not "misconceptions and prejudices"); *Virginia*, 518 U.S. at 533 (striking down sex classification that the Court deemed relied on "overbroad generalizations" rather than "enduring" or "inherent" differences between men and women). Indeed, it is unlikely that the proposed ban on semiautomatic firearms could even pass rational basis review. *See City of Cleburne v. Cleburne Living Center, Inc.*, 473 U.S. 432, 448 (1985) (requiring a special use permit for a home for the mentally disabled failed rational basis review when there was no "rational basis for believing" that the "home and those who would occupy it would threaten legitimate interests of the city in a way that other permitted uses such as boarding houses and hospitals would not"); *Department of Agriculture v. Moreno*, 413 U.S. 528, 537 (1973) (a limitation on food stamp eligibility failed rational basis review when "[m]ost people in the category" targeted by Congress "can and will alter their living arrangements in order to remain eligible for food stamps").

IV. The Ban on 11-Plus Round Magazines Would Also Violate the Second Amendment

1. The principles established by *Heller* and *McDonald* likewise demonstrate that S.150's proposed ban on magazines with a capacity to accept more than 10 rounds of ammunition is unconstitutional. Again, the key question is whether firearms equipped with such magazines are of a kind that are in common use for lawful purposes. Clearly they are.

Americans own tens of millions of magazines fitting this description. *See* Koper, Report to the National Institute of Justice at 65 ("[G]un industry sources estimated that there were 25 million [such magazines] available as of 1995 . . . . [N]early 4.8 million . . . were imported for commercial sale . . . from 1994 through 2000 . . . . During this period, furthermore, importers received permission to import a total of 47.2 million [such magazines]; consequently, an additional 42 million may have arrived after 2000 or still be on their way, based just on those approved through 2000."). Indeed, magazines with a capacity to accept more than ten rounds of ammunition are standard equipment on many popular firearms owned by many millions of Americans for self-defense, hunting, and target shooting. *See* Overstreet Decl. 14 ("Standard magazines for very commonly owned semiautomatic pistols hold up to 17 rounds of ammunition. In 2007, about two-thirds of the 1.2 million pistols made in the United States and not exported were in calibers typically using magazines that hold more than 10 rounds."); *id.* 17 ("More than six million M1 Carbine series rifles have been made since their introduction in the 1940s, and the standard magazines for them hold 15 or 30 rounds. . . . Numerous other rifle makes and models also have the capacity to accept, and are commonly equipped with, magazines holding more than 10 rounds."); *What Should America Do About Gun Violence?: Hearing Before the Senate Comm. on the Judiciary*, 113th Cong. 15-17 (2013) (Written Testimony of David B. Kopel) ("Kopel Testimony").[5]

The defensive utility of having a magazine with more than ten rounds of ammunition is obvious. As an initial matter, while the need for armed self-defense rarely, if ever, arises for the vast majority of people, it can be a matter of life and death when it does. And when life or serious bodily injury is at stake, the prudent person would, obviously, rather have ammunition that she does not need than need ammunition that she does not have. A law-abiding person who runs out of ammunition before her attacker does is very likely to become a crime victim. And a person faced with one or more armed assailants could well need to fire more than ten shots to defend herself and may not be able to change magazines immediately. Because criminals rarely announce their intentions in advance, victims will rarely have more than a single magazine immediately available. And a law-abiding person who is suddenly confronted by an armed assailant may take longer to change magazines under such stress than when calmly shooting the firing range. If she is elderly or disabled, changing magazines may prove to be no easy task.

Defensive utility is also demonstrated by the fact that police officers' duty handguns are typically equipped with magazines capable of holding more than ten rounds. *See* Kopel Testimony at 16. To be sure, a police officer is more likely than a private citizen to face a situation in which he would need to fire more than ten rounds, but private citizens nonetheless reasonably choose to arm themselves with firearms equipped with magazines capable of holding more than ten rounds of ammunition. *Cf.* Overstreet Decl. 15. And S.150 would exempt from its limit on magazine capacity not only active duty law enforcement officers but also, in certain situations, retired officers. *See* § 3(a)(1). "If retired cops need 15 rounds to effectively protect themselves and others, then so do other citizens. Arbitrarily discriminating among Americans in this way is irrational and unconstitutional." Barnett, *Gun Control Fails Rationality Test.*

While some people, including no doubt members of this committee, believe that private citizens do not need these magazines for self-defense, hunting, or other lawful purposes, tens of millions of Americans disagree. And it is the judgment of these law-abiding, responsible citizens, made manifest through the choices they have made in exercising their fundamental, individual right to keep and bear arms for lawful purposes, that matters under the Second Amendment.

2. Because firearms equipped with magazines capable of holding more than ten rounds of ammunition are in "common use" for "lawful purposes," the Constitution guarantees the right of law-abiding, responsible citizens to acquire, possess, and use them. *Heller*, 554 U.S. at 624. But even if a levels-of-scrutiny-analysis were to apply, and even if, contrary to *Heller*, intermediate scrutiny was the applicable standard of review, S.150's magazine ban could not stand.

To be sure, the time it takes to change magazines could, in some situations, make a difference in the outcome of a confrontation. But it is clear that, on balance, restricting magazines to 10 rounds will work to the advantage of criminals, not law-abiding citizens. First, there are many millions of 11-plus round magazines already in circulation, and while most law-abiding citizens will obey any new law restricting the purchase or transfer of such magazines, most criminals will not. And even if one indulges the notion that such a ban will operate equally on law-abiding citizens and criminals alike, it is criminals, not their victims, that generally choose the time and place of an armed confrontation. A criminal can thus plan in advance for the possibility that he will need more than a single 10-round magazine and equip himself accordingly.

Nor does available empirical evidence support a substantial connection between a ban on 11-plus round magazines and public safety. As an initial matter, limiting magazine capacity to ten rounds will be simply irrelevant to the vast majority of gun crimes. *See* KLECK, TARGETING GUNS at 123 ("It is unlikely that large-capacity magazines are currently relevant to the outcome of a large number of violent incidents, since few cases involve large numbers of shots fired."). "[A]vailable studies on shots fired show that assailants fire less than four shots on average . . ., a number well within the 10-round limit . . . ." Koper, Report to the National Institute of Justice at 90. While these studies generally did not report how many incidents involved more than ten shots fired, one study that did address the issue reported that only "2.5% of the gunfire cases involved more than 10 shots." *Id.*

Further, it is unlikely that magazine size would have much of an impact even in those rare instances in which more than ten shots are fired. A study of "mass shootings" – *i.e.*, incidents in which "six or more victims were shot dead with a gun, or twelve or more total were wounded" – from 1984 to 1993 found that "[f]or those incidents where the number of rounds fired and the duration of the shooting were both reported, the rate of fire never was faster than about one round every two seconds, and was usually much slower than that." KLECK, TARGETING GUNS at 124-25. Thus, "[n]one of the mass killers maintained a sustained rate of fire that could not also have been maintained – even taking reloading time into account – with either multiple guns or with an ordinary six-shot revolver and the common loading devices known as 'speedloaders.' " *Id.* at 125. Furthermore, as more recent incidents demonstrate, a mass shooter may simply change magazines each time one is spent. *See* Kopel Testimony at 19 ("At Newtown, the murderer changed magazines many times, firing only a portion of the rounds in each magazine. . . . In the Virginia Tech murders, the perpetrator changed magazines 17 times.").

Putting this data to the side, it is not even evident that S.150 would reduce attacks with firearms equipped with magazines capable of holding more than ten rounds of ammunition. Indeed, although the 1994 federal law also limited magazine capacity to ten rounds, research sponsored by the National Institute of Justice found that "it seems unlikely that the federal ban had any such effect." Koper, Report to the National Institute of Justice at 90 n.107. To be sure, S.150 is stricter than the 1994 federal ban, for unlike the 1994 ban, it would prohibit the transfer of grandfathered magazines that were lawfully possessed before the date of enactment. But again, given that "most of the methods through which criminals acquire guns and virtually everything they ever do with those guns are already against the law," JAMES D. WRIGHT & PETER H. ROSSI, ARMED AND CONSIDERED DANGEROUS xxxv (new 2d ed. 2008), it is highly implausible that this distinction will make much of a difference.

V. HELLER II

In *Heller II*, a divided panel of the D.C. Circuit held that the District of Columbia's ban on semiautomatic "assault rifles" did not violate the Second Amendment. I commend to the subcommittee the dissenting opinion of Judge Kavanaugh, which forcefully and compellingly explains why *Heller* and *McDonald* mandate a textual and historical inquiry, not an intermediate scrutiny analysis, and why D.C.'s assault rifle ban – and thus the "assault weapon" ban proposed in S.150 – is unconstitutional under either of these approaches.

Here, though, I would like to address several of the flaws in the *Heller II* majority opinion, for they are indicative of the types of arguments that will be advanced to justify S.150's proposed bans on certain semiautomatic firearms and on ammunition magazines holding more than 10 rounds.

1. *First*, the panel majority acknowledged that semi-automatic rifles are in "common use" (without identifying the purposes for which they are commonly used) and that there is no "longstanding" tradition of prohibiting their use. *See Heller II*, 670 F.3d at 1260-61. Under *Heller*, that should have been the end of the case, and the District of Columbia's ban should have been struck down. But the panel majority instead proceeded to apply a levels-of-scrutiny analysis, with the level of scrutiny turning on the Court's view of "how severely the prohibitions burden the Second Amendment right." *Id.* at 1261. Under the panel majority's analysis, in other words, the level of scrutiny to be applied in Second Amendment cases turns on the very type of balancing of interests assessment that *Heller* forbids.

Second, the panel majority erred by deeming intermediate scrutiny the proper standard. As explained above, the *Heller* majority rejected the test Justice Breyer advanced in his dissent, which essentially was a form of intermediate scrutiny. Indeed, it is telling that in explicating the intermediate scrutiny standard it was applying, the panel majority in *Heller II* repeatedly invoked *Turner*, the very case that Justice Breyer held up as exemplary of the interest-balancing approach he was advocating, and indeed the panel majority *quoted much of the same language from Turner quoted by Justice Breyer. Compare Heller II*, 670 F.3d at 1259, *with Heller*, 554 U.S. at 704-05 (Breyer, J., dissenting). *Heller* prohibits application of this standard to a ban on possessing arms protected by the Second Amendment.

Third, the panel majority's reasoning for applying intermediate scrutiny cannot be squared with *Heller*. In particular, the panel majority reasoned that "the laws at issue here do not prohibit the possession of 'the quintessential self-defense weapon,' to wit, the handgun," *id.* At 1261-62 (quoting *Heller*, 554 U.S. at 629), and thus that "the ban on certain semi-automatic rifles [does not] prevent a person from keeping a suitable and commonly used weapon for protection in the home or for hunting," *id.* at 1262. "But that's a bit like saying books can be banned because people can always read newspapers. That is not a persuasive or legitimate way to analyze a law that directly infringes an enumerated constitutional right." *Id.* at 1289 (Kavanaugh, J., dissenting). And under *Heller*, it is not the government's prerogative to pick and choose which constitutionally protected arms may be used for lawful purposes; rather, that right is reserved to the law-abiding citizens of this Nation. Thus, in *Heller*, "[i]t [was] no answer to say . . . that it is permissible to ban handguns, so long as the possession of other firearms . . . is allowed." 554 U.S. at 629. And in *Heller II*, it likewise should have been no answer to say that it is permissible to ban some semiautomatic rifles so long as the possession of other firearms is allowed.

Fourth, the panel majority's application of intermediate scrutiny cannot be reconciled with *Heller*. *Heller* concluded, as noted earlier, that the District of Columbia's handgun ban would "fail constitutional muster" under "any of the standards of scrutiny the Court has applied to enumerated constitutional rights," 554 U.S. at 571, including intermediate scrutiny, which is applied in some situations in which an enumerated right is burdened in an incidental or marginal way. *See, e.g.*, *Barnes v. Glen Theatre, Inc.*, 501 U.S. 560, 566 (1991) ("expressive conduct within the outer perimeters of the First Amendment, though . . . only marginally so"); *Ohralik v. Ohio State Bar Ass'n*, 436 U.S. 447, 456 (1978) (commercial speech, which has a "subordinate position in the scale of First Amendment values"). If the District of Columbia's ban on handguns could not pass intermediate scrutiny (*i.e.*, was not substantially related to public safety), it follows that its ban on certain semiautomatic rifles likewise could not pass this level of heightened scrutiny. For while the panel majority attempted to build a case that criminals could misuse "assault weapons," *see Heller II*, 670 F.3d at 1262-63, the far more prevalent misuse of handguns by violent urban criminals could not save the District of Columbia's handgun ban. *See, e.g.*, *Heller*, 554 U.S. at 697-99 (Breyer, J., dissenting) ("From 1993 to 1997, 81% of firearm-homicide victims were killed by handgun. . . . Handguns also appear to be a very popular weapon among criminals. . . . [T]he linkage of handguns to firearms deaths and injuries appears to be much stronger in urban than in rural areas.").

This points to another flaw in the panel majority's reasoning: its focus on ways in which certain firearms may be misused by criminals, rather than on ways in which they may be put to lawful defensive use by law-abiding citizens. Unlike the *Heller* dissenters, the Supreme Court's majority opinion focused on the latter, not the former, explaining that a handgun "is easier to store in a location that is readily accessible in an emergency; it cannot easily be redirected or wrestled away by an attacker; it is easier to use for those without the upper-body strength to lift and aim a long gun; it can be pointed at a burglar with one hand while the other hand dials the police." 554 U.S. at 629. Many of these attributes, of course, likely also explain why criminals prefer to use handguns, but that is not what the *Heller* majority deemed relevant. Conversely, many of the attributes of "assault weapons" that the *Heller II* panel majority deemed pernicious enhance their fitness as defensive, *anti-assault* weapons when in the hands of law-abiding citizens. *See Heller II*, 670 F.3d at 1262-63 (*e.g.*, features that "help stabilize the weapon during rapid fire").

The Supreme Court's approach is authoritative, of course, but it also makes more sense. Criminals are by definition much less likely than law-abiding citizens to abide by restrictions on the types of guns that may be owned. Thus, to the extent a certain weapon gives one party to a confrontation an advantage, banning that weapon will on the whole work to the benefit of the criminals, not the law-abiding.

At any rate, the panel majority's intermediate scrutiny analysis ultimately is at war with itself. For recall the panel majority's reasoning for applying intermediate scrutiny in the first place: that the ban would not "prevent a person from keeping a suitable and commonly used weapon for protection in the home or for hunting." *Id.* at 1262. Of course, it is also true that the ban would not prevent a criminal from simply substituting for a banned semiautomatic "assault rifle" another equally lethal semiautomatic firearm just as "suitable and commonly used" for criminal purposes.

As explained above, it is therefore simply irrational to expect that dubbing a subcategory of semiautomatic weapons "assault weapons" and banning their possession will improve public safety.

Fifth, and finally, the panel majority erred by likening semiautomatic "assault weapons" to fully automatic firearms. According to the panel majority, "*Heller* suggests 'M-16 rifles and the like' may be banned because they are 'dangerous and unusual.' " *Heller II*, 670 F.3d at 1263 (quoting *Heller*, 554 U.S. at 627). Citing the *Staples* decision, the panel majority then concluded that the two firearms are essentially equivalent: "The Court had previously described the 'AR-15' as 'the civilian version of the military's M-16 rifle.' " *Id.* (quoting *Staples*, 511 U.S. at 603). But *Staples* was not *equating* the AR-15 with the M-16; to the contrary, it held that the AR-15, *unlike* the M-16, is among weapons that "traditionally have been widely accepted as lawful possessions." 511 U.S. at 612. The key distinction between these two firearms, of course, is that the AR-15 is semiautomatic, while the M-16 is fully automatic, and thus has long been effectively restricted to military use. The panel majority acknowledged this difference, but instead of recognizing its importance, sought to diminish it: "Although semi-automatic firearms, unlike automatic M-16s, fire only one shot with each pull of the trigger, semi-automatics still fire almost as rapidly as automatics." 670 F.3d at 1263 (quotation marks and citation omitted). There are two problems with this argument. Not only does "the majority opinion's data indicate that semi-automatics actually fire two-and-a-half times slower than automatics," *id.* at 1289 (Kavanaugh, J., dissenting), but, taken to its logical conclusion, the majority opinion's reasoning would justify a ban on *all* semiautomatic weapons.

This cannot possibly be right under *Heller*, given that semiautomatic firearms are ubiquitous and used by tens of millions of Americans for self-defense and other lawful purposes.

2. The plaintiffs in *Heller II* also challenged the District of Columbia's ban on magazines capable of holding more than ten rounds of ammunition. The *Heller II* panel majority also rejected this challenge. (Judge Kavanaugh would have remanded for further proceedings on this issue.) Given that the panel majority addressed both bans together, the panel majority's ruling on the magazine ban is subject to many of the same criticisms as its ruling on the semiautomatic "assault rifle" ban. For example, like "assault rifles," the panel majority found it "clear enough" that "magazines holding more than ten rounds are indeed in 'common use.' " *Heller II*, 670 F.3d at 1261.

That should have been the end of the matter, yet rather than striking down the law, the panel majority proceeded to apply intermediate scrutiny. And in applying intermediate scrutiny, the panel majority invoked testimony that "the '2 or 3 second pause' during which a criminal reloads a firearm 'can be of critical benefit to law enforcement' " without acknowledging the fact that a 2 or 3 second pause during which a victim reloads a firearm can be of equally critical benefit to a criminal.

Heller II, 570 F.3d at 1264. And the panel majority did not address the evidence discussed above showing that banning magazines capable of holding more than ten rounds of ammunition is unlikely to promote public safety.

CONCLUSION

In sum, the principles established by the Supreme Court's decisions in *Heller* and *McDonald* must guide Members of this body as it considers various proposals intended to reduce gun violence. In applying these principles to S.150's proposed ban on what it calls "semiautomatic assault weapons" and on magazines capable of holding more than ten rounds of ammunition, I have concluded that these provisions would violate the Second Amendment by prohibiting the use of arms that are in common use by ordinary Americans for self defense and other lawful purposes.

End Notes

[1] I have spent much of my professional life working on issues relating to the meaning of the United States Constitution. Shortly after serving as law clerk to Judge Paul Roney of the Fifth (now Eleventh) Circuit Court of Appeals and to Justice William H. Rehnquist, I joined the Civil Rights Division of the U.S. Department of Justice in 1981. In 1985 President Reagan appointed me to serve as Assistant Attorney General for the Office of Legal Counsel. I reentered private practice in 1988, and in October 1996 I became a founding partner of Cooper & Kirk, PLLC.

In private practice, I have litigated numerous cases involving the meaning of the Second Amendment. Long before the Supreme Court's decision in *Heller*, I was appointed a Special Assistant Attorney General for the State of Alabama for the purpose of presenting oral argument as an amicus in *United States v. Emerson*, 270 F.3d 203 (5th Cir. 2001). *Emerson* was a seminal case because the Fifth Circuit agreed that the Second Amendment guaranteed an individual right to keep and bear arms and decided the case based on the Founding-era history surrounding the adoption of the Second Amendment. In *District of Columbia v. Heller*, 554 U.S. 570 (2008), I submitted an amicus brief on behalf of former officials in the Department of Justice arguing that the Second Amendment guarantees an individual right to keep and bear arms. Subsequent to *Heller*, the State of Oklahoma appointed me a Special Assistant Attorney General for the purpose of presenting oral argument in defense of its statute allowing employees to keep a firearm locked in their vehicles in their employers' parking lots. *See Ramsay Winch Inc. v. Henry*, 555 F.3d 1199 (10th Cir. 2009). I am currently litigating cases on behalf of individuals and organizations, including the National Rifle Association, seeking to vindicate rights under the Second Amendment, including a case in which the Seventh Circuit recently struck down the State of Illinois's ban on carrying operable firearms in public for self-defense. *See Moore v. Madigan*, 702 F.3d 933 (7th Cir. 2012).

[2] *See id.* at 592, 594 ("[T]he Second Amendment codified a *pre-existing* right. . . . It was, [Blackstone] said, 'the natural right of resistance and self-preservation, and 'the right of having and using arms for self-preservation and defence.' ") (original emphasis, citation omitted); *id.* at 599 ("Justice Breyer's assertion that individual self-defense is merely a 'subsidiary interest' of the right to keep and bear arms is profoundly mistaken. . . . [S]elf-defense . . . was the *central component* of the right itself.") (original emphasis); *id.* at 628 ("[T]he inherent right of self-defense has been central to the Second Amendment right."); *id.* at 630 ("[T]he District's requirement . . . that firearms in the home be rendered and kept inoperable at all times . . . makes it impossible for citizens to use them for the core lawful purpose of self-defense and is hence unconstitutional."); *McDonald*, 130 S. Ct. at 3026 (all citations to controlling opinion of Alito, J.) ("Two years ago, in *District of Columbia v. Heller*, . . . we held that the Second Amendment protects the right to keep and bear arms for the purpose of self-defense . . . ."); *id.* at 3036 ("Self-defense is a basic right, recognized by many legal systems from ancient times to the present day, and in *Heller*, we held that individual self-defense is 'the *central component*' of the Second Amendment right.") (original emphasis); *id.* ("[W]e concluded [in *Heller* that] citizens must be permitted 'to use [handguns] for the core lawful purpose of self-defense.' "); *id.* at 3047 (*Heller* "stressed that the right was also valued because the possession of firearms was thought to be essential for self-defense. As we put it, self-defense was 'the *central component* of the right itself.' ") (original emphasis).

[3] Despite the Supreme Court's clear guidance on this issue, a number of lower courts in the wake of *Heller* have resolved Second Amendment claims by applying a levels-of-scrutiny analysis, often settling on an

intermediate scrutiny approach that resembles Justice Breyer's rejected interest-balancing test. These decisions fly in the face of *Heller* and *McDonald*. *See, e.g.*, Allen Rostron, *Justice Breyer's Triumph in the Third Battle Over the Second Amendment*, 80 GEO. WASH. L. REV. 703, 706-07 (2012) ("The lower courts . . . have effectively embraced the sort of interest-balancing approach that Justice Scalia condemned . . . ."); Darrell A.H. Miller, *Text, History, and Tradition: What the Seventh Amendment Can Teach Us About the Second*, 122 YALE L.J. 852, 855 (2013) ("Some judges . . . have simply ignored the Court's rejection of balancing tests. Instead they have allowed the right to keep and bear arms to be gobbled up by intermediate scrutiny or similar tests that weigh serious, important, or compelling government interests against Second Amendment commands."). *But see, e.g.*, *Moore v. Madigan*, 702 F.3d 933, 939, 941 (7th Cir. 2012) (recognizing that "the Supreme Court made clear in *Heller* that it wasn't going to make the right to bear arms depend on casualty counts," and striking down the State of Illinois's ban on publicly carrying firearms "not based on degrees of scrutiny, but on Illinois's failure to justify the most restrictive gun law of any of the 50 states"); *Heller v. District of Columbia*, 670 F.3d 1244, 1271 (D.C. Cir. 2011) ("*Heller II*") (Kavanaugh, J., dissenting) ("*Heller* and *McDonald* leave little doubt that courts are to assess gun bans and regulations based on text, history, and tradition, not a balancing test . . . ."); *Houston v. City of New Orleans*, 675 F.3d 441, 448 (Elrod, J., dissenting) (5th Cir. 2012), *withdrawn and superseded on rehearing on other grounds*, 682 F.3d 361 (5th Cir. 2012) (agreeing with Judge Kavanaugh that "*Heller* and *McDonald* rule out scrutiny analysis").

4 This is the distinction Judge Silberman adopted in the D.C. Circuit decision that was affirmed by *Heller*. *See Parker v. District of Columbia*, 478 F.3d 370, 394-95 (D.C. Cir. 2007). This distinction is "fairly supported by the historical tradition of prohibiting the carrying of 'dangerous and unusual weapons,' " 554 U.S. at 627 – a tradition that did not bar "Persons of Quality [from] wearing *common Weapons* . . . for their Ornament or Defence, in such places, and upon such Occasions, in which it is common Fashion to make use of them, without causing the least Suspicion of an intention to commit any Act of Violence or Disturbance of the Peace." 1 HAWKINS, TREATISE OF THE PLEAS OF THE CROWN 136 (1716) (emphasis added). And this distinction is rooted in founding-era militia practices: "Ordinarily when called for militia service able-bodied men were expected to appear bearing arms supplied by themselves and of the kind *in common use* at the time." *Heller*, 554 U.S. at 625 (quoting *United States v. Miller*, 307 U.S. 174, 179 (1939)) (emphasis added, brackets omitted).

5 A review of the most recent edition of Gun Digest, a standard reference work that includes specifications of currently available firearms, indicates that about two-thirds of the distinct models of semiautomatic centerfire rifles listed are normally sold with detachable magazines that hold more than ten rounds of ammunition. (Even many rifles normally sold with magazines of smaller capacity are also capable of accepting standard magazines without modification.) GUN DIGEST 2013 455-64, 497-99 (Jerry Lee, ed., 67th ed. 2012). The same book indicates that about one-third of distinct models of semiautomatic handguns listed – even allowing for versions sold in different calibers, which often have different ammunition capacities – are normally sold with magazines that hold more than ten rounds of ammunition. *Id.* at 407- 39. In both cases, but especially for handguns, these figures underestimate the ubiquity of magazines holding more than 10 rounds of ammunition, because they include many minor variations of lower-capacity firearms offered by low-volume manufacturers.

In: Mass Shootings and Gun Violence in America
Editor: John C. Zandler
ISBN: 978-1-62618-893-8

Chapter 19

TESTIMONY OF SUZANNA HUPP. HEARING ON "PROPOSALS TO REDUCE GUN VIOLENCE: PROTECTING OUR COMMUNITIES WHILE RESPECTING THE SECOND AMENDMENT"*

I want to thank you ladies and gentlemen for asking me to testify today. I am speaking for myself and not in any official capacity. Many of you have heard my story before and, of course, it really hasn't changed. I didn't grow up in a house with guns. But I did grow up in a house where my father was an expert on the founding of the country and the meaning of the Second Amendment. So it amazes me that we are back here having the same discussions that we have had several years ago.

When I was 21 and moved out on my own, I was given a gun and taught how to use it. After I became a chiropractor, one of my patients (who was an assistant district attorney in Houston) convinced me to carry it with me at all times. Please understand that at that time in the state of Texas it was illegal to carry a gun, except in your car. We did not have a permitting system.

In 1991, on a beautiful October day, my parents and I went to a local cafeteria to have lunch with a friend of mine who was managing the cafeteria. It was Boss' Day and the day after payday, so the place was packed. We were unable to sit in our usual position by the front window. As we finished lunch and my friend got up to check on things in the kitchen, this pickup truck came crashing through the floor-to-ceiling window where we normally sat. It came to rest about 15 feet from us after knocking over a number of tables and injuring several people. Of course, we all thought it was an accident, and I began to rise to go help the people that he had knocked over. But as I began to stand up, we heard gunshots. Immediately, my Dad and I got down on the floor and turned the table up in front of us. Mom got down behind us. I continued to hear shooting on the opposite side of the truck. Remember, this was 1991 and the type of mass shootings we have seen since were not yet occurring on a regular basis. I kept waiting for him to say something like, "Everyone put your wallets up on the tables!" But the gunshots continued. It took a good 45 seconds...which is an eternity, to realize that he was just there to execute people. As he made his way around the front of the truck, I watched as

* This is an edited, reformatted and augmented version of testimony given on February 12, 2013 before the Senate Judiciary Committee, Subcommittee on the Constitution, Civil Rights and Human Rights.

he leveled his gun on the head of a person crouched beneath him. He pulled the trigger. Then he calmly walked to the next person, pointed the gun and pulled the trigger. It was then that I thought, "I've got him!" I reached for my purse on the floor next to me. I had a perfect place to prop my shooting hand, and I have hit much smaller targets at much greater distances. Could I have missed? It's possible. But it sure would have changed the odds. Then I realized that a few months earlier I had made the stupidest decision of my life. I had begun to leave my gun in my car because at that time, in the state of Texas, concealed carry laws did not exist. I was concerned about getting caught with it. I did what most normal people would do: I wanted to obey the law and certainly didn't want to lose my license to practice my livelihood. I never thought I'd need it in the middle of a crowded restaurant. I remember looking around for something to use as a weapon, and thinking, “Great...what do I do now? Throw a salt shaker at him?” I can't begin to get across to you how incredibly frustrating it is to sit there, like a fish in a barrel, and wait for it to be your turn, with no hope of defending yourself.

It was then that my father took my attention. He began to rise up and said, "I've got to do something! I've got to do something or he's going to kill everyone in here!" I turned to him and tried to hold him down by the shirt collar. But when he saw what he thought was a chance, he stood up and ran at the guy, who at that point was about a dozen feet from us. But the gunman had complete control of the room. He simply turned, and shot my father in the chest. My father fell in the aisle maybe 7 or 8 feet from me. And although he was still alive and conscious, I saw the wound and as awful as this may sound, wrote him off at that moment.

The good news is that it made the gunman change directions slightly, and he went off to my left. That was the first time I had gotten a good look at him. He was a tall 30 something year old man. And I remember wondering what could be so terribly wrong in this man's life that he would be committing this horrible act. At that point, I heard another window crash toward the back of the restaurant. I thought, "Oh my God, here comes another one!" But when I looked, I realized that someone had broken out a window at the back of the restaurant and people were pouring out through it. I peeked over the top of the upturned table, and when the gunman's back was to me, I stood up, grabbed my mother by the shirt collar and said, “Come on, come on! Let's go! We've got to get out of here!” And then my feet grew wings. I was one of the only ones from that front area to make it out that back window. As I stumbled through the broken window I ran into my manager friend who had come out a side, kitchen door. He said, “Thank God you're all right!" I told him, “Yes, but Dad's been hit and it's bad.” Then I turned to say something to my Mom, and realized she had not followed me out. Because it was glass three quarters of the way around the restaurant, I could not see the interior due to the backlighting. And I had no idea where my mother was.

In the interest of time, I will spare you details of the next several minutes. However, I will tell you that several of the first responders were patients of mine. A week or so after the event they took me and my siblings to lunch and filled in some gaps. They told us that they had been in a conference at a hotel one building away when the shooting occurred. In an odd twist of gun control fate, the manager of the hotel asked them to leave their weapons in their vehicles so as not to make her customers uncomfortable. So precious minutes were lost as they retrieved their weapons from their locked trunks and made their way to the restaurant. They told us that as they worked their way through the broken window, they weren't sure who the gunman was. They saw a lot of bodies, and a woman, on her knees in the aisle, cradling a mortally wounded man. They said that a man walked up to her, she looked up at him, he put a gun to her head, she looked down at her husband, and he pulled the trigger. That's how they knew who the gunman was. All they had to do was fire a shot into the ceiling, and this guy immediately rabbitted to a back bathroom alcove area. He exchanged some gun fire with them, and then put a bullet in his own head. 23 people were killed that day, including my parents. Mom and Dad had just had their 47th wedding anniversary 2 weeks prior to this. And although it didn't occur to me at the time, Mom wasn't going anywhere without Dad.

Now it may sound odd to you, but I wasn't angry at the guy that did it. That's like being mad at a rabid dog: you don't be mad at it. You might take it behind the barn and kill it, but don't be mad it. I told the newspapers the next day that I was mad as hell at my legislators because they had legislated me out of the right to protect myself and my family. The *only* thing the gun laws did that day was prevent good people from protecting themselves.

Since that time, we have seen dozens of these mass shootings. Isn't it interesting that nearly all have occurred *in places where guns were not allowed.* If guns are the problem, then someone explain to me why we haven't seen these mass shooting at skeet and trap shoots, or NRA conventions, or the dreaded gun show. We will never know if lives could have been saved at Sandy Hook if a teacher or two been armed.

Look, guns are just a tool. They are tools that can be used to kill a family, or tools that can be used to protect a family. It merely depends on whose hands that tool is in. You may wonder why I take issue with an assault weapons ban. That is simple. It is because there's no logic involved with the proposed ban. I believe that the public and much of the media have been misled to believe that assault weapons are rapidfire, automatic, machinegun-like weapons. I know this from the many interviews I have done on television, radio and newspaper. Automatic weapons have been illegal for regular use in this country since the 1930s. And yet, that is what much of the media and public believe you are trying to ban. In fact, the proposed ban is being based almost entirely on cosmetics. So you are talking about guns that shoot in the exact same manner as the guns I have at home. So it becomes perfectly clear to me that this is merely a gun grab that is based on nothing but the desire to strip citizens of their rights.

Universal background checks? That is no more than a means to register all gun owners. And registration is *always* the first step to confiscation.

Prohibiting people with a diagnosis of PTSD? I believe you would be starting down a very slippery slope if you begin to single out those with emotional problems and strip them of their constitutional rights. Would ADHD or depression be next? We already have a system in place by which those deemed mentally unstable may be stripped of their rights.

I have heard many pundits and legislators say, "Why would anyone *need* this type of gun or a magazine that carries this many bullets?" Well, in this Land where Freedom hangs by a thread, I hate to think we are going to begin having government committees determining what each citizen *needs*. They may decide you don't *need* to drive a particular car, or *need* send your child to private school.

And in this Land of Liberty, it is not only our right to keep and bear arms, I would go so far as to say it is our duty.

With that, I would like to leave you with something to ponder. Can you imagine leaving these chambers and going to a local café with your family, perhaps your children or grandchildren? And as you're quietly finishing your meal you notice a man come in and who pulls a weapon from his overcoat, and calmly begins executing people...people who have no means of defending themselves. As the gunman works his way around the room and gets closer to you, imagine the frustration that you have not having any chance of defending yourself against him. As he levels his weapon on your child or grandchild's forehead, even if you have chosen not to have a gun with you, don't you hope the guy behind you has one and knows how to use it at that point? It makes me physically ill to think of being in that position with my children, and having no way of protecting them.

If you really want to make a difference, and eradicate mass shootings, there are a couple of things that you can do:

1. Rid the country of gun free zones. Don't get me wrong, you won't be able to stop someone from going into a workplace and shooting his estranged wife and the person sitting next to her. But you will prevent the high body bag counts we are seeing now.
2. Encourage, not legislate, but encourage the media to quit using the murderers' names in all of their follow-up reporting. I would love to see them never show the creep's picture after the first day. If the killer is still alive and going to trial, wouldn't it be great if they fuzzed out their names and faces as if it were obscene? We all know they have to report the news. But they could be part of the solution and help take the glory out of their horrendous acts.

I am proud of my Texas Capitol. While visitors wait to go through a metal detector, we have a fast-track queue that allows concealed carry permit holders to zip right through. Many legislators carry on the House and Senate floors and committee hearings, while permitted citizens with guns sit in the gallery. There would be no high body bag count there. Our State government trusts its' people. With that, I would like to say that if I had it to do over again, I would much rather be in prison with a felony offense on my head, and have my parents alive to know their grandchildren.

Thank you for your time.

INDEX

C

F

G

H

I

Q

R

T

U

V

W

Y

Z